ROMAN CATHOLICISM

AFTER

VATICAN II

ROBERT A. BURNS, O. P.

Georgetown University Press / Washington, D.C.

Georgetown University Press, Washington, D.C.
© 2001 by Georgetown University Press. All rights reserved.
Printed in the United States of America

10 9 8 7 6 5 4 3 2 1   2001

This volume is printed on acid-free offset book paper.

All excerpts of the New Testament are reprinted from
The New Testament of the Jerusalem Bible, Readers'
Edition (Garden City, NY: Image Books, 1969).

Library of Congress Cataloging-in-Publication Data

Burns, Robert A., 1934–
   Roman Catholicism after Vatican II / by Robert Burns.
     p. cm.
   Includes bibliographical references and index.
   ISBN 0-87840-822-3 (cloth: alk. paper) — ISBN 0-87840-832-1 (pbk.: alk. paper)
     1. Catholic Church—History. 2. Church history. I. Title.

   BX945.2 .B87 2001
   282'.09'045—dc21

                                                     00-061021

Dedication and Acknowledgments

For my "families": the Burnses, the Costellos, the Gugginos, the Otharts, the Bradels, the Krewedls, and the Kolins.

I would like to thank Suzanne Tumblin, Adele Barker, and Cynthia White for their help in editing the manuscript.

Table of Contents

Introduction

The Second Vatican Council ended in December 1965. The decrees of the council inaugurated a process that is far from complete. The Catholic Church is presently in a continuing state of reformation. Many questions are still debated, perhaps the most important being the question of authority. The centralization of power in Rome and the lack of collegiality at all levels continue to irritate many Catholics. This is especially true because Vatican II favored the sharing of authority and also taught the principle of subsidiarity, which maintains that nothing should be done by a larger and higher institution that can be done equally well by a smaller and lower institution. Part of the problem is that never before in the history of Catholicism have so many and such sudden changes been introduced in the life of the Church, often without adequate explanation, at least at the local level. A further difficulty results from the general nature of the council's documents, which leaves them open to conflicting interpretations.

Vatican II was a unique council. In fact, it can be argued that it was the first truly global council, including many indigenous representatives of six continents. The previous 20 councils were much more provincial in style and content, whether they were held in Asia Minor (the first eight councils) or in Europe (the last 12 councils). Also, until the council of Trent (1545–1563) the deliberations and decisions of the councils were solely the private concern of the bishops in attendance, at least while the councils were in session. With the invention of the printing press, Trent and especially Vatican I (1870) were subjected to more rapid diffusion of information by the media. But never in history did an ecumenical council have the same kind of intensive scrutiny as did Vatican II, when there was massive coverage by the print media as well as by radio and television.

The uniqueness of Vatican II can be seen in the number of participants who had the right to vote on conciliar decisions, at least three times more than at Vatican I and perhaps 20 to 30 times the number of those who voted at the Council of Trent. And the number of working hours, not only during the council but those carried out by the various commissions between the four sessions of the council, far surpasses the labor of any previous council. Furthermore, never had a council been so broadly represented biblically and theologically, including in its membership not only Catholics but also Protestant experts.

The documents of the council dealt with the reform of the Church, with *aggiornamento*, a term used often by Pope John XXIII, which served as a guiding principle. The word means updating and implies the need to make changes in the Church to bring it into alignment with the present day. The documents seem clearly to imply an openness to the future. Vatican II can certainly be placed in the tradition of previous reform councils such as the Council of Constance, the Fifth Lateran Council, and the Council of Trent.

Another distinctive feature of Vatican II was its awareness of human experience, cultural differences, and historical conditioning of all things human. Both of these notions, despite some ambivalence, are critical in the treatment of the various documents and in teachings concerning the Bible and Church history.

Pope John XXIII, who convened Vatican II and whose spirit pulsates throughout the council's documents, inspired not only Catholics but all who heard or read his words. In his five years as pope (1958–1963) John XXIII witnessed to the Gospel in a humble and therefore powerful fashion. He called the council with a sense of Christian hope and refused to be frightened by the risks of such an undertaking. With him began a new epoch of Church history, an epoch of new vitality and of new promise. The process of reformation continues, and in this book some of the important ongoing and debatable aspects of the process will be investigated.

Chapter 1 presents an overview of the Roman Catholic understanding of Jesus Christ. It examines the New Testament portrayal of Jesus in the light of present-day scholarship. It also reviews the teachings of the first six ecumenical councils on Christology. I follow this with a summary of the teachings concerning Jesus of St. Anselm of Canterbury and St. Thomas Aquinas. As will be seen, from the time of St. Thomas's death in the thirteenth century until the middle of the twentieth century, his Christology dominated Catholic thinking. St. Thomas's Christology for the most part dealt with questions concerning Jesus's inner makeup: his intellect, his soul, his knowledge, his subjection to the Father, and so on. Catholic Christology in the second half of the twentieth century has made considerable advances over its medieval and neoscholastic predecessor. Physical, historical, and linguistic methods, known to us only for approximately the past 125 years, have produced a scientifically critical study of the Bible—a study, according to Raymond Brown in *Crisis Facing the Church*, that has "revolutionized views held in the past about the authorship, origin, and dating of the biblical books, about how they were composed and about what their authors meant" (1975, p. 8). The most significant development in contemporary Christology has been a recovery of the *full humanity* of Jesus in a manner that at the same time respects His divinity, as we shall see. Other late twentieth-century studies in liberation, feminist, and ecological Christologies will be briefly presented. Finally, I will analyze negative criticisms of the traditional understanding of Jesus, especially in the work of the Jesus Seminar, together with appropriate Catholic responses to their methodology and conclusions.

Chapter 2 discusses the question of the exercise of authority in the Church and the desire of many Catholics for a more collegial sharing of it. It is evident that authority is under attack in the Catholic Church, at least from the viewpoint of a shared authority. Although the Church is not a democracy, neither is it an absolute monarchy. Rather it is a community comprising both ordained and lay members. The question asked by many Catholics is how the Church can better express a shared authority. In answer to this question I present a brief historical review of papal authority. I will illustrate that the basic problem concerning authority for many of today's Catholics lies in the centralization of authority in Rome and the lack of shared decision making by the pope in relation to the bishops of the Church and to the entire Catholic community. The meaning of *collegiality* at all levels of the Church will be discussed, including the role of the bishops in relation to the pope, episcopal conferences, the selection of bishops, priests' senates, and diocesan and parish councils. The chapter continues with the question of authority as it pertains to the priesthood, including priestly celibacy; women and ministry; the permanent diaconate; religious orders and congregations; the laity; and the local parish. Finally, I will discuss the demands of many Catholics who are urging greater democratization of the structures of Church governance.

Chapter 3 deals with Catholicism as a global church together with the problem of inculturation—in other words, recognition that the Church must be rooted in the various cultures of the world and not only in the culture of Europe or North America. In becoming Christian the peoples of the world are expected to be fully themselves in their respective historical contexts and to enrich the universal Christian community with their particular cultural heritage. I will consider examples of inculturation from earlier periods in Church history, such as the accomplishments of Saints Cyril and Methodius among the Slavic people and of the Jesuit Matteo Ricci in China. I will then address recent Church teachings on inculturation, as well as the problem of cultural relativism and the meaning of contextualization as it is manifested in liberation theology. Finally, I will present the history of inculturation and of multiculturalism in the United States, with special emphasis on Hispanics in this country and their relation to both American culture and the Catholic Church. Chapter 3 concludes with a brief overview of Hispanic–American theology.

Chapter 4 deals with the validity of other religions in relation to the Christian claim that salvation through Jesus is unique and final. The future of Roman Catholicism and its relationship to the world religions will be strongly tied to the manner in which this question is answered. I will examine earlier Christian attitudes from sacred scripture and tradition, as well as the modern Catholic position concerning world religions, and I will include an analysis of the meaning of salvation together with the Church's present understanding of the meaning of revelation. This is followed by an examination of Karl Rahner's theory of the "anonymous Christian," in which Rahner sees Jesus as the unique savior of the world in a manner that encompasses all of humankind. Rahner (1904–1984), a Jesuit theologian, certainly ranks among the most important theologians of the twentieth century. The center of Rahner's theology is Christology, with Jesus as God's final and unique revelation to the world. Rahner believed that an all-loving God would not condemn members of other religions or persons without a religion, who through no fault of their own do not accept Jesus Christ. He argues that if we are to take seriously the idea that God wills the salvation of all, it follows that somehow God offers His grace not only to those who have heard and responded in faith to the Gospel but to all human beings through their own concrete religions and to everyone who accepts God's grace in the depths of their own souls. I will examine Rahner's position, and follow this with objections to it raised by two noted Catholic theologians—Hans Küng and Henri de Lubac—and the Lutheran scholar George Lindbeck. I will then give a brief rejoinder to their objections. Chapter 4 continues with an analysis of the position of Roman Catholicism as highlighted at Vatican II. I will finish the chapter with a discussion of the council's insistence on the need of interfaith dialogue and the meaning, purpose, and expectation of such dialogue.

CHAPTER 1

Jesus in Contemporary Catholic Thought

Because the foundation of the Church's life and teachings center on Jesus Christ, we will begin with an examination of the Church's understanding of Jesus as the Son of God. This chapter will present the current methodology of Catholic scriptural scholarship; a brief historical survey of the Church's teachings about Jesus, including the early Church, ecumenical councils, the medieval period, and advances in contemporary Catholic scholarship that deepen one's understanding not only of Jesus's divinity but also of His humanity. I will then present other developments in post-Vatican II studies concerning Jesus, such as liberation, feminist, and ecological Christologies. Finally, I will discuss the problem of the *Jesus of history* and the *Christ of faith* in light of the recent and highly publicized writings of the Jesus Seminar and others who have attacked the reliability of the New Testament portrayal of Jesus. I will complete the chapter with responses to these critics from notable Catholic scholars such as John Meier, Luke Timothy Johnson, and Raymond Brown.

JESUS: THE SON OF GOD

The Catholic faith proclaims that Jesus Christ is the Son of God, the second person of the Trinity. Jesus, who is recognized by Christians as the Christ, was crucified on a cross and Christians believe He rose from the dead. He is understood to be personally active in the Church and in the world today. At Vatican II the centrality of Christ to the Church was stressed. Though the council was primarily concerned with a renewal of the Church, it was animated in part by a refocusing of the primary role of Jesus in the life of the Church.

Many of the documents of Vatican II are based on strong Christological statements. For example, the *Pastoral Constitution on the Church in the Modern World* states that Christ is "the goal of human history, the focal point of the desires of history and civilization, the center of mankind, the joy of all hearts, and the fulfillment to all aspirations."[1] *The Constitution on the Sacred Liturgy* described the Paschal Mystery of Christ as the norm that guides the revision of the liturgy.[2] Similar Christological statements are presented throughout the documents of the council.

The Christological focus was not developed in any detail at Vatican II, but in subsequent years more has been written by Catholic scholars on the person and meaning of Jesus Christ than in the previous three centuries combined. Christology, it should be noted, is the study of the person of Jesus Christ and who he is, past and present. The sources of Christology are the New Testament, in particular the four Gospels, as well as Christian tradition and contemporary human experience. The proper object of Christology is not simply the historical Jesus or the Gospels but also the crucified and risen Christ who is present in the Christian community and in the world by means of Christian preaching and scholarship, the sacraments, Christian practice, and human experience.

THE NEW TESTAMENT

The historical life of Jesus of Nazareth is given in the New Testament. Problems associated with an understanding of the historical life of Jesus, such as the intervening years between his Resurrection and the actual writing of the New Testament books, should not lead to a position of historical skepticism. Nor can the Gospels be read in a literal fashion. A middle ground between historical skepticism and fundamentalism recognizes that some historical data can be discovered in the Gospels by means of the historical–critical method. In this regard a helpful guide, but by no means an exhaustive one, was given in the 1964 instruction from the Pontifical Biblical Commission. The document is titled *The Historical Truth of the Gospels* and indicates the presence of at least three stages of tradition within the Gospels that must be taken into account in searching for the historical foundations of the life of Jesus. These stages include (1) the original words and deeds of Jesus, (2) the oral proclamation of the apostles and disciples following the Resurrection, Ascension, and Pentecost experience, and (3) the writing of the New Testament books.[3] The commission makes clear that we do not have in the written Gospels the words and deeds of Jesus as exactly and as completely as when they were first spoken or performed. Nor do we have the exact record of what was communicated orally between the Resurrection of Jesus and the actual composition of the Gospels. What we do have is the finally edited versions given by the evangelists.

The *first stage* of tradition, which deals with the original words and deeds of Jesus, is discovered through *historical criticism,* which is a rather late development in the history of Christian theology and of biblical interpretation. Until the Enlightenment of the eighteenth century it was generally assumed that the Gospels gave a clear and reliable account of the words and deeds of Jesus. This assumption was first challenged by Herman Reimarus (1694–1768), an Enlightenment scholar, and by many subsequent writers. With the use of the tools of modern biblical research scholars continue to get behind the testimonies of faith to the basic historical foundation of Jesus's life and ministry. Recently John Meier, a noted Catholic biblical scholar, who is a professor of New Testament Studies at Notre Dame University, used this method in *A Marginal Jew: Rethinking the Historical Jesus.* Volume 1 was published in 1991 and deals with "The Roots of the Problem and the Person." Volume 2 was published in 1994 and deals with "Mentor, Message, and Miracles."[4] Meier is presently working on Volume 3. In these volumes he deals with the four canonical Gospels, which he argues offer the historian the best opportunity to achieve a genuinely historical picture of Jesus.

Meier's treatment is solid and moderate. He is a careful scholar and considers every opinion and weighs every option. In his first volume he reconstructs what can be known concerning Jesus's origins, family, language, and social status. He then considers issues pertaining to the chronology of Jesus's ministry. In the second volume he turns more directly to Jesus's ministry, considering in turn Jesus's relationship to John the Baptist ("Mentor"), Jesus's message concerning the future and future arrival of the Kingdom of God ("Message"), and Jesus's wonder-working ("Miracles"). Meier searches for those pieces of the Gospel narratives that can, by the strict canons of scientific inquiry, be verified with a high degree of probability. His approach is to locate the pieces that best satisfy all the criteria of science and then to argue in search of a "pattern." In arriving at such patterns Meier must make assumptions, and it is for these instances that he receives some criticism from scholars such as Luke Timothy Johnson, a Catholic who is a New Testament scholar at Emory University in Atlanta, Georgia. Johnson believes that Meier makes some false inferences when he moves from the demonstration concerning specific instances of Jesus's life to the larger patterns. Though Johnson respects Meier's great industry and erudition, he argues that the limits of Meier's approach stem from the limits of the historical–critical method, however valuable that method might be. Johnson argues that "Christian faith has never—either at the start or now—been based on historical reconstructions of Jesus, even though Christian faith has always involved some historical claims concerning Jesus.

Rather, Christian faith (then and now) is based on religious claims concerning the present power of Jesus."[5]

The *second stage* of tradition, which deals with the oral proclamation of the apostles anddisciples following the Resurrection, Ascension, and Pentecost experience, was discovered through a method known as *form criticism,* which was developed in Germany between 1918 and 1940. It is concerned primarily with the formation of the Gospel tradition that occurred after Jesus's Resurrection, chiefly by means of preaching and liturgical expression. The chronology of this stage covers roughly the years between 35 and 60 A.D. It is essentially a means of analyzing typical features of biblical passages such as hymns, sermons, instructional material, sayings of Jesus, dialogues, and so forth, to relate them to their original "situation in life." The development of form criticism made evident the fact that a long period of oral tradition preceded all of the New Testament books.

The *third stage* of tradition, the writing of the New Testament books, is studied by means of *redaction criticism,* the origin of which is in the mid-1950s. This method seeks to discover the dominant ideas that governed the final writing and editing of the Gospels as we have them today. In other words, it seeks to discover the peculiar purpose of each evangelist. Redaction criticism stresses the previous existence of both oral and written traditions from which the New Testament authors worked and that they creatively transformed to suit their particular theological and catechetical intentions.

THE LIFE OF JESUS

Jesus's early years were spent in Nazareth, a city in Galilee, in the northern section of Palestine. With the exception of a brief appearance at the age of 12 in the temple in Jerusalem, his first 30 years were lived in relative obscurity. Jesus's public life began when he was baptized by John the Baptist. His message at this time was, "The time has come, he said, and the kingdom of God is close at hand. Repent and believe the good news" (Mark 1:14). The announcement of the reign of God is central to Jesus's ministry and His mission. The *reign of God* is a symbol of the transforming presence of God in individuals and in the world at large, renewing and reconciling all things. It is both a process (reign of God) and the reality toward which the process is moving (the Kingdom of God).

Jesus used *parables* to introduce His audience to the meaning and the implications of the Kingdom of God. Some of His parables stress the reversal of values that the reign of God brings (Matt. 13:44–46); others are an invitation to live a new kind of life (Matt. 25:31–36). The *miracles* performed by Jesus are expressions and signs of the triumph of the reign of God in the present. This is especially true of His healing miracles. They point to the final arrival of the Kingdom at the Second Coming of Jesus, when total harmony will be inaugurated. Also central to Jesus's preaching concerning the reign of God is His call to *faith* or *conversion*. Jesus also set up a new *table fellowship,* the Eucharistic meal, among the socially and religiously marginalized people of Palestine, notably tax collectors and sinners. This new table fellowship symbolizes the inclusive character of the Kingdom of God. Through the Eucharist, Jesus invites his followers to a table of fellowship that is an anticipation of the heavenly banquet itself, one that is open to everyone.

Jesus issued a *call to discipleship* and formed communities of equality among women and men, rich and poor. His Kingdom-centered mission is animated in particular by His personal experience of God or *Abba* (Father), described by some scholars as the source and ground of Jesus's ministry.

Jesus's preaching and actions eventually led Him into conflict with the religious and political leaders of His day. He became a serious challenge to the status quo. For example, He was criticized for breaking the Sabbath, for claiming to forgive sins, for calling God His father, for eating and drinking with sinners, for setting Himself above the authority of Moses, for casting out demons, and for promising salvation. This conflict came to a head in Jerusalem when Jesus cast the money changers out of the temple (Mark 11:15–17). This event was followed by his Last Supper, his arrest and condemnation, and finally his death on the cross.

Jesus's crucifixion shattered the hopes of his disciples. However, on the third day Jesus rose from the dead. This event restored and transformed their faith. They were empowered by the Holy Spirit and sent forth to preach the good news.

THE RESURRECTION

The Christian faith stands or falls on Jesus's Resurrection from the dead. As St. Paul wrote, "and if Christ has not been raised, your faith is in vain; you are still in your sins. Then those also who have fallen asleep in Christ have perished" (1 Cor. 15:17–18). But Jesus was raised from the dead. And just as "death came through a human being" so "the resurrection of the dead came also through a human being. For just as in Adam all die, so too in Christ shall all be brought to life" (1 Cor. 15:21–22).

No one witnessed the actual moment of Jesus's Resurrection. Was it, then, a historical event? The answer is no, at least not in the ordinary sense of the term *historical event,* which implies the action is open to scientific investigation and verifiable by neutral witnesses. But this does not mean that the Resurrection was not a *real* event for Jesus, with historical implications for others. The disciples were convinced that they had seen Him, so for them the appearances are historical. Nevertheless, it would seem better to speak of the Resurrection as *transhistorical* or *metahistorical* rather than *unhistorical*, because many would understand the term to imply that it never happened. As Richard McBrien wrote,

> It is transhistorical, or metahistorical, in the sense that it refers to an event which lies beyond the confines of space and time. Similarly, the reality of the risen Lord is also *a reality which transcends history as we know it* [emphasis mine]. By the resurrection Jesus enters a completely new universe of being, the end-time of history, beyond the control of history and beyond the reach of historians.[6]

The question of the *bodiliness* of the Resurrection is very important. There is no justification for reducing the meaning of Jesus's Resurrection, as some have done, to something like "the continuing significance of Jesus" or "the disciples' realization that Jesus's message could not die." By "Resurrection" the early Christians meant, as the New Testament time and again reiterates, that something happened *to Jesus himself*. God had raised *him*, not merely reassured *them*. He was alive again. The bodily element is clear in the description of some of the post-Resurrection appearances of Jesus to His disciples. The evangelists speak of touching (John 20:27), eating (Luke 24:41–43), and conversing (John 21:15–22) in relation to Jesus. This makes clear the underlying unity between the Jesus of history and the risen Lord.

Yet there is something radically different about Jesus's *bodiliness* following the Resurrection. New Testament writers present different conceptions of what a "resurrected body" is. In Luke's account Jesus's resurrected body is very physical: Jesus Himself says, "Look at my hands and my feet, that it is I myself. Touch me and see, because a ghost does not have flesh and bones as you can see I have" (Luke 24:39). Paul, however, makes a clear distinction (1 Cor. 15: 42–46) between the body of this life (*sarx* = physical body) and the resurrected body (*soma pneumaticon* = spiritual body). There is something *radically different* about Jesus's *body* following the Resurrection. The Resurrection was not simply the resuscitation of a dead body. It is noteworthy, for example, that the disciples did not recognize Him as He stood before them (Luke 24:16; John 20:14, 21:4). He also is portrayed as coming and going in a manner unlike that of any mortal body (Luke 24:31; John 20:19, 26). Mark explicitly wrote that he appeared "in another form" (Mark 16:12). Though the resurrected body is a "spiritual body," Paul made clear that there is a continuity between the person that was and the person that will be. But there is a difference as evidenced in Jesus's resurrected body, and Paul used the analogy of the relation between the *body* of the seed and the *body* of the plant, an analogy of continuity but also of difference between different bodies. In 1 Corinthians 15:35–38 Paul wrote, "But someone may say, 'How are the dead raised? With what kind of body will they come back?' You fool! What you saw is not brought to life unless it dies. And what you saw is not the body that is to be but a bare kernel of wheat, perhaps, or of some other kind; but God gives it a body as he chooses, and to each of the seeds its own body."

The Christian claim concerning the Resurrection of Jesus is not that He returned to His former manner of living but rather that after His death He entered into an entirely new form of existence, one in which He shared His power as God with others. The Resurrection experience is not simply something that happened to Jesus: It is something that was shared by His followers. The sharing in Jesus's new life through the power of the Holy Spirit is an essential dimension of the Resurrection. The Spirit proceeds from the "Lord of the Spirit, and through Jesus' Resurrection has become a life-giving spirit" (1 Corinthians 15:45). The risen and exhalted Lord releases the Spirit and the Spirit builds the Church. Experience and conviction together form the primordial *Resurrection experience* that founded the Christian movement and continues to inform it today.

On the basis of their experience of the Resurrection Jesus's disciples saw the life and death of Jesus in a whole new light. They reinterpreted everything He had said and done, recalling and reconstructing it to the best of their ability. Brown discussed this reinterpretation in light of titles attributed to Jesus in the New Testament. He believes the main Christological distinction among contemporary New Testament scholars is centered on the kind of Christology detectable in the ministry of Jesus, which he refers to as explicit or implicit Christology.[7] Brown deals expressly with the titles attributed to Jesus in the New Testament. It is evident that the complete picture of how Jesus thought of Himself and how others thought of Him goes beyond the question of His titles. At the same time, however, the titles are valuable pointers to what others thought of Jesus and possibly to what he thought of himself.

EXPLICIT CHRISTOLOGY

Explicit Christology is a Christology that evaluates Jesus in terms of the titles known to the Jews from the Old Testament or from the period between the completion of the Old Testament and the beginning of the New Testament. Brown observes that it would be difficult to find contemporary support for the thesis that Jesus used Himself or accepted the higher titles of later New Testament Christologies such as "Lord" in the full sense, "Son of God," or "God." This does not mean that scholars who deny Jesus's use of these titles are saying that Jesus was not Lord, Son of God, or God. It means that they regard the application of such designations to later (post-Resurrection) Christian reflection on the mystery of Jesus. But there are many exponents of explicit Christology who think that during His ministry Jesus referred to Himself or accepted the designation of Messiah, or Prophet, or Servant of God, or Son of Man, the "lower" titles of Christology. According to Brown, most Roman Catholic writers of the 1960s were adherents of explicit Christology.[8]

IMPLICIT CHRISTOLOGY

In recent years there has been more acceptance of *implicit Christology* by most Roman Catholic scholars. Adherents of implicit Christology maintain that Jesus did not express His self-understanding in terms of titles or accept titles attributed to Him by others. Rather He conveyed what He was by speaking with unique authority and by acting with unique power. By His words and deeds he proclaimed that the reign of God was making itself present in Him in such a way that a response to His ministry was a response to God. Yet this implicit claim to uniqueness was not phrased in titles reflecting the traditional expectations of Judaism. As Brown observes, for example, those scholars who think Jesus did not use or accept the title "Messiah" are not necessarily detracting from the greatness of Jesus. He writes,

> Indeed, a greater claim can be made for Jesus if he did not find the title "Messiah" acceptable. It may mean that his conception of himself was so unique that the title did not match his uniqueness—the Church was able to call him Messiah successfully only when it reinterpreted the title to match Jesus' greatness. Thus the ultimate tribute to what and who Jesus was may have been that every term or title in the theological language of his people had to be reshaped by his followers to do justice to him, including the title "God" itself.[9]

Gerald O'Collins, S.J., in *Christology: A Biblical, Historical, and Systematic Study of Jesus,* deals clearly and succinctly with the question of titles attributed to or accepted by Jesus. This book is highly recommended for anyone interested in understanding the major issues of Christology today.[10]

THE EARLY CHURCH

Jesus, the One who proclaimed the Kingdom of God in His own lifetime became, after His death and Resurrection, the One proclaimed. Catholic scholars trace a *discernible continuity* between the evaluation of Jesus during His ministry and the evaluation of Him in the New Testament writings. The idea that St. Paul was the *inventor* of Christianity ignores Paul's own testimony of his relationship to the Christian community. Paul reported that he went twice to Jerusalem, once three years after his calling to "report to Cephas" (Gal. 1:18) and again 14 years later, when the three leaders of the Jerusalem church, Peter, James, and John, reached an agreement about the mission to the Gentiles (Gal. 2:7–9). He speaks of his own mission to the Gentiles, in fact, as extending "from Jerusalem to Illyricum" (Rom. 15:19), immediately before declaring his intention to travel back to Jerusalem with his collection for the members of that community (Rom. 15:25).

As for the content of his preaching in 1 Corinthians 15:1–13, Paul insisted that he proclaimed to his communities what he had also received, and that his preaching was in agreement with the other apostles: "Whether it was I or they, so we preach, and so you believed" (1 Cor. 15:11). The historian who wants to construct a version of Christian origins on a basis totally other than this must actively suppress Paul's own explicit declarations.

THE EARLY CHRISTIAN PERIOD

From the outset the driving force behind theological inquiry and official teaching about Jesus was clearly the experience of salvation. Having experienced through Him the forgiveness of sins, the gift of the Holy Spirit, and the new life of grace in the community, Christians asked themselves, What questions does this experience of salvation raise about Jesus, His being, and His identity? What does Christ experienced by me say about Christ Himself? These questions were inevitable and were further stimulated by the challenge of dissident opinions and by the need to communicate the Christian message across cultural lines.

Exaggerations concerning Jesus's divinity or His humanity soon appeared among some Christian thinkers. One group, the Docetists (from the Greek, *dokein*, "to seem, appear") taught that the body of Christ only appeared to be real; Jesus only "seemed" to have a human body. This teaching was explicitly condemned by Ignatius of Antioch early in the second century. The roots of Docetism seem to be linked to a belief that materiality, including human flesh, is evil. The doctrine found many allies among Gnostics of the second and third centuries and among Pelagians of the fifth century. Among the strongest adversaries of Docetism were those early Christians who defended the orthodox view of the full humanity of Jesus Christ, such as Polycarp, Irenaeus, and Tertullian. Another group, the Adoptionists, basically denied the divinity of Jesus and taught that He was only human but became the *adopted* Son of God. Some early Christian communities, known as Ebionites, espoused this position and spoke of Jesus being *adopted* as Son of God because of His moral perfection. This position was quickly condemned by Christian writers.

CHRISTOLOGICAL COUNCILS

Beginning in the fourth century and continuing through the seventh, six ecumenical councils were held to articulate an understanding of the Church's belief in Jesus Christ, especially as this belief is conveyed in scripture and creeds. Ecumenical councils are exercises of the collegial authority of the bishops of the Church in tandem with the pope.

The Council of Nicaea (325 A.D.)

Arius (c. 260–c. 336), who was born in Libya and became a presbyter (priest) in Alexandria, was the primary reason Emperor Constantine convened the first general (ecumenical) Church council in 325 A.D. Arius taught that the Son was not coeternal with the Father but was the only creature directly created by the Father. In turn, the Son carried out the will of the Father by creating everything else. Jesus was understood as a created intermediary between the Father and the human race. The Son was not truly God and not equal to God the Father. There was a time when the Son did not exist. (Arius had practically nothing to say about the Holy Spirit.) The Council of Nicaea condemned Arius, rejected the subordination of the Son to the Father, and stated as part of the Nicene Creed that the Son "is true God from true God, begotten not made, of one substance/being [Greek: *homoousios*] with the Father." Nicaea spoke out clearly for Christ's divinity, but the issues raised by Arius caused continuing controversy.

The First Council of Constantinople (381 A.D.)

The First Council of Constantinople condemned Apollinarius of Laodicea, who denied that Jesus had a human intellect or rational soul. Apollinarius held that the divine logos (word) became embodied in human flesh but that Jesus had only one nature, the divine. The First Council condemned him as a heretic, because Jesus was understood to have *two natures, the divine and the human*. In fact the council did not produce any new Christological dogma. However, it did accept the Nicene Creed, which was formulated in 325 A.D. with certain modifications. The creed issued at the Council of Nicaea is not the creed popularly known as the Nicene Creed, however. What is commonly called the Nicene Creed is the creed affirmed by the Council of Constantinople in 381 and is formally called the Nicene–Constantinopolitan Creed. Longer than the creed issued at Nicaea, the creed of Contantinople includes a fuller treatment of the Holy Spirit, which certain Christian groups had denied. Constantinople put Trinitarian language firmly in place. The identification of the creed of Constantinople with that of Nicaea occurred at the Council of Chalcedon (451 A.D.), when the bishops understood the Council of Constantinople as essentially affirming the faith of Nicaea with an expanded teaching on the Holy Spirit.

The Council of Ephesus (431 A.D.)

The third ecumenical council condemned Nestorius, who was patriarch of Constantinople from 428 A.D. until he was deposed by the Council of Ephesus in 431 A.D. He was condemned as a heretic for teaching there were *two separate persons* in Christ, one divine and the other human, in contrast to the orthodox teaching that in Christ there is only one divine person. Because of his failure to understand the unity of the two natures in the one divine person, Nestorius refused to speak of Mary as the Mother of God, another orthodox position; thus he was condemned by the Church.

The Council of Chalcedon (451 A.D.)

The fourth ecumenical council was the greatest of the first four general councils of the Church. The Council of Chalcedon expressed in clear terms the Church's scriptural understanding and traditional faith in the unity (one person) and distinction (two natures) of Christ. The immediate occasion of the council came from Eutyches, the head of a monastery in Constantinople, who apparently taught that the unity in Christ was such that only one nature remained in Christ after the Incarnation, the human nature being absorbed or overshadowed by the divine nature. This position is known as Monophysitism (Greek: *mono* = "one"; *physis* = "nature"). The council affirmed the one person of Christ in His two natures, the divine and human, and held that the two natures existed "without confusion or change, and without division or separation" while belonging to only one person. In other words, the unity of Christ exists on the level of person, the duality on that of His natures. The council also stated, quoting Hebrews 4:15, that Jesus was "like unto us in all things but sin."

Nearly 600 bishops attended the Council of Chalcedon, including three papal legates and two representatives of Latin Africa. It was by far the largest and most important Council of the early Church. In affirming that the unity of Christ exists on the level of person and the duality on that of His natures, the council proved a lasting success in regulating language

about Christ. The terminology "one person in two natures" became normative even into the twentieth century and beyond, into the twenty-first century. Chalcedon provided a logical conclusion to the first three councils.
Against Arianism, the First Council of Nicaea reaffirmed that Christ is divine. Against Apollinarianism, the First Council of Constantinople affirmed
that Christ is fully human. Against Nestorius, the Council of Ephesus professed that Christ's two natures are not separated. And against Eutyches,
Chalcedon taught that, although belonging to one person, the two natures
are not merged or confused. One can appreciate the way the first four councils became acknowledged as representing the essential and orthodox norm
for understanding and interpreting the Christological (and Trinitarian)
faith of the New Testament.

One of the key definitions from Chalcedon is worth noting. It states,

> Following, therefore, the holy fathers, we confess one and the same Son,
> who is our Lord Jesus Christ, and we all agree in teaching that this very
> same Son is complete in his deity and complete—the very same—in his
> humanity, truly God and truly a human being, the very same one being
> composed of a rational soul and body, coessential (*homoousios*) with the
> Father as to his deity and coessential with us—the very same one—as
> to his humanity, being like us in every respect apart from sin (cf. Heb.
> 4:15). As to his deity, he was born from the Father before all ages, but as
> to his humanity, the very same one was born in the last days from the
> Virgin Mary, the Mother of God, for our sake and for the sake of our sal-
> vation: one and the same Christ, Son, Lord, Only Begotten, acknowl-
> edged to be unconfusedly, unalterably, undividedly, inseparably in two
> natures, since the difference of the natures is not destroyed because of
> the union, but on the contrary, the character of each nature is preserved
> and comes together in one person and one hypostasis, not divided or
> torn into two persons but one and the same Son and only begotten God,
> Logos, Lord Jesus Christ—just as in earlier times the prophets and also
> the Lord Jesus Christ himself taught us about him, and the symbol of
> our Fathers transmitted to us.[11]

The Second Council of Constantinople (553 A.D.)

The fifth ecumenical council basically repeated the definition of Chalcedon
and reiterated its condemnation of Nestorianism. It condemned Theodore of
Mopsuestia (d. 428 A.D.), Ibas of Edessa (d. 457 A.D.), and Theodoret of
Cyrrhus (d. c. 958 A.D.) on the grounds of Nestorianism.

The Third Council of Constantinople (680–681 A.D.)

The sixth ecumenical council condemned Monothelitism (Greek: *mono* =
"one"; *theleis* = "will"), which taught that Jesus had only a divine will. In an

effort to reconcile the Monophysites with the Church, Pope Honorius I followed the advice of Sergius, the patriarch of Constantinople (610–638), and spoke of Christ possessing "one will." Such a teaching threatened belief in Christ's full humanity, as if the human nature of Christ lacked an essential faculty, its will. The council declared that Christ possesses two wills, one divine and one human, as well as two natures. The council also excommunicated the late Pope Honorius.

Doctrinal development of Christology stopped at the Third Council of Constantinople. When Christological dogma was dealt with by subsequent councils of the Church, it was always simply a matter of reiterating the teachings of one of these earlier councils, especially Nicaea, Ephesus, and Chalcedon. This is still the case in various papal encyclicals and decrees of Roman congregations in recent years.

CHRISTOLOGY IN THE MIDDLE AGES

In the Middle Ages, questions about the identity and mission of Jesus were treated by such scholars as St. Anselm of Canterbury and St. Thomas Aquinas in a systematic manner. Following are brief reviews of both.

St. Anselm of Canterbury

St. Anselm of Canterbury (c. 1033–1109) made significant contributions to Christological discussion. He was a monk, theologian, and became archbishop of Canterbury in 1093. His *Cur Deus Homo?* (Why Did God Become Man?), written after he became archbishop, describes Christ's death on the cross as an act of "satisfaction," returning to God the honor stolen by human sin. "Satisfaction," a nonbiblical term drawn from Roman law and applied by Tertullian (c. 160– 225 A.D.), a Latin Christian writer and Apologist from Roman Africa, took pride of place in Anselm's theory of redemption. Anselm proposed that satisfaction required more than the Incarnation. Jesus *had to do* something that He as a human being was not required to do. Because all sin offends the honor of the infinite God, the reparation must have infinite value. Only the God–man can offer something of infinite value. Because Jesus was sinless, He was not bound to die. But He endured death nonetheless as a payment of the debt incurred by our sins. In doing so He compensated for those sins.

Anselm's theory of satisfaction has often been criticized for being juridical and Roman. In fact, its cultural roots were found instead in the feudal society of northern Europe. So far from being a legal and private matter, the "honorable" service owed by vassals to their lords was a social factor that guaranteed order, peace, and freedom. Denying honor to the lords

meant chaos. A demand for satisfaction, therefore, is not for the sake of ap-
peasing the lord's personal sense of honor but for the sake of restoring order
to the "universe" (the feudal system) in which and against which the sin
was committed. As McBrien observes, "The feudal lord cannot simply over-
look the offense, because the order of his whole economic and social world
is at stake. So, too, with God."[12]

Anselm's "inculturation" of the theology of redemption was more vul-
nerable on other grounds: its nonbiblical version of justice and sin. Concerning this O'Collins writes,

> Rather than expressing God's fidelity to all creatures and, especially, to
> human beings, Anselm's commutative notion of justice seemed to pic-
> ture God as so bound to an abstract order of things that it would be "un-
> thinkable" simply to grant forgiveness without requiring reparation.
> Likewise, instead of interpreting sin very clearly as an infidelity and
> disobedience which bring a break in personal relationship with a loving
> God, Anselm understood it more as an infinite dishonour that upset the
> just order of things. Although elsewhere he richly recognized the role of
> God's merciful love, *Cur deus homo* contained only a brief closing refer-
> ence to the divine mercy.[13]

St. Thomas Aquinas

St. Thomas Aquinas (c. 1225–1274), in his *Summa Theologica*, modified
Anselm's theory, arguing that it was *fitting* for God to act in the manner described by Anselm but it was *not necessary,* as Anselm had insisted.[14] St.
Thomas mitigates Anselm's thesis by maintaining that God could pardon
sin even though adequate satisfaction was not made, and he goes on to say
that Christ's suffering and death was a meritorious sacrifice that was accepted by God as being inspired by love.[15] Unfortunately St. Thomas understood the specific point of sacrifice to be that of placating God and in general
dealt with Christ's suffering and death in light of satisfaction as the part of
a particular form of justice—namely, penance, which involves a punitive element. This opened the way in subsequent years to the idea of propitiating
an angry God by paying a redemptive ransom. Thus altered, Anselm's theory entered the wider stream of medieval and then postmedieval theology.
Over the years many Catholics have incorrectly assumed it to be a matter
of doctrine, even dogma, which it is not. Through Luther and Calvin, Protestantism accepted Anselm's theory in a severe form—namely that Christ
died as our *substitute,* in *punishment* for our sins. However, it should be
noted that St. Thomas himself denies that Christ's work of reconciliation
means that God began to love us again only after the ransom was paid.
God's love for us is everlasting; it is *we who are changed* by the washing
away of sin and the offering of a suitable compensation.[16]

From the medieval period until the middle of the twentieth century (specifically, the 1500th anniversary of the Council of Chalcedon in 1951) Catholic Christology is really a series of commentaries on St. Thomas's *Summa Theologica*, even retaining the *Summa's* basic structure.

O'Collins argues that any summary of St. Thomas's Christological achievement should include the following five ideas: (1) Christ is not pictured as a merely passive victim but freely consented to His suffering and death. (2) Though one may wonder whether Aristotelian thought really shaped and structured Aquinas's Christology or simply remained a useful language and surface terminology, it is clear that he followed the Church fathers in doing theology by combining the best biblical exegesis of his time and the best philosophy he could find. (3) In discussing the different facets of Christ's mediatorship, Aquinas endorsed the helpful scheme of priest–prophet–king. (4) His great attention to the "mysteries" of Christ's life stood in judgment over many subsequent Christologies and their neglect of Jesus's human story. (5) Aquinas highlighted the Incarnation but he did not allow an all-absorbing theology of the Incarnation. Unlike many of his predecessors and successors he treated Christ's Resurrection at considerable length.[17]

St. Thomas's Christology dealt for the most part with questions concerning Christ's inner makeup: his intellect, soul, knowledge, grasp of the beatific vision, powers, capacity for suffering, subjection to the Father, and so on. However, he also dealt with Christ's meaning for the human race and for Christians as His sons and daughters. But the Christologies of subsequent centuries focused on Christ *as He is in Himself* rather than *for us*. Christology and Soteriology grew farther and farther apart. Soteriology literally means "the study of salvation." It is that area of theology that focuses on the suffering, death, Resurrection, and exaltation of Christ insofar as they bring about the salvation of the human race.

CONTEMPORARY CATHOLIC CHRISTOLOGY

Recent Advances

Catholic Christology in the second half of the twentieth century has made considerable advances over its medieval and neoscholastic predecessors. Physical, historical, and linguistic methods, known to us for only approximately the past 125 years, have produced a scientifically critical study of the Bible, "a study that has revolutionized views held in the past about the authorship, origin, and dating of the biblical books, about how they were composed, and about what their authors mean."[18] In the early years of the twentieth century (1900–1940, approximately) the Catholic Church strongly opposed such biblical criticism because of what was perceived as its misuse by a number of scholars who were called Modernists. But in the 1940s, under the leadership of Pope Pius XII, the Church reversed its position. Pope Pius XII's encyclical *Divino Afflante Spiritu* (Inspired by the Holy Spirit; 1943) instructed Catholic scholars to use the methods formerly forbidden to them. In 1964 the Church moved beyond the position of Pope Pius XII when the Pontifical Biblical Commission's *The Historical Truth of the Gospels* made clear to Catholics that the Gospels are *not* literal, chronological accounts of the words and deeds of Jesus but are the product of a development through years of preaching, selection, synthesizing, and explication.[19] Biblical scholarship has affected theology in a number of ways, not the least of which is Christology.

Christology "From Above"; Christology "From Below"

The distinction between Christology "from above" and Christology "from below" did not come into general use until after Vatican II and was explicitly defined by Karl Rahner in a lecture given in Munich in 1971.[20]

Christology "from above" begins with *the preexistent Word of God* in heaven, who "comes down" to earth to take on human flesh and to redeem us by dying on the cross, rising from the dead, and returning to enjoy an exalted state as Lord in heaven. This was the dominant form of Catholic Christology from the medieval period until Vatican II. Notable scholars in this group include Teilhard de Chardin, Piet Schoonenberg, Parimundo Pannikar, and Hans Urs von Balthasar.

Christology "from below" begins with the Jesus of history, a *human being like us in all things except sin,* who stands out from the rest of the human race by His proclamation of, and commitment to the Kingdom, or Reign, of God. His life of dedicated service to others led Him to the cross, from which God raised Him up and exalted Him. As will be seen in the following sections, this is the dominant approach of Catholic Christology today as found in the writings of Catholic writers such as Leonardo Boff, Anne Carr, Elizabeth Johnson, Hans Küng, Karl Rahner, Edward Schillebeeckx, and Jon Sobrino, among others.

The Humanity of Jesus

The most significant development in contemporary Christology has been a recovery of the full humanity of Jesus in a manner that at the same time respects His divinity. Although Christianity has always taught that Jesus reveals God to the world, Vatican II states in the *Pastoral Constitution on the*

Church in the Modern World that the same Jesus "fully reveals man to himself and brings to light his most high calling."[21] The document also directs attention to the humanity of Jesus, noting that "[h]uman nature, by the very fact it was assumed, not absorbed, in him . . . He acted with a human will, and with a human heart he loved."[22] The council also discussed the relationship between Christology and eschatology (in this context the Second Coming of Christ) by emphasizing that Christ is the ground and goal of humanity, history, and creation, and that the Paschal Mystery (Easter) is the key to the future of the world.[23] Another very significant teaching shifts from an exclusivist Christology (only Christianity brings salvation) to an inclusivist Christology by acknowledging the spiritual and moral values of other world religions.[24]

During the past 25 years Catholic biblical scholars and theologians have dealt with the humanity of Jesus in many books and articles. The difficulties in defining His humanity have been a result, at least in part, of the stress placed by Christian thinkers on His divinity. This emphasis of Jesus as divine has been done to the extent that many Christians find it hard to understand Jesus as fully human. The Church stressed Jesus's divinity because opposition to this belief has been more prevalent through the centuries than denial of His humanity, especially among scholars. In stressing divinity, not enough appreciation has been given to the Chalcedonian view (and biblical teaching) that Jesus is truly human as well.

In regard to Jesus's nature, insufficient attention was paid to many biblical passages that reveal His humanity. Paul, for example, pointed out in Philippians 2:6–7, "Who, though he was in the form of God, did not regard equality with God something to be grasped. Rather, he *emptied himself,* taking the form of a slave, *coming in human likeness;* and *found human* in appearance, he *humbled himself* becoming obedient to death, even death on a cross" [emphasis mine]. Scholars are paying attention to this passage, because it refers to Jesus's *kenosis* (emptying), whereby He emptied Himself from a condition in which divine attributes, including omniscience, were fully operative, to a state in which He took on a fully human nature. And yet from the very beginning of His earthly life he was indeed divine as well as human. Therein lies the mystery of the Incarnation.

Among solidly orthodox Catholic theologians, two basic theories are offered in an attempt to show the relationship between Jesus's divinity and humanity. A particular concern is the question of whether or not Jesus was limited in His human knowledge—that is, in regard to His own self-knowledge.

Some theologians maintain that because of the *hypostatic union* (the union of the divine and human natures in the one infinite person) or because of special enlightenment given to him by the *beatific vision* (the clear, immediate sight of God) or infused knowledge, Jesus simply could not be limited in human knowledge. Certainly there were no limitations in matters of religion, or of the future, or in matters regarding Himself. This attitude was long held by Catholicism. In 1907, for example, Pope Pius X maintained that no scholar could teach that Jesus did not have unlimited knowledge.[25] For most Catholics there is an instinctive distaste, therefore, regarding any discussion that maintains that Jesus's human knowledge was in any way limited. It seems to imply a degrading of Christ and certainly violates Catholic sensitivities.

And yet adherents to a second theory on the relationship of Jesus's divinity and humanity argue, and offer solid biblical evidence for their reasoning, that neither the hypostatic union nor other possible privileges necessarily granted Jesus extraordinary knowledge. Proponents of this theory tend to attribute to Jesus an intuitive knowledge or immediate awareness of who He was, but they maintain that He had gradually to acquire the ability to express this to Himself and then to others over a period of time, not of necessity but because He willed freely out of love to *empty Himself* and truly become a human being. It is at the very core of human experience that one grapples with the question of self-identification and that only through trial and error, often mixed with pain, does an individual really come to terms with a clear sense of his or her essence. So, too, did Jesus, who was human as well as God.

It will be useful to present a few of the many scriptural insights offered in support of the second theory. In regard to Jesus's knowledge of the ordinary affairs of life, there are texts in the Gospels that seem to indicate that He shared normal human ignorance about everyday matters. There are other texts that attribute to Him extraordinary and even superhuman knowledge about such affairs. Two texts that indicate ordinary human knowledge, for example, are Mark 5:30–33 and Luke 2:46–52. In Mark 5:30–33, a woman in a crowd touches Jesus's garments and is healed by His miraculous power. When Jesus perceives that miraculous power has gone forth from Him, He asks who touched Him. His disciples think this a rather odd question because there was so much jostling by the crowd, but the woman understands and confesses it was she. The narrative seems clearly to presuppose ignorance on Jesus's part regarding who touched him and who was healed. In Luke 2:46–52 Jesus is described in the Temple at the age of 12 astounding the rabbis with His intelligent questions and His knowledge. Then in Luke 2:52 we are told that following the incident Jesus went home with His parents and grew in wisdom, as well as in stature and in favor with God and humankind. The evangelist did not seem to think it was strange that Jesus should ask questions or grow in wisdom.

The Church teaches that Jesus had a human soul and thus a human intellect. Many modern biblical scholars ask if the Church can admit that Jesus's intellect was *tabula rasa* (literally, a blank slate) when he was born. They also ask whether it is possible to maintain that Jesus's intellect was not activated by infused knowledge but by human experiences, as is true of all other human beings. Their response is that scriptural evidence points in this direction. If so, it would have taken Jesus time to formulate concepts, and He might have found some of the prevalent ideas of His day—such as the notion of Messiah—inadequate to express what He wanted to say. One would then be able to say that His knowledge was limited, but such limitation would not exclude an intuitive consciousness of who He was and His unique mission to humankind. His life struggle would have been to discover the proper concepts and words to adequately express Himself, both to Himself and to His followers.[26]

What is being proposed is that Jesus, though "true God of true God" from the beginning of His earthly experience, was also a true human being in the fullest sense of the words. He was not *acting* as though he were a mere man—in other words, He was not performing a charade throughout His life but He was truly a human being, learning as all people do, while at the same time conscious of His divinity. Thus in the Garden of Gethsemane, even though by then Jesus was fully aware of His divinity, He was indeed terrified and, thus, experienced the bloody sweat. And on the cross, when He cried out, "My God, my God, why have you forsaken me?" (Matt. 27:46), he was not simply quoting the first verse of Psalm 22:1 as though calling attention to an earlier prophecy but He actually *felt* abandoned by the Father. Nevertheless, He submitted Himself to His Father's will. Such an evaluation of the Gospel evidence, if correct, does nothing to detract from the dignity of Jesus. If anything, it shows just how loving God is to become fully human in all ways except sin, and it allows Christians to identify even more perfectly with Jesus as a brother who took on the nature of humankind and willingly submitted Himself to the trials and tribulations of the human condition. From the Christian perspective, in reaching out to Jesus one really does touch a brother, but in touching Him one is, at the same time, touching and being embraced by God Himself. With such an understanding, Christianity also avoids any danger of making Jesus appear as some kind of mythical, divine being. All danger of Docetism can be laid to rest when one takes the Scriptures as literally as possible and teaches that Jesus was not only true God but was also truly a human being, just as any one of us. Such an understanding can deepen one's personal relationship with Jesus and, at the same time, can produce a great effect on Christian moral life.

OTHER DEVELOPMENTS IN POST-VATICAN II CHRISTOLOGY

There is a pronounced difference between medieval and contemporary Christology. Catholic Christology assumed a new shape as it assimilated not only the advances of twentieth-century New Testament scholarship but also newly emerging liberationist, feminist, and ecological consciousness.

Liberation Christologies

Liberation theologies developed in Latin America. Gustavo Gutierez and the other liberation theologians argue that the primary task of theology and Christology is not to convince the nonbeliever of the *truths* of the Christian faith but rather it is to help free the oppressed from their inhuman living conditions. *Liberation* is used in three senses. First, *liberation* refers to freedom from oppressive economic, social, and political systems. Second, *liberation* means that human beings should take control of their own destiny. Third, *liberation* means being emancipated from sin and accepting a new life in Christ. Liberation Christology focuses on the primacy of practice, especially the practice of liberation within the life of Jesus. The cross of Christ is perceived to symbolize the solidarity of God with the suffering of humanity and the Resurrection reveals the triumph of that divine solidarity. Two of the leading Latin American theologians who have written from this perspective are the Brazilian theologian Leonardo Boff and Jon Sobrino. Boff's best known work on Christology is *Jesus Christ Liberator: A Critical Christology for Our Time.*[27] Sobrino, a Jesuit theologian from El Salvador, is known for his *Christology at the Crossroads.*[28]

Feminist Christologies

Related to liberation Christology is the rise of *feminist Christology,* the adherents of which have studied the New Testament in a way that is liberating for women and men alike. Authors such as Anne Carr and Elizabeth Johnson have made important contributions in this area. Feminist Christology retrieves the neglected presence of women in the ministry of Jesus and exposes the presence of a critique of patriarchy implicit in the preaching and practice of Jesus. Above all, Paul's statement in Galatians 3:28 is singled out: "There is neither Jew nor Greek, there is not male and female; for you are all one in Christ Jesus." In *Transforming Grace: Christian Tradition and Women's Experience,* Carr points out that the classical formulation of the Council of Chalcedon spoke only of the divinity and humanity of Jesus, not His maleness. The symbol of *headship*—good in itself, Carr insists —is one of many that have functioned in a false, ideological, and oppressive way.[29] The starting point for feminist theology is women's *present experience* in the Church—their experience of its communal life, of the sacraments, of the preaching of the Gospel, and of "the corporate and graced awareness of critical Christian feminism."[30] What women find in the Jesus of the Gospels is a person of remarkable freedom and openness to women as seen in His inclusion of women among His disciples, His friendship with Mary Magdalene, His positive use of women in His parables, His breaking of taboos in speaking with the Samaritan and Syro-Phoenician women, and the role of women as the first witnesses of the Resurrection. Carr writes, "The theological symbols of Christian tradition are interpreted today by women within this narrative context that the New Testament stories provide."[31]

Elizabeth Johnson's Christology is situated in the wider context of a theology of God. This is evident in *She Who Is: The Mystery of God in Feminist Theological Discourse*.[32] Johnson uses the same approach in *Consider Jesus: Waves of Renewal in Christology*.[33] Johnson points out that Jesus's maleness poses a problem for feminist theology—not his maleness as such but the distorted manner in which it has been interpreted and used in official androcentric theology and practice. For Johnson the basic elements of a feminist Christology are rooted in the life, death, and Resurrection of Jesus and in the Wisdom tradition of Sacred Scripture. Among these elements are (1) Jesus's preaching, which proclaimed justice and peace for all, women and men alike; (2) the Spirit of the risen Christ was poured out on all who believe, women as well as men, thereby breaking down all artificial divisions between people; and (3) Jesus was identified soon after His Resurrection as *Sophia*, a Wisdom—that is, as one who is "revelatory of the liberating graciousness of God imaged as female. . . ." As a consequence, "Women, asfriends of Jesus—Sophia, share equally with men in his saving mission throughout time and can fully represent Christ, being themselves, in the Spirit, other Christs."[34]

Ecological Christologies

Another development in Christology is a focus on the possibility of an ecological Christology. This perspective highlights the Wisdom Christology of Paul's epistle (Phil. 2:6–11; Rom. 8:19–23; Eph. 1:3–14; Col. 1:15–10); the synoptic Gospels; and the Logos Christology of the Gospel of John. Paul Knitter, a professor of theology at Xavier University in Cincinnati, Ohio, argues that the reformation of Christianity, as can be seen in liberation theology, begins by hearing the cry of the oppressed people or the *oppressed earth*. This must be done in common with members of other religions, and all must respond to those needs. He argues, as do many other theologians, that dialogue with the world religions is critically important. In *One Earth, Many Religions,* published in 1995, Knitter proposes a "multi-normed, soteriocentric" (salvation-) oriented approach to dialogue "based on the common ground of global responsibility for eco-human well-being."[35] In doing so he is following the example of those who posit the *salvation* of humankind and of the *earth* as the common ground and starting point for all to share and understand their religious experiences and their ideas of that which is ultimately important. In taking this approach Knitter maintains that it will be clear that "this soteriocentric or globally responsible model for a theology of religions is not a rejection but rather a revision and a reaffirmation of the 'God-centeredness' and 'Christ-centeredness' that are essential to the way Christians live and talk about their religious truths."[36] In *One Earth, Many Religions,* Knitter elucidates the specter of environmental and social injustice that looms over any discussion of humankind's future, and he notes the complex structures—economic, social, and political, as well as religious—that face those who approach this task. He brilliantly articulates a "this-worldly soteriology" that is necessary to overcome eco-human plight, and he offers practical advice on projects and actions that have been undertaken to put an end to human and environmental suffering.

THE JESUS OF HISTORY AND THE CHRIST OF FAITH

In recent years a number of scholars have attacked the reliability of the New Testament. Some declare that *Jesus never said* most of what is recorded of Him in the Bible, and others maintain that *Jesus never did* most of what Scripture says He did. Such claims are receiving considerable media coverage in the United States, and it is important for Catholics and for all orthodox Christians to understand what is taking place.

Such critics of the Bible argue that the Jesus of the New Testament must be stripped of ancient myths that surrounded Him about what He said and did, so that a modern person can understand His true message. These writers argue that the Jesus of Nazareth we find in the pages of the New Testament is a fictitious creation of the early Church, and He must be exposed for who He truly is if He is to have any "value" for people who face the twenty-first century. The Christ of creed and dogma in the early Church and in the Middle Ages is thus said to be visible no longer for people who have experienced the scientific revolution. Opinions such as these are certainly not new. They have been a staple of debate since the Enlightenment brought new approaches to the study of Jesus. What is new is that scholars who have subjected Jesus to scrutiny in their private studies and disclosed their conclusions in closed academic circles are now waging their battle through the public media. *Time* and *Newsweek*, television reports and discussions, newspaper articles, and many books authored by skeptical critics have proliferated. What makes this use of the media so unfortunate is that most of the American public, apart from isolated pockets, do not read Scripture extensively or in the critical manner that would allow them to clearly understand the arguments presented. Thus a great deal of confusion about Christology ensues among the general public.

THE JESUS SEMINAR

One group of people that has been at the forefront of this endeavor calls itself the Jesus Seminar. It was founded in 1985 by Robert Funk together with John Dominic Crossan, then a professor at DePaul University in Chicago. Both have notable credentials in New Testament scholarship. Funk is not only a well-established New Testament scholar but is also the former executive secretary of the Society of Biblical Literature, the most important learned society for biblical studies in the United States. When this book went to press Funk was still the president of the Seminar, whose headquarters are located at the Westar Institute in Sonoma, California. The stated reason for the existence of the Seminar is to examine all the sayings attributed to Jesus in the New Testament and in other early Christian documents. The task of the Seminar, as stated by Marcus Borg, a noted New Testament scholar and professor of religion and culture at Oregon State University, is "to assess the degree of scholarly consensus about the historical authenticity of each of the sayings of Jesus."[37] However, the Jesus Seminar also has an agenda other than the academic one, an agenda for the people of the Church whom they claim they want to "liberate" from the "dark ages of theological tyranny" by liberating Jesus. Funk says, "We want to liberate Jesus. The only Jesus most people know is the mythic one. They don't want the real Jesus, they want the one they can worship. The cultic Jesus."[38] The Seminar primarily opposes the teachings of fundamentalist Christians and the "dictatorial tactics of the Southern Baptist Convention."[39] But it is difficult to avoid the impression that the Seminar also opposes all those who subscribe to any traditional understanding of Jesus as defined by the historic creeds of Christianity—that is, in some sense as risen Lord and Son of God.

There are 74 members, or fellows, belonging to the Seminar, together with perhaps another 100 who agree with the approach to sources taken by the Seminar. This is an impressive number but quite small in relationship to the 6,900 biblical scholars who are members of the Society of Biblical Literature and thousands of others with substantial scholarly training in the New Testament who for personal or ideological reasons do not take part in the Seminar's activities. The two leading academic organizations for biblical study, the Society of Biblical Literature and the Society for the Study of the New Testament, have no official association with the Jesus Seminar.

The Seminar understands itself to be the third "quest" of the histori-cal Jesus in this century. The first quest is found in Albert Schweitzer's *The Quest of the Historical Jesus,* which was published in 1906 when he was a lecturer in New Testament at the University of Strasbourg. The second quest is described in James M. Robinson's *A New Quest of the Historical Jesus,* published in 1959.

In fact the quest for the historical Jesus dates to the Enlightenment of the eighteenth century. Enlightenment thinkers taught that empirical-ly verifiable truth, and in the case of the Bible, historical truth, was the only sort of truth worth considering. As a consequence of Enlightenment thought, for the first time a distinction was made between the human being Jesus of Nazareth (the Jesus of history) and the Christ of Church tradition (the Christ of faith). Theologians looked behind creeds and dog-mas for the "real" Jesus, the man of Nazareth who had lived among the Jews in the first century. After centuries of Church history, these scholars hoped to rediscover the "undogmatic" Jesus, freed from Church dogmas. In theological literature of this kind the term *the historical Jesus* became a synonym for the "real Jesus." Enlightenment scholars denied the existence of the supernatural realm, and so events in Jesus's life could be described as historical only if they were tangible and perceptible events devoid of su-pernatural intervention.

Enlightenment thought created the quest for the historical Jesus, and the moment when this occurred can be fixed precisely. In May 1778, the philosopher Gotthold Ephraim Lessing (1729–1781) caused a great scandal with the posthumous publication of the last part of the work of Hermann Samuel Reimarus (1694–1768). Little is known of Reimarus's life. He was not a theologian, but he taught oriental languages. The ideas of the En-lightenment attracted him and brought him into conflict with traditional Christianity. Probably for fear of reactions from orthodox Christians, he never published the writing that contained his fierce criticisms. Lessing knew Reimarus personally and thought his ideas so valuable that some years after his death Lessing published Reimarus's work. Lessing worked for some time in the city of Wolfenbüttel. Between 1774 and 1778 he pub-lished a selection of Reimarus's writings, which quickly became known as the "Wolfenbüttel Fragments." In wide circles these "fragments of an un-known" were regarded as an extremely sharp attack on the Christian faith.[40]

Reimarus argued that the origin of Christianity rests on deceit. Dur-ing His lifetime Jesus had a different intention from that of His disciples after His death on the cross. According to Reimarus, He saw Himself pri-marily as a political messiah who regarded it as His most important task to liberate the Jewish people from Roman oppression. However, He failed, and with His cry on the cross, "My God, my God, why have you forsaken me?" (Mark 15:34), Reimarus argues that He acknowledged His failure. But His disciples refused to recognize the destruction of their dreams and therefore they created belief in the Resurrection of Jesus and exalted Him to be the Son of God. Reimarus believed that from the perspective of historical scholarship, even the Gospels must be regarded as suspect. Jesus Himself left no writings. The Gospels were written by His disciples, who manipulated history and created a new image of Jesus. According to this argument, the result was that the Jesus whom we meet in the Gospels is someone other than the "historical" Jesus of Nazareth who lived among the Jews at the beginning of the first century and was executed for His revolutionary attitude on the authority of the Roman procurator, Pontius Pilate.

Reimarus introduced a notion that since then has become one of the most important issues in the discussion of the historical Jesus. Whereas for centuries the continuity between the life of Jesus and the preaching of the early Christian community had been taken for granted, Reimarus emphasized what he considered to be the discontinuity: In reality Jesus was a totally different Messiah from the Christ figure who is described in the Gospels. The question of continuity and discontinuity is critical today in the position of the Jesus Seminar, the adherents of which argue for discontinuity, and of Roman Catholic and other orthodox Christian biblical scholars and theologians, who argue in favor of the continuity of Jesus's life and teachings with the New Testament presentation.

Reimarus's writings provoked many biblical scholars and theologians in the nineteenth century into writing accounts of the life of Jesus. An excellent book by C. J. den Heyer, *Jesus Matters*, traces scholarship regarding "the historical Jesus during the past two centuries."[41] He analyzes the various "Lives of Jesus," written in the nineteenth century, as well as the development of Christology in the twentieth century. He points out that the world changes but the New Testament does not. Because the "canon" (the list of authoritative books) was established during the fourth century, den Heyer notes, no books have been added to the list or removed from it. The Bible has not changed, but it is now read with different eyes. Since the nineteenth century our knowledge of the world in which Jesus lived has increased considerably. The development of historical criticism has deepened our understanding of the first stage of the Gospel tradition, the original words and deeds of Jesus. Form criticism has helped to uncover the second stage of the tradition—namely, the oral proclamation of the apostles and disciples (catechesis, prayers, hymns, and so on). Form criticism is a method that was developed in Germany between 1920 and 1940. It deals primarily with the formation of the Gospel tradition that occurred through preaching and liturgical expressions roughly between 35 A.D. and 60 A.D. It is essentially an analysis of typical features of biblical texts such as hymns, sermons, prayers, sayings of Jesus, dialogues, and descriptive narratives to place them in their original context. The development of form criticism has made clear that a period of oral tradition preceded the writing of the New

Testament. And redaction criticism has helped to uncover the third stage of the tradition, the actual composition of the Gospels by the evangelists. The Church for centuries had left no doubt that *high* Christology was the best way of describing the meaning of Jesus Christ: He is the unique Son of God; gradually the *humanity* of Jesus came more markedly into the foreground. During the second half of the twentieth century, the discovery of the humanity of Jesus has been followed by a deeper understanding of his Jewishness. The exalted Jesus of dogma underwent a far-reaching metamorphosis. Anyone who sets out to sketch a profile of Jesus today no longer begins *above* in heaven, but *below*—in Jesus of Nazareth, a Jew living among Jews in Palestine at the beginning of the first century.

Catholicism and the Historical–Critical Method

Catholic scholarship is heavily involved in the use of the historical–critical method, and many are engaged in the quest for the historical Jesus. They include in their studies scholarly work on the social, political, and economic realities at the time of Jesus. Perhaps, as was pointed out at the beginning of this chapter, the best known of these works is Meier's *A Marginal Jew: Rethinking the Historical Jesus*. Meier observes that everyone who writes on the historical Jesus writes from some ideological vantage point. No one is exempt, including Meier, who works out of a Catholic context. He attempts to write as a *neutral historian* by merely describing the "facts" and declining to explain and evaluate the purpose of Jesus's life. He recognizes that the "historical Jesus" should not be confused with the "real Jesus." The historical Jesus is but a reconstruction based on available evidence.[42] Historical reconstructions, he also repeatedly recognizes, are fragile and have to do with what is probable rather than what is certain.[43] Meier takes into account all the Greco–Roman and Jewish testimonies concerning Jesus.[44] Luke Johnson points out two aspects of Meier's analysis that deserve particular attention. He writes,

> The first [aspect] is that his argument for the eschatological dimension to the mission of both John and Jesus stands in stark contrast to the tendency (found in the Jesus Seminar, Borg, Crossan) to eliminate the eschatological from Jesus' ministry in favor of the image of a (only slightly Jewish) cynic philosopher. In my view Meier gives a better account of the evidence. Second, the five hundred pages of his second volume that he devotes to the traditions concerning Jesus the miracle worker are a useful counterbalance to scholars (in this case, excluding Borg and Crossan) who find such traditions embarrassing.[45]

Meier's conclusions, in many instances, are in sharp contrast to those found in the Jesus Seminar. This can be seen by comparing the work of Meier and other Catholic scholars with that of the Seminar.

The Five Gospels of the Jesus Seminar

The Jesus Seminar is an association of New Testament scholars who meet twice a year to debate the question of the historical Jesus. The purpose of the Seminar is to uncover the actual historical words and deeds of Jesus as distinguished from embellishments of the early Christian community and of the authors of the Gospels. The Seminar has attracted great attention, and the writings produced by members such as Funk, Crossan, Marcus Borg, and others are found in every major bookstore and library.

Four Distinctive Aspects and Critiques of Each

The first extended publication of the results of the Jesus Seminar appeared in 1993. It was given the evocative title *The Five Gospels: The Search for the Authentic Words of Jesus*. It presents new translations of the four canonical Gospels, as well as a translation of the Gospel of Thomas. As Luke Johnson observes, there are four aspects of this book that make it distinctive.

Iconoclastic Translation   The first distinctive aspect is that the translation is deliberately iconoclastic. Jesus does not tell the leper, "I will it, be made clean" but "Okay—you're clean!" (Mark 1:40). The "salt of the earth" does not have "savor" but "zing" (Matt. 5:13). The Sabbath is not "made for man" but "made for Adam and Eve" (Mark 2:27–28). The translation presents itself as "more historical" and in closer touch with ancient social realities than more "ecclesiastical" translations. Johnson writes,

> In some cases this may be so. In other cases, the colloquial and slang seem to be chosen for their own sake—and reflect the deliberate irreverence of the Seminar's press conferences. The result is not always greater accuracy. "Adam and Eve," for example, may be a politically correct rendering of "man," but it obliterates the specific symbolic background of this Gospel expression.[46]

Color-Coding of Jesus's Sayings   A second feature of *The Five Gospels* is the color-coding of Jesus's sayings. Approximately 30 fellows of the Seminar went through the four canonical Gospels and the Gospel of Thomas and tried to determine the authenticity or lack thereof of Jesus's sayings. Each member voted by using colored beads to indicate the likelihood of a particular saying as authentic. The votes were then tallied and weighted to determine how to color-code each saying of Jesus. Unlike a traditional red-letter edition of the Bible, where the words of Jesus are marked in red, the Jesus Seminar used four colors to highlight Jesus's words, with each color corresponding to the likelihood that Jesus really said what is claimed for Him. Each color had its own interpretation.

Red: Definitely said by Jesus

Pink: Probably Jesus said something like this

Grey: Probably not from Jesus but from the Christian
community

Black: Definitely not from Jesus but from the Christian
community

Of the 1,500 sayings attributed to Jesus very few are marked in red (15), with about 75 more marked in pink. A saying that appears only in the Gospel of Thomas (the fifth gospel), for example, ended up in the grey category but had exactly as many members of the Seminar voting that it was red/pink as it did voting that it was grey/black. In other words, what is represented as a "scholarly consensus" is in fact a plus-50 percent result in a ballot involving 30 electors. If 16 voted a particular saying was authentic, for example, and 14 that it was not, then it was assigned *pink*. The fifteen *red* sayings, in contrast, all have 75% of the votes or more.

The introduction to *The Five Gospels* explains the voting procedure:

> The Seminar did not insist on uniform standards for balloting. The ranking of items was determined by a weighted vote. Since most Fellows of the Seminar are professors, they are accustomed to grade points and grade-point averages. So they decided on the following scheme:
>
> red = 3
> pink = 2
> grey = 1
> black = 0
>
> The points on each ballot were added up and divided by the number of votes in order to determine the weighted average. We then converted the scale to percentages—to yield a scale of 1.00 rather than a scale of 3.0. The result was a scale divided into four quadrants:
>
> red = .7501 and up
> pink = .5001 to .7500
> grey = .2501 to .5000
> black = .000 to .2500.[47]

It is interesting to note that the inclusion of the Gospel of Thomas side by side with the four canonical Gospels does not result in a significantly higher number of red sayings (five) for the former. In fact, the five sayings are found in the canonical Gospels as well. The point of including this "fifth gospel" seems to be that even here, in what the members of the Seminar believe contains even earlier sources than the canonical Gospels, very few authentic sayings of Jesus are identified.

The Gospel of Thomas   A third aspect of the book is its inclusion of the *Gospel of Thomas*, which was discovered by a citizen from the village of Nag Hammadi in Upper Egypt in 1945. The find comprised the remains of an ancient Coptic library. (Coptic is the latest form of the ancient Egyptian language. It came into use in the second century A.D. and developed as an almost exclusively Christian language with numerous Greek words.) *The Gospel of Thomas* is filled with examples of Greek vocabulary. Included in the library are 12 codices (books) plus eight leaves from a 13th codex, all written in the fourth century A.D. The find was truly a "library," because the codices contain everything from a fragment of Plato's *Republic* to Roman works such as the *Sentences of Sextus*, as well as Christian works that reflect a range of Gnostic views. *The Gospel of Thomas* is a collection of 114 sayings of Jesus, with no narrative framework. Scholars debate whether the *Gospel of Thomas* is Gnostic in its theology. Gnosticism (Greek *gnosis* = "knowledge") is a system of religious belief according to which salvation depends on a singular knowledge or inner enlightenment about God, which liberates a person from the ignorance and evil that characterize the created order. It denies the full humanity of Jesus. Gnosticism has assumed different specific forms and has been embraced by a variety of distinct religious groups. Whether or not the *Gospel of Thomas* should be regarded as Gnostic, there is a fairly wide agreement that it should be dated at the very earliest to the mid-second century. The main point of the debate for most scholars is whether the *Gospel of Thomas*'s sayings are dependent on the Gospel tradition or represent, in some cases, a tradition as early or earlier than that found in the canonical Gospels. A number of scholars argue that it represents an independent tradition that in fact is as early, if not earlier, than that of the Synoptics—that is, the Gospels of Matthew, Mark, and Luke. They are referred to as Synoptics ("seeing together") because of their similarity in structure, albeit sharing many differences in content. Others, such as Meier, disagree. Having presented his arguments, he writes

> Since I think that the Synoptic-like sayings of the Gospel of Thomas are in fact dependent on the Synoptic Gospels and that the other sayings stem from 2nd-century Christian gnosticism, the Gospel of Thomas will not be used in our quest as an independent source for the historical Jesus.[48]

The inclusion of the *Gospel of Thomas* by the Jesus Seminar, side by side with the four canonical Gospels, does not include a significantly higher number of red sayings (five), as we have seen. Concerning this Luke Johnson writes,

> Its inclusion seems to make primarily a political or "cultural wars" point: the Gospels are to be considered of value only insofar as they are

sources for the Historical Jesus, and the Christian Canon should be re-constructed on that basis.[49]

Dedication to Galileo, Thomas Jefferson, and David Strauss   The fourth aspect of *The Five Gospels* is the dedication of the book to Galileo, presumably as an example of revolutionary thinking that is oppressed; Thomas Jefferson, who wrote *The Life and Morals of Jesus of Nazareth*, which sought to distill the essential Jesus from "the corruptions of Christianity"; and David Strauss, who wrote *The Life of Jesus Critically Examined* in 1835. The implication is plainly that this book shares both the radical and the controversial character of such antecedents.

Specific Criteria and a Critique of Each

In the introduction to *The Five Gospels* the historic creeds of Christianity are attacked. "The Church appears to smother the historical Jesus by superimposing this heavenly figure on him in the creed: Jesus is displaced by the Christ, as the so-called Apostles' Creed makes evident."[50] The creed came about as a result of the influence of Paul, "who did not know the historical Jesus" and for whom "Jesus the man played no historical role."[51] These assertions not only lack demonstration, but they identify the creed of Christianity as a form of "theological tyranny."[52]

Scholars distinguish three historical periods of stages in the production of the New Testament. The first stage pertains to the actual words and deeds of Jesus—roughly 28 to 30 A.D. The second stage, roughly 30 to 70 A.D., was created by the oral tradition of the early Church. The third stage, roughly 70 to 100 A.D., was produced by the editorial work of the evangelists. How, then, can we determine what comes from Jesus, from Stage 1? Rules of judgment are needed to make such decisions, as, for example, in deciding what material comes from the historical Jesus. The introduction to *The Five Gospels* lists seven pillars or assumptions on which the book is based.

The first pillar is the distinction between "the historical Jesus, to be uncovered by historical excavation, and the Christ of faith encapsulated in the first creeds."[53] Adherents of the Jesus Seminar repeatedly assert that scholars cannot believe in the historical Christian doctrines and remain real scholars. This, however, is much disputed by large numbers of academically trained Christian biblical scholars who teach and publish in the area of New Testament studies.

The second pillar is the belief that Matthew, Mark, and Luke "are much closer to the historical Jesus than the Fourth Gospel (John), which presents a 'spiritual Jesus.'"[54]

The third pillar is the belief that the Gospel of Mark was written before the other canonical Gospels.

The fourth pillar is the belief that Luke and Matthew both depended on a common source for the material they have in common, which is not found in Mark. This hypothetical source of sayings of Jesus is called *Q* (which stands for the German word for source, *Quelle*.)

With the exception of the first pillar, the pillars are basically accepted by Catholic and other orthodox New Testament scholars. By no means has critical biblical scholarship been resisted by the Church, especially since the publication of Pope Pius XII's encyclical *Divino Afflante Spiritu* (With the Divine Spirit Blowing) in 1943, which encouraged Catholic scholars to use all the tools of modern scholarship in studying the Bible.

The fifth pillar maintains that modern biblical scholarship has dispensed with a Jesus who spoke of a final judgment and the end of the world. In other words, Jesus was not an eschatological figure and His understanding of the Kingdom of God was noneschatological. The adherents of the Seminar present this view as being in the mainstream of New Testament scholarship, when in reality, far from representing a consensus of scholarship, this is one "assumption" of the Jesus Seminar fellows that puts them most at odds with other researchers into the historical Jesus. Something so fundamental as the eschatological character of Jesus's ministry and speech—that Jesus acted in view of a future triumph of God's will—is simply dismissed without significant argument. Concerning this Luke Johnson writes,

> The introduction insists ... that although John the Baptist had an eschatological mission, and although the earliest Christian traditions understood Jesus eschatologically, Jesus the disciple of John (the Baptist) and teacher of the Church had a completely noneschatological and indeed countereschatological understanding of God's kingdom. A less sophisticated logic might naturally conclude just the opposite: if Jesus' mentor was eschatological and Jesus' followers were eschatological, it would seem logical to suppose that Jesus was eschatological.[55]

Many Catholic authors write about the eschatological message of Jesus. One of the most impressive scholars is Edward Schillebeeckx, who has written *God the Future of Man* and *Jesus: An Experiment in Christology*.[56] Rudolf Schnackenburg's *God's Rule and Kingdom*[57] and Benedict T. Viviano's *The Kingdom of God in History*[58] also contain exceptional arguments concerning the eschatology of Jesus's message.

The sixth pillar is the separation of the written culture of our day from the oral culture of Jesus's time. The result is that we should not expect an ancient oral culture to have preserved very much of the real words and actions of Jesus by the time the material was finally written down as

a Gospel: "The Jesus whom historians seek will be found in those fragments of tradition that bear the imprint of orality: short, provocative,
memorable, oft-repeated phrases, sentences, and stories."[59] Besides being
enormously speculative, this assumption falsely assumes that oral cultures were incapable of preserving large amounts of detailed information
and ignores the substantial evidence for the careful preservation of oral
material within Judaism. If the role of oral tradition was important to the
ancients in general, it was especially important to Jewish culture. As early
as the book of Deuteronomy, the importance of oral instruction and memory regarding divine teaching is stressed (Deut. 6:4–9). Moreover, Jewish
rabbis developed elaborate means by which to communicate the tradition
orally from generation to generation, finally codifying the tradition in
writing toward the end of the second century A.D. in the *Mishnah*. Rab-
binic schools, which specialized in the study of law, taught the importance
of careful memory work. To the Jew, if something reflected the Word of
God or the wisdom of God, it was worth remembering.[60] Thus the long history of passing on oral tradition through skilled experts discounts the
sixth pillar.

The seventh pillar insists that the burden of proof of any Gospel saying now falls on the side of authenticity. This means that each statement
must be justified historically to be considered to have its origin in Jesus
Himself. This insistence that material in the Gospels be considered guilty of
unhistorical fabrication until proven valid by scholars is necessary because
"the gospels are now assumed to be narratives in which the memory of
Jesus is embellished by mythic elements that express the Church's faith in
him, and by plausible fictions that enhance the telling of the gospel story for
first-century listeners."[61] Again the adherents of the Seminar assert their
own views and not those of New Testament scholarship in general, which
are far less pessimistic about the nature of the Gospels. If historians were
to adopt such extreme skepticism regarding ancient sources, our knowledge
of all aspects of the remote past would be very sketchy, to say the least.

Some of the specific criteria used by the Seminar adherents in reaching their decisions on historicity are also given in the introduction to *The
Five Gospels*. Several of these are in fact the common criteria of New Testament scholars in general. The criterion of multiple attestation is inar-
guable and focuses on those sayings or deeds of Jesus that are attested in
more than one literary source (e.g., Mark, *Q*, John) or in more than one literary form or genre (e.g., parable, dispute story, miracle story, prophecy).
Also, the criteria of dissimilarity and embarrassment are widely used by
other scholars. The criterion of dissimilarity focuses on words and deeds of
Jesus that cannot be derived either from Judaism at the time of Jesus or
from the early Church that followed him. Such sayings or deeds are logi-
cally more likely to be from Him than not. Examples often given are Jesus's
sweeping prohibition of all oaths (Matt. 5:34, 37) and His total prohibition

of divorce (Mark 10:2–12). The criterion of embarrassment focuses on actions or sayings of Jesus that would have embarrassed or created difficulty for the early Church. For example, Jesus says He does not know the exact day or hour of the end in Mark 13:32. Jesus said, "But as for that day or hour, nobody knows it, neither the angels of heaven, nor the Son; no one but the Father" (Mark 13:32). Yet in Mark 13:24–27 Jesus claims that He is the Son who can predict the events at the end of time, including His own coming on the clouds of heaven. It is not surprising that a few later Greek manuscripts dropped the words "nor the Son" from the saying in Mark. It is highly unlikely that the Church would have taken pains to invent a saying that emphasized the ignorance of its risen Lord.

Compartmentalizing of Evidence

A serious problem with the approach of *The Five Gospels* is its compartmentalization of evidence. Other than the four Gospels, the rest of the New Testament evidence concerning Jesus is casually dismissed. L. Johnson writes,

> Paul is caricatured as "having no interest in Jesus." The narratives of Acts and the Gospels are tossed out as mystical fabrications based on faith. More than that, any sayings that are "developed" must also be dismissed from the reconstruction. What is left is a small pile of pieces. But on this basis, Jesus is declared to have "really" been one way rather than another. And this is announced *before* [emphasis mine] the Seminar takes up its (equally portentous) work of figuring out which deeds attributed to Jesus "really" came from him. This is not responsible, or even critical, scholarship.[62]

In a lengthy review of *The Five Gospels*, Professor Richard Hays of Duke University concluded the following:

> [T]he case argued by this book would not stand up in any court. The critical study of the historical Jesus is an important task . . . but the *Five Gospels* does not advance that task significantly, nor does it represent a fair picture of the current state of research on this problem. Some of its purported revelations are old news, and many of its novel claims are at best dubious.[63]

The Jesus Seminar is not alone in its "quest" for the historical Jesus. In *The Real Jesus*, L. Johnson describes and briefly critiques Barbara Theiring, who wrote *Jesus and the Riddle of the Dead Sea Scrolls: Unlocking the Secrets of His Life Story;*[64] Episcopal Bishop John Spong, who wrote *Born of a Woman: A Bishop Rethinks the Birth of Jesus;*[65] Borg, who wrote *Jesus: A New Vision: Spirit, Culture and the Life of Discipleship;*[66] and John Dominic

Crossan, who wrote *The Historical Jesus: The Life of a Mediterranean Jewish Peasant*.[67] Johnson also examined other authors and gives a brief critique of their work. His book serves as an excellent introduction to the best-known authors in this third quest for the historical Jesus.[68]

HISTORICAL METHODOLOGY AND THE RESURRECTION OF JESUS

A critical issue in the historical study of Jesus is the question of methodology. As we have seen, some scholars examine particular Gospel sayings or events and analyze them in an *objective* fashion, wrenching them apart from the world of Jesus and His followers and reducing them to their smallest elements, as if such deconstruction were *the* way to know and understand Jesus. Historical reconstruction goes astray when, in the name of getting at the facts behind the texts, it leaves the Gospels in fragments and ignores both the overall theological intention of the evangelists and the literary intention of their texts. The theological and literary whole is greater than the sum of its historical parts. What the evangelists wish to proclaim and witness about Jesus for their particular readership emerges not just from a mass of specific details but also from the entire scope of their Gospels. Each Gospel is a complete narrative to be evaluated in its own literary right.

To be sure, the Gospels serve as the chief sources for a reconstruction of the historical Jesus; but to speak of the Gospel writers as presenting or intending to present the historical Jesus transports them in an exegetical time machine to the Enlightenment. As Meier writes,

> The real Jesus is not available and never will be. This is not because Jesus did not exist—he certainly did—but rather because the sources that have survived do not and never did intend to record all or even most of the words and deeds of his public ministry—to say nothing of the rest of his life.[69]

We cannot know the *real* Jesus through historical research, whether by this we mean His total reality or just a reasonably complete biographical portrait. The Gospels do present us with *the earthly Jesus*—in other words, a picture, however partial and theologically colored, of Jesus during his time on earth. Thus we can know the *historical Jesus* or the *Jesus of history*. The Jesus of history is a modern abstraction and construct. The Jesus of history is the Jesus we can *recover* and examine by using the scientific tools of modern biblical research. But it is important to reiterate that the historical Jesus is not the real Jesus, but only "a fragmentary hypothetical reconstruction of him by modern means of research."[70]

It is also important to note that the constantly changing, often contradictory portraits of the historical Jesus presented by various scholars, however useful in academia, cannot be the object of faith. In this regard Meier writes,

> [T]he proper object of Christian faith is not and cannot be an idea or scholarly reconstruction, however reliable. For the believer, the object of Christian faith is a living person, Jesus Christ, who fully entered into a true human existence on earth in the 1st century A.D., but who now lives, risen and glorified, forever in the Father's presence. Primarily, Christian faith affirms and adheres to this person—indeed, incarnate, crucified, and risen—and only secondarily to ideas and affirmations about him. In the realm of faith and theology, the "real Jesus," the only Jesus existing and living now, is this risen Lord, to whom access is given only through faith. . . . This presently reigning Lord is accessible to all believers, including all those who will never study history or theology for even a single day in their lives.[71]

In other words, even though the Christian faith has always involved some historical claims concerning Jesus, it nonetheless has been based on religious claims concerning the present power of Jesus. And this power is clearly related to Jesus's Resurrection from the dead, which is denied by the fellows of the Jesus Seminar.

Tracing modern biblical criticism back through David Strauss, the introduction to *The Five Gospels* notes,

> Strauss distinguished between what he called the "mythical" (defined by him as anything legendary or supernatural) in the gospels from the historical. . . . The choice Strauss posed in his assessment of the gospels was between the supernatural Jesus—the Christ of faith—and the historical Jesus.[72]

The Jesus Seminar fellows have clearly aligned themselves with Strauss: "[T]he distinction between the historical Jesus . . . and the Christ of faith" is deemed the first pillar in "scholarly wisdom" and "modern biblical criticism."[73] For them Jesus's Resurrection from the dead is not a live option even to be considered as a possible explanation for the relevant data. Their view becomes explicit when the Seminar comes to the words of the risen Jesus: "By definition, words ascribed to Jesus after his death are not subject to historical verification."[74] But because words spoken during

Jesus's life are sometimes transferred to the resurrected state, "the Jesus Seminar decided in some instances to evaluate such words as though they were spoken by a historical figure.[75] It could not be plainer that the Seminar rules out the risen Jesus as a historical figure and that it does not do so on the basis of the evidence but *by definition.* There is no justification for reducing the meaning of "the Resurrection of Jesus" to something like "the continuing significance of Jesus" or "the disciples' realization that Jesus's message could not die." By *Resurrection* the evangelists and Jesus's early disciples clearly meant that something happened *to Jesus Himself.* God had *raised Him,* not merely reassured His followers. But an event that was not witnessed by the human eye and that by definition breaks through the bounds of history is an event that goes beyond the capacity of human description.[76] The problem, then, is that no one saw *the actual Resurrection.* Is it a historical event, therefore? The answer is no if by *historical* one means something open to scientific investigation and verifiable by neutral witnesses. However, this does not mean that the Resurrection was not a *real* event for Jesus with *historical implications* for others.

Behind the apostolic confession of faith in the risen Lord lies the experience of having witnessed Him at some time and in some way. The disciples were convinced that they had indeed seen Him, so that *for them* the appearances are *historical.* As McBrien writes,

> [I]t would have been very difficult from a purely psychological point of view to synchronize such a wide range of individual experiences of the risen Lord unless there was some basis in reality for them. Furthermore, the appearances are not to people in general, but to particular individuals, in particular places, at particular times.[77]

A passage quoted earlier in this chapter is worth repeating. McBrien states,

> Nonetheless, it would seem better to speak of the resurrection as *transhistorical,* or *metahistorical,* rather than *unhistorical* [emphasis mine]. The average person will translate unhistorical simply to mean it never happened at all. It is transhistorical, or metahistorical, in the sense that it refers to an event that took place on the other side of death and, therefore, which lies beyond the confines of space and time. Similarly, the reality of the risen Lord is also a reality which transcends history as we know it. By the resurrection Jesus enters a completely new universe of being, the end-time of history, beyond the control of history and beyond the reach of historians.[78]

The Christian claim concerning the Resurrection of Jesus is not that He resumed His former manner of life but rather that after His death He entered into an entirely new form of existence, one in which He shared the power of God and in which He could share that power with others. The Resurrection experience, then, is not simply something that happened just to Jesus but it is equally something that happened to His followers. The sharing in Jesus's new life through the power of the Holy Spirit is an essential dimension of the Resurrection.

The question remains: Can there be a "nonhistorical" event that has historical effects? Yes, of course, it happens often even if seldom as dramatically as in the case of nascent Christianity. This can be seen in religious founders such as Mohammed and Siddhartha, whose own formative–originative experiences are inaccessible on the historical plane as well as in the many instances of artists, poets, and mystics whose *effects* are obvious but whose *causes* remain inaccessible to historical inquiry.

L. Johnson's reaction to the Jesus Seminar's insistence on dealing with the Resurrection of Jesus only on the historical level and therefore denying that it occurred is insightful. He writes,

> Insistence on reducing the resurrection to something "historical" amounts to a form of epistemological imperialism, an effort to deny a realm of reality beyond the critic's control. This, however, is not even good history. It is instead an ideological commitment to a view of the world that insists on material explanations being the only reasonable explanations, that reduces everything to a flat plane where not even genius, much less the divine, can be taken into account. Such an ideological commitment begins with the assumption that Christianity *cannot* have anything distinctive about it.
>
> For the responsible historian, however, the recognition of forces and realities beyond the ken of strict historical method is what makes the doing of History exciting and ennobling. When a so-called historian uses the historical method to deny, in effect, the reality of anything beyond what the method can demonstrate, we suspect a certain defensiveness to be at work. When such denial is practiced by someone also claiming to be a Christian, something still more curious is happening.[79]

MODERN HISTORICAL RESEARCH AND THE JESUS OF HISTORY

We cannot know the *real* Jesus through historical research, whether by "real Jesus" we mean His total reality or just a reasonably complete biographical portrait. But we can pursue a deeper understanding of the Jesus of history, the Jesus whom we can *recover* and examine by using the scientific tools of modern historical research. In fact, it is important to do so.

Meier believes that such an enterprise serves the interests of the Christian faith in at least four ways.

1. It acts against any attempt to reduce faith in Christ to a contentless cipher, a mythic symbol, or a timeless archetype. Historical research underlines the fact that there is a specific content to Christian faith, content connected with specific persons and events in past history. While historical research cannot supply the essential content of faith, it can help theology give greater depth and color to that content.

2. Historical research affirms that the risen Jesus is the same person who lived and died as a Jew in first-century Palestine, a person as truly and fully human as any other human being.

3. Such research has acted against any attempt to "domesticate" Jesus for a comfortable, respectable, bourgeois Christianity and from its inception "has tended to emphasize the embarrassing, nonconformist aspects of Jesus: e.g., his association with the religious and social 'lowlife' of Palestine, his prophetic critique of external religious observances that ignore or strangle the inner spirit of religion, his opposition to certain religious authorities, especially the Jerusalem priesthood."[80]

4. The historical Jesus is not easily coopted for programs of political revolution. Compared with the classical prophets of Israel, the historical Jesus is remarkably silent on many of the burning social and political issues of His day. "Like good sociology, the historical Jesus subverts not just some ideologies, but all ideologies. . . ."[81]

Properly understood, historical research is a bulwark against the reduction of Christian faith in general and Christology in particular to relevant ideology of any kind. It is a constant stimulus to theological renewal. For this reason alone, knowing the Jesus of history is worth the pains of the pursuit.

SUMMARY

The first six ecumenical councils analyzed Scripture and defined the Church's understanding of Jesus, the Christ. He is understood to be one divine person with two distinct natures, human and divine. Until the mid-twentieth century Jesus's divine nature was accentuated, but today the fullness of His human nature is being examined as well, with no detriment to His divinity. Feminist, liberation, and ecological Christologies present new approaches to the study of Jesus.

A number of biblical scholars, the most notable being the fellows of the Jesus Seminar, have seriously questioned the traditional understanding of Christology. They argue that the creeds of the Church are false and are based on ideas that Jesus never taught and events, such as his Resurrection, that never occurred. Catholic scholars, such as Meier and especially L. Johnson, have taken exception to the manner in which the Seminar uses the historical–critical method and to several key assumptions the fellows of the Seminar make. Meier, L. Johnson, and most Catholic and Protestant scholars, using the same methodology but not the same assumptions, present strong cases in defense of traditional Christian beliefs while at the same time deepening and enriching the belief in Jesus on which the Church is grounded.

Study Questions

1. What are the three stages within the Gospel according to the Pontifical Biblical Commission? Explain what is meant by *historical criticism; form criticism;* and *redaction criticism.* How do these methods affect the study of Christology?

2. Explain "implicit" Christology and "explicit" Christology.

3. What is meant by Christology "from above" and "from below"?

4. Explain the key teachings of the councils of Nicaea, First Constantinople, and Ephesus. Why were these councils held?

5. How does the teaching of St. Thomas Aquinas concerning the atoning death of Jesus differ from that of St. Anselm of Canterbury? Give a critique of both theories.

6. Name the "seven pillars" of the Jesus Seminar. Which of these are criticized by L. Johnson? Do you agree with Johnson's criticisms? Explain.

7. What is the *Gospel of Thomas*? Why is it used in *The Five Gospels*? How important is it to gaining a deeper understanding of Jesus?

8. List some of the main tenets of feminist Christology. In what ways does this approach offer valid insights into an understanding of Jesus?

9. What is meant in saying that the Resurrection of Jesus was transhistorical? How does this differ from saying the Resurrection was a historical event?

10. What are the four reasons given by Meier in his support of using the scientific tools of modern historical research in studying the Jesus of history? Is the Catholic Church supportive of the use of such research? If so, does this research present a challenge to orthodox Catholic belief?

CHAPTER 2

Authority in the Church

The question of how authority is exercised in the Catholic Church will likely be disputed for years to come. In fact, most Christian churches today are experiencing, in one form or another, a crisis in authority. Martin Marty, the eminent Church historian at the University of Chicago, maintains that in each historical epoch a particular question tends to predominate, such as Christology, grace, or the sacraments. He maintains the present question is that of authority[1]: "The fact that papal 'infallibility' and Protestant biblical 'inerrancy' came to be defended in the nineteenth century and used as weapons between the parties in the twentieth century is an indicator of their issue of authority." It is certainly evident that authority is under attack in the Catholic Church, at least from the viewpoint of the need for a shared authority. There are many issues that the Church must face honestly, including the shortage of priests, the role of women in the Church, and sexual morality, to name a few. Although the Church is not a democracy, neither is it an absolute monarchy. Rather it is a community comprising both ordained and lay members. The question asked by many Catholics today is how can the Church better express a shared responsibility? In other words, how can the concept of collegiality be put into practice in relation to papal authority?

In addition, there are two diametrically opposed interpretations of papal authority. One such group, generally referred to as *progressive*, regards certain papal and curial pronouncements to be culturally and historically conditioned and open to investigation and to possible change. A second group, in the words of John A. Coleman, appeals to "a literal, ahistorical, and nonhermeneutical reading of papal and curial pronouncements as a sure bulwark against the tides of relativism, the claims of science, and other inroads of modernity."[2] This latter group is generally known as *integralist* and is represented by some well-known organizations such as Catholics United for the Faith (CUFF) and Opus Dei, which was founded in Spain in 1928 by Father Josemaria Escriva de Belaguer (1902–1975). Both CUFF and Opus Dei have strong representation in the United States. Pope John Paul II leans strongly in the direction of the integralist viewpoint.

Eugene Kennedy addresses the two major groupings in the Church today in an interesting fashion. He depicts "Culture One" Catholics, the "integralists," as those who stand by and work diligently to protect the papacy and its lines of control over the Church at large.[3] Culture One is intrinsically dependent on the Church *as institution* for its existence. "Culture Two" Catholics, the "progressives," according to Kennedy, are intrinsically dependent on the Church *as mystery* and only extrinsically dependent on it as institution. This group sees papal and curial pronouncements as historically conditioned and open to investigation.

The difference between Catholicism's two cultures is not that of a "divided Church," as is often maintained by the media. Nor is the difference neatly summed up by referring to them as "left-wing" and "right-wing" Catholics. Both groups belong to the institutional Church and are loyal to the Church, although with clear differences on some issues. As Kennedy observes,

> It [the Church] may appear riven by disagreements but that does not shatter its unity or its integrity. As noted, its subgroupings may argue opposite sides of the questions that the media may describe as significant in present-day Catholic life: celibacy, birth control, the possibility of married or women priests, a long agenda of social issues. But these groupings can only differ because they accept and embrace so much that is the same: the Church as an ongoing institutional presence in history, the pope, the bishops and clergy as its leaders and teachers, the familiar issues that seem natural to it because they are classically institutional in nature.[4]

Culture Two Catholics are neither hostile nor indifferent to their faith. They see themselves as deeply committed Catholics. They also strongly support the vision of Vatican II. They understand Vatican II as an event that broke Culture One open to the movement of the Holy Spirit and in doing so brought about many needed reforms in the Church. Despite the fact that the documents of Vatican II contain many ambivalent statements because of their compromise nature, they nevertheless made Culture Two Catholicism possible and inevitable.

It is important to note that believers in both Cultures One and Two recognize the sensible place of healthy authority in any well-ordered or productive human life. But when is healthy authority present? A partial answer to this question is discovered when authority takes into consideration the moral judgment of ordinary people. In fact, the official Church has always acknowledged the sensus fidelium (sense of the faithful) as a reliable moral guide. Patrick Granfield's study shows that the "sense of the faithful" is one of the traditional balances to the excessive use of papal authority.[5] Culture Two Catholics feel that papal authority today is not taking into consideration the sense of the faithful in any meaningful way, be it the question of birth control, the ordination of women, or any number of other considerations.

The basic problem with authority for many Catholics is the centralization of authority in Rome and the lack of shared decision making on the part of the pope in relation to the bishops of the Church. There is also concern that the *sensus fidelium* is too often ignored. To understand the monarchical mode of the papacy today a brief historical review of the development of papal authority will be useful.

THE DEVELOPMENT OF PAPAL AUTHORITY

During the first 300 years of its existence, Christianity witnessed a Church constituted rather collegially as an assembly of local churches, each determining their local leaders. The fourth century marked the beginning of a clerically controlled institutionalization of the Church. When Emperor Constantine signed the Edict of Milan in 313 a.d. Christianity became legally secure. The emperor granted certain privileges to the Christian clergy and in doing so inaugurated an officially sanctioned class status between Church and state. When Rome was sacked by Alaric in 410 A.D. the Roman Empire in the West effectively was left without an emperor, and clerics stepped in and took the reins of authority. They were led by the bishop of Rome. By the time of Pope Gelasius (492–496 A.D.) the notion of papal primacy as a dominating civil force had developed into a full theoretical justification for clerical dominance in the West. With Gelasius, the word *pope* as applied to the bishop of Rome became normative. Later the Eastern Emperor Justinian (527–565 A.D.) reasserted power over the West, but only for a short period of time. After Justinian's death the pope and bishops again assumed the functions of civil authority, and clerics became the custodians of the Roman law.

On Christmas day in the year 800 A.D. Charlemagne was crowned emperor by Pope Leo III, and so was created, at least in theory, a Christian empire. Following this, and until the latter part of the eleventh century, ultimate control of the empire was in the hands of secular rulers. During this period many kings appointed bishops who were unsuitable for the task.

In 926 A.D. Pope John XII crowned Otto I emperor. Emperor Otto and his successors tended to appoint people who were indeed more suitable to be bishops. They in turn made some valiant efforts at reform but were hindered by clerical corruption that would remain a serious problem until the reign of Pope Gregory VII (1073–1085 A.D.). Pope Gregory brought about important Church-wide reforms. Gregory's efforts were directed at freeing the Church from domination by secular rulers. However, the struggle to keep kings from interfering with the Church by appointing their own bishops pushed Gregory to exalt the power and authority of the papacy.

In the next century Gratian's *Decrees* (1140 A.D.), the forerunner to Canon Law, represented an effort to achieve some degree of uniformity in the life of the Church. Its laws, probably unconsciously, also brought about an even greater concentration of clerical control in the Church. One of the main results of the Fourth Lateran Council, which was held in 1215 A.D., was the strengthening of episcopal power as well as making absolute the papal control that would predominate throughout the Middle Ages to the present day. In addition, canonists promoted a pyramidal model of the Church, with each lower rank humbly obeying the higher rank and the pope reigning at the pinnacle.

During the fourteenth and fifteenth centuries conciliarists, such as Marsilius of Padua, objected that the dominant papal monarchy of the high Middle Ages was an aberration or at least a historical accident that required correction.[6] Cardinal Nicholas of Cusa, who was engaged in the struggles of the Council of Basel, restated the ancient principles of consent and of authority deriving from the whole people, especially when these principles were endangered by the claims of centralizing monarchies.[7] But the objections of such individuals to the dominance of the papacy were to no avail. Nor should we see the conciliar movement as a representation, even theoretically, of a more collegial papacy. It was a highly clerical endeavor that virtually excluded the laity from the councils.

In the period from the conclusion of the Council of Trent (1563) until Vatican II, authority in the Church became even more clerically understood and more centralized in the papal office. The Protestant Reformation questioned authority not only in its corrupted forms but in principle. The Council of Trent in response insisted on the authority of the hierarchy. The pope was now regarded as a "universal bishop." Catholics were directly under the pope, even more than to the individual's own bishop. The shift of all significant power to Rome accelerated thereafter.

In the nineteenth century the papacy attained its highest power. This was achieved by Pope Pius IX at the First Vatican Council (1870) with the dogmatic definition of papal primacy and of papal infallibility. Papal primacy refers to the authority that the pope has over the whole Church as its leading bishop, or primate. Infallibility, which literally means "immunity from error," is the charism, or gift, by which the Church is protected from fundamental error in formulating a specific teaching regarding a matter of faith or morals. It can be exercised by the pope and by an ecumenical council. Vatican I did not use the term "monarchy," but in fact it did give a monarchical description of the papal office. There are solid theological reasons to avoid calling the Church a monarchy. For example, the notion of a monarchy seems to indicate unilateralism in decision making and an excessive centralization in government. Also, papal monarchism tends to stress the juridical at the expense of the spiritual, and often neglects the charismatic gifts in the Church at large. As Patrick Granfield points out, if the Church is called a monarchy it must be considered a unique one because it is neither hereditary nor absolute, but rather constitutional. At Vatican I, in 1870, Gregory II, Youssef, the Milkite Patriarch of Antioch, recommended unsuccessfully that the council should state clearly that the Church is not an absolute monarchy. Other prelates made similar suggestions with the same result. As Granfield writes, "The pope is not an absolute monarch because he does not have unlimited authority. He is bound by the constitution of the Church and by certain doctrinal and structural restraints."[8]

There is a very important text from Vatican II, which is pertinent to the discussion of papal monarchism. In Chapter 3 of *The Dogmatic Constitution on the Church* there is a discussion of the papacy. When this chapter was being written Pope Paul VI suggested the phrase "accountable to the Lord alone" be added to the text describing the exercise of papal primacy. The Theological Commission, which was preparing this section of the *Constitution,* rejected the pope's amendment. A text from Vatican I notes there are limitations on papal authority. At that council Bishop Zinelli of the Deputation on the Faith stated,

> From all the sources of revelation it is clear that full and supreme power in the Church was conferred upon Peter and his successors, full in the sense that it cannot be limited by any greater human power but only by the natural and divine law.[9]

The Theological Commission then presented its own objection:

> It is an oversimplified formula. The Roman Pontiff is also bound to revelation itself, to the fundamental structure of the Church, to the sacraments, to the definitions of earlier councils, and other obligations too numerous to mention. Since such a formula would also require long and complicated explanations, the Commission has decided that it is better not to use it. There is also a psychological reason, lest in appeasing some we cause anxiety among others, especially in our relations with the East, as is clear in the history of another formula *"ex sese et non ex consensu ecclesiae"* [by himself and not by consent of the church].[10]

Although these two texts do not possess formal conciliar authority, they are significant. They indicate that neither Vatican I nor Vatican II held that the papacy has absolute power, but rather is limited by the very constitution of the Church.

THE MEANING OF "COLLEGIALITY": THE ROLE OF BISHOPS

The term "collegiality," made popular in the 1950s by the French Dominican theologian Yves Congar in his writings on the theology of the laity, was not used in the documents of Vatican II. However, it was later adopted by theologians and by the magisterium of the Church to describe the unique relationship that exists within the College of Bishops under the leadership of the pope. Vatican II portrayed the Church as "collegial" by introducing a mode of decision making in the Church that emphasizes coresponsibility among the bishops with the pope as expressed in ecumenical councils, synods, and episcopal conferences. "Collegial" also refers to the principle that the Church is a communion (college) of local churches, which together constitute the Church universal. For centuries, as we have seen, the Church was governed and directed by the papacy and the Roman curia in a noncollegial fashion. (The term "Roman curia" refers to persons and officers who assist the pope in matters of service and governance of the Church.) Vatican II said the Church is realized and expressed not only at the universal level but also at the local level.[11] There is a dialectical balance between the Church as a worldwide community and the local congregation.

In regard to the College of Bishops, Vatican II stressed the unity between the papal and episcopal offices. Bishops are believed to be successors of the apostles, and the pope the successor of St. Peter. The pope is the head of the College of Bishops and works with the bishops to promote the Gospel. At least theoretically, collegiality does not endanger papal authority, because the pope can always exercise his supreme power freely.[12] At the same time, the notion of collegiality at one level includes the need for the pope to be in continuous dialogue with his bishops and to take their opinions to heart. Thus collegiality *is* a challenge to any pope. It is the pope who determines the success or failure of collegiality.

Collegiality differs from both monarchy and democracy. An absolute monarch can certainly seek advice but would not have to take it. In a democracy the majority opinion of the people is the final word, and an official who opposes the will of the community can be voted out of office. In the Catholic Church, collegiality means that the head of the Church, or for that matter a local pastor, must take ultimate responsibility for decisions that are made but act in a consultative manner with the people of God.

To promote collegiality Pope Paul VI established the Synod of Bishops in 1965. In doing so he hoped to establish a closer relationship with the bishops of the world and to avail himself "of the consolation of their assistance, the help of their prudence and experience, the support of their counsel, and the benefit of their authority."[13]

Many theologians debate the collegial nature of these conferences, because only 200 bishops—at most—out of the more than 3,000 prelates worldwide are invited. Nevertheless, any session of the Synod of Bishops has a consultative function, which is to advise the pope, even though it does not possess decision-making powers. A synod is a very useful collective action of the bishops, and its actions may help to lead the worldwide episcopate in particular matters.

A number of problems exist with the structure of the Synod of Bishops, the most notable among them being the objection that because the pope not only determines the agenda of the synod and also ratifies those bishops who are allowed to attend, the range of acceptable theological opinions appears to be too narrow.

The Episcopal Conference—in other words, a regular meeting of bishops in a particular nation or territory—is another expression of collegiality. Such conferences have been held for centuries, dating back to the early Church, and have been very influential in the life of the Christian community. In 1966 Pope Paul VI in his *motu proprio Ecclesiae Sanctae* (Personal letter on the Holy Church) mandated that each nation or territory establish a permanent conference of bishops if one did not already exist. Such conferences are marvelous examples of the spirit of collegiality and have been of critical importance in recent years throughout the Catholic world. For example, the U.S. Bishops' Conference has issued many important pastoral documents covering a variety of topics such as Communism, ecumenism, the parish, priestly formation, the laity, war and peace, and the U.S. economy.

Two of the most important documents of the U.S. Bishops' Conference are *The Challenge of Peace: God's Promise and Our Response* (1983) and *Catholic Social Teaching and the U.S. Economy* (1985). Both letters are in fact collegial in nature and are the result of dialogues not only with the Catholic community but also with the American public at large. In producing the letter on peace, for example, the bishops went through a long process of consultation with a variety of groups: biblical scholars, moralists, arms-control experts, top officials in the Reagan administration, two former secretaries of defense, military leaders, peace activists, and others. A similar process was used in writing *Catholic Social Teaching and the U.S. Economy*. As for the binding power of these pastorals, the bishops have stated that not everything within them contains the same moral authority. For example, in *The Challenge of Peace* the bishops conclude,

> The moral judgments we make in specific cases, while not binding in conscience, are to be given serious attention and consideration by Catholics, as they determine whether their moral judgments are consistent with the Gospel.[14]

The pastoral *Catholic Social Teaching and the U.S. Economy* concludes similarly. What the American bishops are trying to do is to awaken American Catholics and other Americans to the problems of social injustice and get them involved in the struggle for peace and human rights. Because these pastorals are collegial in nature and involve the expertise of so many, their impact has been much greater than would be similar nonconsultative letters. The role of the bishops is discussed in Vatican II's *Decree on the Bishops' Pastoral Office in the Church*.[15] In its earlier stages this document represented the preconciliar ecclesiology that tended to make bishops entirely subordinate to the pope and curia, thus making the episcopacy more a jurisdictional than a sacramental reality. However, the final version of the decree reflects the teaching of *The Dogmatic Constitution on the Church* regarding collegiality. Bishops are said to exercise their episcopal office, which they have "received through episcopal consecration."[16] They exercise that office at three levels: over their own diocese, or "local church"; in collaboration with other bishops on a regional or national level (episcopal conferences); and as a worldwide body in union with the pope (college of bishops). Bishops, therefore, are not simply the delegates or vicars of the pope, as had been proposed by a rigid hierarchical model in effect before Vatican II. Rather, they are "the proper, ordinary, and immediate pastors" of their own dioceses.[17] That pastoral office, which includes preaching the Gospel, presiding at worship, and ministering to those in need must always be exercised in the mode of a servant.[18] The bishop must carry out his episcopal duties in a manner that encourages communication and integration among the various apostolates.[19] In other words, he must act in a collegial manner.

Vatican II also asserted unequivocally that the diocesan bishop "possesses all the proper, ordinary and immediate power which is required for the exercise of his pastoral office."[20] The diocesan bishop is thus presumed to have all the authority needed to exercise his pastoral authority *unless* a particular cause has been reserved to a higher authority, namely the pope or the curia.[21] Perhaps it is not too much to hope that continued systematic reflection on the constitutional structure of the Church will lead to a satisfactory resolution of the as yet unresolved theoretical and practical tensions between the papacy and the episcopacy, between the bishop of Rome and the diocesan bishops throughout the world.

The Dogmatic Constitution on the Church (n. 22) teaches that the pope has "full, supreme, and universal power over the Church," but the bishops are no longer perceived as simply the pope's vicars or delegates. They govern their diocese not as "vicars of the Roman Pontiff, for they exercise an authority which is proper to them" (n. 27). However, a bishop's authority in his own diocese became a highly publicized issue in October 1986 in the case of the archbishop of Seattle, Raymond Hunthausen. This incident illustrates the problems that can occur between the bishop of a particular diocese and the Vatican. Bishop Hunthausen fell into disfavor with Rome for his liberal positions on a number of issues. He allowed children to receive first communion before making their first confession. He also permitted general absolution from sins without individual confession when there was a shortage of priests. He allowed the national convention of the gay Catholic group Dignity to have a special Mass in his cathedral. Other concerns were raised by the Vatican, including Hunthausen's liberal attitude regarding divorce and remarriage. Archbishop Hunthausen also refused to pay his taxes in protest against nuclear weapons, though the Vatican said this attitude was not the reason for the subsequent action it took.

The Vatican's response to the situation, on December 3, 1985, was to appoint an auxiliary bishop, Donald Wuerl, to serve with Archbishop Hunthausen and in a real sense to monitor him. Later Rome instructed Hunthausen to put Bishop Wuerl in charge of liturgy, priestly formation, discipline, and the archdiocesan tribunal that handles marriage annulments and ministry to homosexuals. Finally Wuerl was put in charge of priests who were leaving the ministry or were already laicized. Archbishop Hunthausen was shocked and disturbed by this action, because by right such obligations were his as the chief pastor of the archdiocese. Many fellow American bishops and the great majority of Seattle's Catholic community were also dismayed. But to his credit Hunthausen, out of deference to the pope, obediently gave up his authority in those areas requested by Rome even though they were a major function of his office.

The tension was between the bishop's authority in his own diocese and his duty to submit to the authority of the pope. The archbishop recognized the latter as more important. Finally, after protests lodged by the people of Seattle and interventions with Rome carried out by several American bishops, Archbishop Hunthausen's full authority was restored in June 1987, and he was allowed to conduct himself as his conscience dictated. It is clear from this case that although Vatican II clarified many points concerning the relationship between the pope and the bishops, many issues are yet to be decided.

THE SELECTION OF BISHOPS

The selection of bishops by the clergy and people of their dioceses is a venerable and authentic Catholic tradition. However, the Church's mechanisms for choosing bishops have changed many times, usually in response to changes in the secular world. For centuries kings and other national leaders played a decisive role in the appointment of bishops. At present bishops are appointed by the pope, but this practice is relatively recent, a product of the centralization that followed Vatican I.

The question of how bishops are selected is a critical one. In the ancient Church, bishops were elected by the Christians within their own communities. The pope was informed of the election and he formally recognized and approved the new bishop. In this way the visible communion between the local churches and the pope, which constituted the Church as catholic or universal, was both expressed and maintained.

In the early period of the Church the election of bishops by members of their diocese was common, and Pope Leo I's (440–461 A.D.) principle, that the bishop who is to preside over all should be elected by all, remained the norm rather than the exception.[22] From earliest times the election of a bishop expressed the awareness that the Church is not simply a clerical domain but rather encompasses the whole people of God. Great bishops, such as St. Ambrose in Milan and St. Augustine of Hippo, were elected by the clergy and people. Gradually the right of the local church to choose its bishop was eroded both by the secular government and by the centralized papacy, until the 1917 *Code of Canon Law* (Canon 329, #2) asserted that bishops are freely nominated by the pope. Canon 377 of the new *Code of Canon* Law (1983) restates this canon.[23]

The pope's selection of all bishops worldwide was more tenable in an age in which diocesan bishops were treated in practice, if not in theory, as little more than delegates of the pope to a particular diocese. But, as John Beal writes,

> The rehabilitation of the theology of the particular church as a portion of the people of God and of the diocesan bishop as representative of that church renders the current law for the selection of bishops increasingly untenable from an ecclesiological and, therefore, canonical perspective. It is rather difficult to see how a bishop imposed from above, without any meaningful consultation with the local church as a community of faith . . . can be considered a legitimate representative of that church.[24]

Although the present *Code of Canon Law* does not permit meaningful consultation with the members of a particular diocese concerning the selection of its bishop, no significant theological or canonical principles stand in the way of a change from the present procedure to the establishment of a more democratic process for the selection of bishops.

There is a more positive side to the system of the pope making the appointments because it makes bishops more independent of governments who in the past often demanded a say in their appointments. For the most part, however, such governmental imposition has ceased to exist. In fact there is a significant and growing demand today to reinstitute the practice of the local elections of bishops. A notable example of this desire for change occurred in Germany on January 27, 1989, when 163 German-speaking theologians from Germany, Switzerland, Austria, and the Netherlands signed the *Cologne Declaration. A* large number of theologians from Spain, Italy, Belgium, France and Brazil later ratified this *Declaration,* in which they objected that vacant dioceses were unilaterally filled without regard for the recommendations of the local church and declared that the Vatican's autocratic methods were in contradiction to the Gospel spirit of brotherhood, to the positive postconciliar experiences of freedom, and to the collegiality of the bishops. The catalyst in this declaration was the appointment of Cardinal Joachim Meisner as archbishop of Cologne, in opposition to the recommendation of the Cologne Cathedral Chapter, which was made up of the priest-electors of bishops in their diocese.

Vatican II gave the Church new directions in its authoritative structures in calling on the pope to work more closely with the bishops within the principles of collegiality and subsidiarity. It is subsidiarity in particular that is in question concerning the election of bishops. The principle of subsidiarity as applied to the Church means that the pope should not do for local churches that which they can well do for themselves. Both the local church and the pope should agree on the appointment of the bishop. This decision should be made on the basis of authentic dialogue carried on between the two. Will the selection process change? Only time will tell.

THE PRIESTS' COUNCIL (SENATE)

Just as the pope and the bishops constitute one college, so the local bishop and his priests form another.[25] The Priests' Council or senate does not limit the authority of the bishop in any way, but the priests do offer their opinions on many fronts. According to Canon Law, the purpose of such a council is to "aid the bishop in the governance of the diocese according to the norm of law, in order that the pastoral welfare of the portion of the people of God entrusted to him may be promoted as effectively as possible" (Canon 495, #1). The Priests' Council should be representative of the priesthood in a diocese in all of its diversity, including various ministries, regions, and age groups. Canon Law specifies, toward that end, that about half the members are to be freely elected by their fellow priests (Canon 497, #1).

The Priests' Council has a continuous existence and is a legal effort to give structural expression to the rights of priests to be heard by their bishop in what pertains to the good of the Church. As Eugenio Corecco writes,

> The hearing the bishop is to give to the presbyters does not reflect simply a moral, legal, or vaguely communional obligation, but flows from the ontological structure of communion itself which implies an immanence of the component parts. . . . It follows that the obligation to have a presbyteral council is not justified by corporative principles, but has its *raison d'etre* in the fact that the ministry of the diocesan bishop is not purely personal but essentially synodal.[26]

Despite the fact that the Priests' Councils are consultative in nature, they have the potential to give the governance of a local diocese a more participatory style. Unfortunately, the experience of such councils since Vatican II has not been uniformly good. The relationship of members of these councils to their bishops has run the full spectrum, from excellent to very poor. In some dioceses personality conflicts have made the councils symbols of disunity rather than of unity. In other dioceses, councils such as these have been mutually helpful to priests and bishops, and therefore to the diocese as a whole. Whatever the result, the place of the Priests' Councils in the life of the Church is quite important for the full development of Christian life in every diocese.

PASTORAL COUNCILS (DIOCESAN AND PARISH)

The laity in the United States today are highly educated, and most of those who have not had the advantages of formal study at the college or university level are nonetheless people of common sense who have an enormous body of information and a rich fund of diverse experience. All who are baptized, laity as well as clergy, belong to the people of God. For this reason *The Dogmatic Constitution on the Church* states, "Thus every layman, by virtue of the very gifts bestowed upon him, is at the same time a witness and a living instrument of the mission of the church herself, according to the measure of Christ's bestowal (Eph. 4:7)."[27]

Because all the laity are directly involved in the mission of the Church, Vatican II urged that a pastoral council be established in each diocese.[28] It is also the reason why *The Dogmatic Constitution of the Church* urges pastors to promote parish councils by stating that they should "recognize and promote the dignity as well as the responsibility of the layman" and to "willingly make use of his prudent advice."[29] Diocesan and parish councils are not matters of hierarchical largesse. They exist because the mission of the Church is the responsibility of each member, ordained or not. Because the Church is a single community with a single mission, its life and work must be reflective of this. If all are responsible for the mission, however differently, then all must have a proportionate share in those decisions whereby the Church commits itself to the work of Christ. A parish without a council is a parish without a broadly representative outlet for this universal missionary obligation.

The new *Code of Canon Law* recognized the right and at times the duty of all the faithful as individuals "to manifest to their sacred pastors their opinion on matters which pertain to the good of the church and . . . to make their opinion known to the other Christian faithful" (Canon 212, #3). What is lacking, however, are *structures* to translate that right and duty from rhetoric to reality. And such structures are clearly needed. The diocesan pastoral councils are *recommended* for every diocese, and *permitted* at the discretion of the bishop for every parish, *but they are not mandated.*

An excellent suggestion about how the diocesan and parish councils might be interrelated is found in *The Directory on the Pastoral Ministry of Bishops,* the writers of which observe,

> To make the [diocesan pastoral] council's work more effective, the bishop can order, if the good of the faithful requires it, that in every parish pastoral councils be set up and that these be aligned with the diocesan council. These councils, grouped together according to areas, could choose their representatives to serve on the diocesan council, so that the whole diocesan community may feel that it is offering its cooperation to its bishop through the diocesan council.[30]

If implemented, this suggestion might help to dispel the parochialism that too often characterizes parish councils and might also give the members of the diocesan council a stronger sense of the constituency they represent.

In regard to parish life, it is important to note that a parish council is not a panacea for all problems encountered. But decisions of such bodies can be enormously helpful to the life of the local congregation. The success of a parish council depends on the attitude of the pastor. No matter how open-minded and benign the pastor of a parish without a council might be, his ministry will be one exercised *on* rather than *in conjunction with* his parishioners. On the other hand, if he is truly committed to having such a council, and appoints members and allows them to function with an open spirit, the council will be successful. Otherwise it is doomed to fail. The same can be said of the bishop and his diocesan council. A bishop or priest with a monarchical notion of authority will find such councils onerous at best. Those who understand collegiality and the need to share the gifts of the Holy Spirit will strongly support such organizations. The recognition of the coresponsibility of all members of the people of God is the key to the successful future of the Church.

THE PRIESTHOOD

The shortage of priests in the Catholic Church in the late twentieth and early twenty-first centuries has reached alarming proportions. The problem is not simply the number of priests but rather that number relative to the entire Catholic community. In the United States, for example, the Catholic population has been growing steadily, but the ratio of priests to laity has been declining steadily. In 1942 the priest-to-laity ratio was 1 to 617; in 1962, 1 to 771; and in 1990, 1 to 921. The bishops of the United States have projected that by 2005 the ratio will be 1 to 2,200. These ratios pertain to the number of priests in relation to the actual number of parishioners. The ratio is (and will be) much higher in other parts of the world.[31] These numbers are clearly reflected by the decline in the number of diocesan seminarians in the United States over the past 30 or so years. In 1968, there were 22,334 diocesan seminarians preparing for the priesthood. In 1978, the number had dropped to 9,560. In 1988, the total number was 4,981 and in 1999 the number was 3,302. Alarming figures indeed, especially when it is estimated that by the year 2005, 46 percent of the active diocesan clergy in the United States will be 55 years of age or older, and only 12 percent will be 34 years or younger.[32]

The status of the priesthood within the Catholic community was secure before Vatican II. This is no longer the case, at least in part because the fundamental concept that has characterized the priestly vocation has been called into question—in particular, that of a special, "sacral" priesthood. A priest was understood to be a sacred person, set apart by ordination and in possession of special sacramental power. Often referred to as "another Christ," the priest was understood as a mediator between God and His people. This sacral model of priesthood dominated the Roman Catholic understanding of ordained ministry from the twelfth century through to Vatican II. A review of the development of the sacral model shows its problematic character. What becomes clear is that the sacral model is not evident in the New Testament but rather reflects a medieval sacralization of the role of the priesthood.

The New Testament evidence is complicated. It does not speak of Christian ministers as priests, be they apostles, prophets, teachers, presbyters, or any other form of ministry. Jewish priests are referred to often and Jesus is referred to as a high priest in Hebrews 8:1. The entire Christian community is referred to as a royal priesthood in 1 Peter 2:9. But the word *priest* is never used in the New Testament to describe ordained ministers.

As the apostles disappeared from the scene and false teachers emerged (1 Tim. 4:1–3; Titus 1:10–13) a growing need for Church order became apparent. Presbyters (elders) were appointed in each Christian community and became Church leaders, in charge of the religious and moral behavior of the people of their community. They also ministered to needy individuals and stressed orthodox doctrine. Pope Clement of Rome, who died c. 100 A.D., put in place the offices of presbyter–bishop, and deacon. He understood the line of authority in the following manner: from God, to Jesus Christ, to the Apostles, to the bishops and deacons, and their successors (1 Clement 42, 44:1). The first letter of Clement was a letter from the church at Rome to the church at Corinth. In the letter Clement says that this Church order is divinely inspired.

During the early decades of the life of the Christian community there is no evidence to suggest that anyone in particular was commissioned to preside over the Eucharist. No explicit mention is made of any of the apostles, including St. Paul, presiding over the Eucharist, although they undoubtedly did so. We simply do not know how a certain individual came to preside over the Lord's Supper. At most it can be said that those who presided did so with the consent of the local church. And we are not told that this was an exclusively male prerogative. It seems most likely that in the "house churches," the host or hostess presided. The New Testament refers explicitly to women whose houses were used for the Eucharist, as in Colossians 4:15, where St. Paul refers to "Nympha and the church which meets in her house." And in Romans 16:3–5, St. Paul sends greetings to Prisca along with her husband Aquila, his "fellow-workers" and leaders of a house church in Rome. As Paul Bernier writes,

> [I]t is not because the New Testament ministers have the power to consecrate the Eucharist that they are ministers of the Christian community: it is because they are leaders that they preside over the community's public prayer. It is ministerial leadership that is emphasized in Acts and the epistles; almost nothing is said of sacramental, much less eucharistic, leadership.[33]

It is important to note that nowhere in the New Testament or in Christian writings of the first century does the Church appear to be leaderless. Early Church ministry is centered on the person who presided over the community, who in turn presided over the Eucharist. By the time of Ignatius of Antioch, whose writings date from the end of the first decade of the second century, it is clear that in his church the bishop presided over the Eucharist. With Ignatius we first find evidence for the so-called monarchical episcopate—in other words, a local church presided over by one bishop.

By the middle of the second century the bishops of the Church were monarchical and were recognized as successors of the apostles. They were understood to be the leaders of the local churches and teachers who could authoritatively interpret the apostolic tradition.

Presbyters during the second century were Christian leaders who worked with the bishop, but they were not priests. The direct application of priestly vocabulary to Christian ministers begins only in the third century. The first real evidence for any kind of ordination comes from the *Apostolic Tradition* of Hippolytus, which contains detailed ceremonies for the ordination of bishops, presbyters, and deacons. Hippolytus wrote at the beginning of the third century, but the practice of ordination probably began in the late second century. As Hippolytus describes the structure of the Church of his day, the bishop was elected by the people of his community, but he was ordained by the imposition of hands from another bishop. The presbyter, or priest, was ordained by the bishop, with other priests joining in with the laying on of hands. These presbyters did not preside at the Eucharist but formed a ring around the bishop as he presided. With the permission of the bishop, a presbyter could preside at the Eucharist. Deacons were ordained by the bishop alone and their responsibilities were determined entirely by their bishop.

Because the Christian community had no formal priesthood of its own during the first two centuries apart from the role of the bishop–presbyter, it drew on the Jewish priesthood as a model during the late second and early third centuries when the office of the priesthood developed. The Old Testament provided a clear prototype within which the Jewish priest was seen as an intermediary between humankind and God, one designated to offer sacrifice to God. All Jewish priests were male by proscription.[34]

The Edict of Milan in 313 A.D. ended the persecution of the Church, and Emperor Constantine promoted freedom of religion for all, including Christianity. The emperor conferred special privileges on the clergy and endowed them as a special caste within the Church. This distinction caused a sharp division between the laity and the clergy, a division that would be accentuated in the Middle Ages with the development of the distinction between *ordo clericorum* and the *ordo laicorum*, the former devoted to the higher things of the spirit, the latter to the lower things of the flesh.[35]

It was during the fourth century that the phenomenon of the diocesan priesthood or the "country priest" came into being. This occurred because with the legitimization of Christianity under Emperor Constantine, Christianity attracted many new converts. The bishops assigned their presbyters to say Mass in outlying areas, because the members had become far too many to allow everyone to gather in the same place at the same time with the bishop. Presbyters now became "Mass priests." This resulted in an increasing emphasis on the relationship between the priest and the Eucharist rather than on the relationship between the Eucharist and the community.

During the sixth century, according to the Dutch Dominican Edward Schillebeeckx, the practice of the private celebration of the Eucharist began in connection with the veneration of relics.[36] The priest was becoming a sacred person whose identity was defined in terms of a cultic function. The sacral model of the priesthood had begun, heightened by the law of abstinence from sexual intercourse for married priests and ultimately the law of celibacy, which became universal in the twelfth century.[37]

As a result of the influence of Canon Law in the twelfth century and under the impetus of Pope Alexander III and the Third Lateran Council (1179 A.D.), the idea of a sacral priesthood was firmly ensconced and remained unchallenged in Roman Catholicism for the next eight centuries. The focus of the sacrament of Holy Orders was the Eucharist, which created a liturgical, or sacral, understanding of the priesthood, one that has endured to the present. Though theologically sound, it is a rather narrow vision of the priesthood, one that basically limits the understanding of Jesus's own priesthood to that of sacrifice. Also, the idea that priesthood was essentially a *power* tended to move theological thought away from the earlier notion of ministry as essentially a *service*. Bernier writes,

> This can (and has) led to the priesthood being seen as sort of a domination over the Christian people, and associated more with the power to rule than to serve. True, for the scholastics, this was a sacred power to bring salvation to sinful humanity. However, it is also true that service, *diakonia*, is not central; rather consecrating the bread and the wine and forgiving sins are the normal ways of expressing this *power*. But it remains a fact that power became the normal way of understanding the sacrament of order.[38]

Vatican II examined this long history of the priesthood, especially the scholastic formulation that Trent had used, and found it wanting. The council produced the *Decree on the Ministry and Life of Priests*. When this document speaks of priestly power it refers especially to the authority to build up the community in truth and holiness and to lead the congregation to maturity, so that each member might be led to the full development of his or her gifts and vocation.[39] Trent presented a theology of priesthood primarily correlated to sacrifice, whereas Vatican II does so in relation to the whole mission of the Church.

The primary role of the priest according to the *Decree on the Ministry and Life of Priests* (nn. 2–6) at Vatican II is to *foster community*. In fact, leadership and service to the community is *the* function of the ordained. All other priestly functions, including the sacramental ones, are to be seen in light of joining the faithful together in the one body.[40] Vatican II places great stress on preaching because without an understanding of Scripture the community cannot grow. Such preaching must not simply be informative or consoling but also challenging, which includes serious questions concerning peace and justice. The council also strongly emphasized the role of the Eucharist in the Church. No Christian community can be built up unless it has the Eucharist at its foundation. Vatican II in the *Dogmatic Constitution on the Church* speaks to the common priesthood of all the baptized and affirms the laity's equal dignity, equal call to holiness, and equal responsibility for the mission of Christ. The ordained and common priesthood are related to one another even though the ordained priest's ministry is unique and is performed publicly, in Christ's name, for the sake of others. The major change of orientation emerging from the council was to shift the emphasis from the sacral or cultic model of ministry to a more ministerial one in response to what was believed to be an unbalanced approach in medieval theology. Now the priest's cultic functions are seen in relation to his ministerial role, which is to build up and preserve the unity and love of the Christian community.

There are those who see the shortage of priests as an opportunity to get more lay people involved and to bring about perceived changes in the structure of parish life. There is some truth in this. However, it still remains true that Catholics want priests not only for presiding at the Eucharist but for preaching, baptisms, and marriages. Any changes in Church policy need to be accompanied by a renewed valuing of the priesthood by Catholics and renewed encouragement of vocations by parents, teachers, the laity in general, and by priests themselves.

PRIESTLY CELIBACY

Before Christianity emerged the idea of perpetual celibacy was not perceived to be a need by members of other religions, and in some instances was forbidden by civil law. Perpetual celibacy was never accepted by Judaism. Christianity introduced a new perspective. For example, Luke 20:36 points to the unmarried state as a reflection of the heavenly kingdom, in which there is no marriage. St. Paul introduced the idea of perpetual celibacy to his communities, but admitted that the grace of celibacy was not given to all and made clear that those who could not live such a life should marry (1 Cor. 7:1–9).

For the first three centuries all bishops, priests, and deacons were permitted to marry. The question of celibacy was raised formally at the first universal council, the Council of Nicaea, in 325. Bishop Hoses of Cordoba, Spain, advocated celibacy as a requirement for all clergy, but the council rejected his proposal. The question may have been raised as the result of the monastic movement, which began toward the end of the third century. The monks, who were greatly admired, lived a celibate lifestyle.

The exact roots of Christian thinking regarding celibacy are not clear. Certainly St. Paul's writings were influential. Yet we know that most of the apostles were married, as was true of the clergy in general in the early centuries of the life of the Church. The preference for celibacy was tied strongly to a deprecation of the body, which is more neo-Platonic than Christian. In theories of asceticism and contemplation that arose during the third century by writers such as Origen, who was greatly influenced by neo-Platonism, sexual abstinence was considered essential for the priestly life. Passion was seen as inimical to the use of reason and therefore to spiritual development. Also, the desire to honor the Eucharist led to the conclusion that it was incompatible with marital sexuality, which was seen as unclean.

The Eastern and the Western churches have taken different positions on the question of perpetual celibacy. The Eastern churches allow priests, deacons, and other clerics to marry, even though bishops must be celibate. The Trullan Synod in 602 supported this legislation and it has remained in force for the Eastern churches (the Orthodox), as well as for Eastern churches in union with Rome (the Uniate). In the West celibacy was effected by a series of local councils and by papal teachings. Before the Council of Nicaea, the Council of Elvira, held in 305, passed a law requiring clerical celibacy. Various popes issued similar decrees in the fourth and fifth centuries. But such laws were never uniformly observed. Pope Gregory VII (1073–1078) and his program of reform are credited with bringing about a more consistent observance of clerical celibacy. Finally, two Church councils, Lateran I in 1123 and Lateran II in 1139, made clerical celibacy a universal law, which has remained in effect in the West to the present day.

The Protestant Reformation brought with it a strong challenge to priestly celibacy. Martin Luther condemned celibacy in 1522. John Calvin was more temperate in this regard. He held that celibacy was an acceptable way to serve God, but believed that it was of no greater value than married life. One of the tragedies of Church history occurred when Lutheran and Catholic scholars met at Augsburg in 1530 to discuss the Augsburg Confession, which is a statement of Lutheran beliefs written by Philip Melancthon and approved by Martin Luther. The meeting was an attempt at reconciliation, and agreements were reached on the most serious theological issues that had previously divided the traditions. The negotiations, however, failed because the two sides were unable to reach agreement on other issues, such as on giving the chalice to the laity, on monastic vows, on the difficult question of the restoration of those Catholic Church properties that had been taken over by Lutherans, and on priestly celibacy.[41]

The Council of Trent (1545–1563) upheld the value of retaining the clerical obligation of celibacy. The council, it is interesting to note, recognized that this was a Church law rather than a divine law and conceded that it could be changed should the Church ever decide to do so.

Today the celibacy question is being discussed, even though Pope John Paul II insists the question is closed. But the problem persists and even intensifies as the number of priests continues to decline. Unfortunately, the open discussion of priestly celibacy frequently takes place in newspapers and magazines and usually the arguments on both sides are superficially presented.

Certainly some serious arguments can be presented in favor of retaining clerical celibacy. One argument maintains that because Jesus himself was celibate, and because the priesthood is a special vocation by which one follows Jesus, such a sacrifice is appropriate. Also, celibacy serves as a sign of total dedication to the kingdom of God, a kingdom in which there will be no marriage: "For at the resurrection men and women do not marry; no, they are like the angels in heaven" (Matt. 22:30). Finally, celibacy functions as a witness that sexual activity, though good, beautiful, and important, is not the absolute necessity it is held to be in Western culture. To change the celibacy requirement would be seen to give in to cultural mores. A number of other arguments in favor of celibacy can also be offered.

Conversely, there are many arguments in favor of eliminating the requirement of celibacy. For example, though it seems clear that Jesus never married, many of his apostles were married men. Further, the law of celibacy is a Church law, not a divine law, and can be changed should the Church deem it necessary. A further suggestion supporting the lifting of the requirement of celibacy states that a married priest would be more pastorally sensitive to the needs of married couples and families if he were married himself. It can also be argued that it is certainly possible to have a total commitment in one's love of God and of one's spouse and therefore serve the Church as a married priest.

Schillebeeckx, and many others, argue the celibacy question in regard to the right of the people of God to celebrate the Eucharist, which is the supreme act of worship for Catholics **as it is for other Christian denominations.**[42] He believes that the shortage of priests in the Catholic Church is tied closely to the law of celibacy, which many are unable to accept, and therefore the lack of vocations. De facto, many Catholics today are able to celebrate the Eucharist only occasionally because of the lack of priests. This is especially true in developing countries. And as the shortage of priests continues in the developed world, including the United States, the availability of Eucharistic celebrations will become problematic in many areas. In 1982 the ratio of priests to the Catholic population of North America was 1 to 886; in Latin America it was 1 to 6,911; and in Africa it was 1 to 17,233. In Brazil, which has the largest Catholic population of any nation, the ratio was 1 to 9,000.[43] The ratio has continued to expand in recent years. Dean Hoge, a Protestant sociologist who teaches at Catholic University in Washington, D.C., argues that the vocation crisis is not the result of a lack of spiritual vitality or a loss of faith in the Catholic Church. His research suggests rather that it is "largely a matter of institutional policies."[44]

One of the consequences of the shortage of priests is that the Catholic Church is increasingly being forced to choose between its tradition of Eucharistic worship and its present requirements for ordination. In this regard John Coleman writes,

> Just who are the real traditionalists? Those who defend no options to celibacy even when it means defining Catholic communities by something other than the Eucharist or those who assume that Eucharist is more central to the Catholic imagination of ministry than any disciplinary condition for ordination?[45]

The notion of a *right* to the Eucharist is stated in *The Dogmatic Constitution on the Church:* "The laity have the right, as do all Christians, to receive in abundance from their sacred pastors the spiritual goods of the Church." And it goes on to say that "participation (in liturgical celebrations) . . . is their right and duty by reason of baptism."[46] The question remains, how can communities of the baptized, who have a divine right to the Eucharist, be deprived of it for ecclesiastical reasons such as the requirement of celibacy for priestly ordination, if that be the case?

WOMEN AND THE PRIESTHOOD

The question of female priests has surfaced frequently in the postconciliar Church, and the refusal of the magisterium to admit women to the priesthood continues to be a serious concern of many Catholics. Mary Jo Leddy, a Sister of Scion and a Canadian social activist, believes that unless the Church comes to terms with the equality of women soon, and in a very fundamental way, "we are going to lose not just one generation of women, but many generations."[47] Increasingly women are treated as equals in society but not in the Church. A number of Protestant churches have been ordaining women as ministers and priests for some years now, but the Catholic Church adamantly refuses to do so. Those advocating the ordination of women reject the arguments of their opponents, especially the idea that because Christ was male, all priests must be male. They maintain that the Church's 2000-year history of an exclusively male priesthood developed out of a patriarchal culture and to continue to support that culture would tie the Church's understanding of Christ and His Church to one time and culture.

Thomas F. O'Meara points out that in the United States, 70 percent of ministry is and has been performed by religious women, "all of whom are officially not in the ministry and who ... have no real public life in the church. They are formally laity."[48] Certainly their vast accomplishments since the nineteenth century show that women are indeed enormously important ministers in the American church. And yet even these women are not officially recognized as such by the Catholic Church. This example of the "second-class treatment" of Catholic women by the official Church illustrates why one of the most critical and potentially explosive questions facing the Catholic Church today is that of the role of women.

Education, especially higher education, has allowed women to assume more public roles in society and in the Church. The number of women in professional theological and biblical societies has increased dramatically in recent years. These women are making significant contributions in theological and biblical studies. Other women are assuming responsibilities that were closed to them in the past. Women serve as hospital chaplains, campus ministers, liturgical administrators, religious educators, and occupy a variety of other important positions. In priestless parishes, which is now more than 10 percent of all parishes in the United States, women perform the ministries of a pastor with two exceptions: They do not say Mass or hear confessions. These parish administrators conduct Bible studies, counsel, visit the sick, and are the liturgical leaders of the community. In some remote areas women have been commissioned by their bishop to preside at weddings and funerals.

In assuming greater leadership in the Church, women are responding not only to their own calling but are supported by many official Church documents. The *Decree of the Apostolate of the Laity* of Vatican II states, "Since in our times women have an ever more active share in the whole life of society, it is very important that they participate more widely also in the fields of the Church's apostolate."[49] Earlier, Pope John XXIII said, in *Pacem in Terris* (1963), that women's participation in public life is one of the most significant "signs of the times" to which the Church should attend. And in 1971 the Third World Synod of Bishops called for women to participate in, and share responsibility for, the life of society and of the Church. But the leadership of the Church stops short when the question of ordination arises.

During the pontificate of Pope Paul VI, in 1972, the ministries of acolyte and lector were restored to the laity when the apostolic letter *Ministeria Quaedam* (Certain Ministries) was published. Women were given permission to serve in both capacities, but formal commissioning to those offices was reserved to men. Because of this discriminatory attitude many dioceses simply discontinued the practice of commissioning.

In 1976 the Pontifical Biblical Commission stated that Scripture alone did not support the exclusion of women from ordination. But in that same year, and despite that report, the Congregation for the Doctrine of the Faith issued the *Declaration on the Question of the Ordination of Women*, which presented arguments against the ordination of women to the priesthood without any mention of the report of the Pontifical Biblical Commission. The main arguments given were that the Church is following Jesus, who chose only men as apostles; that it has been the constant tradition of the Church; and that the "natural resemblance" between Christ and the celebrant of the Eucharist would be difficult to see were the role not assumed by a man. This *Declaration* still remains the most basic presentation of the Vatican position. Of course, voluminous responses have been presented in the past 20 years.

The arguments in the *Declaration* are by no means simplistic and are summarized brilliantly by Dennis Doyle in *The Church Emerging from Vatican II*.[50] Another excellent analysis is given by Bernier in *Ministry in the Church*.[51] Important in this regard, and summarized by Bernier, is the contribution to the literature on this subject made by Sarah Butler. Butler was the head of the Catholic Theological Society of America's task force studying the issue of women's ordination, and is a proponent of women's ordination. In an honest and straightforward analysis of the Vatican's position, Butler, in an article titled "Second Thoughts on the Ordination of Women," points out that many who disagree with the Congregation for the Doctrine of the Faith's position do not always understand the position they are trying to refute.[52] Her article led to an interesting series of articles on the subject in the 1991 issues of *Worship* magazine. Butler makes clear that although one may not agree with the Vatican's position, even after probing the depths of its arguments, it is important to understand the anthropology that forms the basis of those documents, which she explains in these articles.

The *Declaration on the Question of the Ordination of Women* admits that its arguments are not probative. However, it believes that the arguments of those who favor the ordination of women are very speculative and impossible to prove. Because it is a matter of doubt, the *Declaration* says it is better to rely on the tradition itself as most clearly representing the will of God. Despite the conclusions of the magisterium the issue will not go away. Continuing dialogue is necessary, and only with mutual respect will a resolution take place. Many believe that women will be ordained at some time in the future.

THE PERMANENT DIACONATE

The origins of the diaconate are found during the New Testament period. By the time of Ignatius of Antioch at the beginning of the second century, the position of the deacon was already established as a constituent part of the hierarchy. The diaconate flourished in the second and third centuries, and much of the early history of this office can be pieced together from assorted letters, canons of local councils, and theological writings of the day.

The functions of a deacon varied from place to place, but ministries of charity, liturgy, and diverse forms of ministry of the Word were common. In some places deacons were the principal administrative agents of their bishops and often were more powerful than any of the presbyters. Deacons received monies and goods to be dispensed for service to the Church, such as care of widows and those in need. They sought out those in need and distributed aid. They represented the bishop on many occasions and assisted him during the liturgy. Each of these tasks became more involved and more formalized as time passed. Deacons became the bishop's advisor, legal representative, and confidant. They were often the most logical choices to succeed the bishop on his natural death or martyrdom.

In the third and fourth centuries the diaconate in the West began to decline for several reasons. As the Eucharist increasingly became the focus of ministry, the role of the priest, who presided at Mass, became more important than that of the deacon. As the role of the priest increased within the Church, so did rivalry with the order of deacons. To some priests it became more and more intolerable to have deacons exercise the bishop's power. The abuses of power and position by some deacons were all that was needed to justify change in local churches. Church councils during the fourth century emphasized the inferior status of deacons in relationship to priests. By the seventh century the diaconate in the West had become simply a transitional step for candidates to the priesthood. What we know today as the permanent diaconate had ceased to exist.

The Council of Trent in the sixteenth century reaffirmed the place of the diaconate, though its call for an implementation of that office was never realized. In *The Dogmatic Constitution on the Church*, Vatican II restored the diaconate as a permanent order of ministers in the Church. The *Constitution* briefly described the nature and functions of this office and left it to local episcopal conferences to decide, with papal approval, whether or not to restore the diaconate in their own countries.[53] Following the council's closure, Pope Paul VI implemented the council's decision by establishing canonical norms for the permanent diaconate and new rites for the conferral of the ministry. The bishops of the United States in 1968 petitioned the Holy See to restore the diaconate in this country, and permission was granted to do so. In the discussions before and during the council that led to the reestablishment of the permanent diaconate, three primary motives were at work, according to a document titled *Permanent Deacons in the United States*, published by the Bishops' Committee, which dealt with this issue.[54] The first was a desire to restore to the Church the full complement of active apostolic ministries. A second motive was the desire to integrate and strengthen with sacramental ordination and grace those who were, in fact, already exercising deaconal functions. The third goal was to provide ministers in churches in which functions vital to the Church's life could not be carried out.

The diaconate program involves more than three years of study and formation. Because 90 percent of the candidates are married, their wives are encouraged to attend classes with their husbands. On ordination a permanent deacon is understood by Canon Law to be a cleric and is thus required to be attached to a diocese and subject to the laws governing clerics, though with some exceptions, such as the right to marry. However, no one ordained to the diaconate can marry after ordination if he is single at that time, or, if married, he may not remarry on the death of his wife. Ordinarily a deacon derives his own financial support from his secular occupation.

The ministries of a permanent deacon are many. Primarily he is to be a minister of love and justice by serving needy individuals. He is also to be a minister of the Word, proclaiming the Gospel at the liturgy, preaching, giving catechetical instructions, and serving the community in many other pastoral ways. He is greatly involved in the ministry of the liturgy. As has been said, at Mass he can proclaim the Gospel and preach. He can also voice the needs of the people in the general intercessions, assist in the presentation of the gifts, and distribute communion.

The deacon can also perform other liturgical roles, such as baptizing, witnessing marriages, bringing the Eucharist to the infirm and to the dying, and presiding over funerals and burials. In addition to these roles, he can also preside over liturgies of the Word, the Liturgy of the Hours, exposition and benediction of the Blessed Sacrament, lead nonsacramental reconciliation services, and conduct prayer services for sick and dying individuals. According to Vatican II, Pope Paul VI's *Sacrum Diaconatus Ordinem* (The Sacred Order of the Diaconate), and the *Code of Canon Law* (Canon 517), deacons may be given charge over the pastoral care of Christian communities that cannot be provided a pastor in the person of a priest. They may also be involved in pastoral programs aimed at creating and guiding small Christian communities within parishes or in particular sectors of society.

Deacons can and do provide great service in many parishes throughout the United States. However, there are still some priests who will not deal with permanent deacons in any fashion. Many such priests are silent about their dislikes. Those who do speak out often recall specific incidents to which they took exception. Some freely admit they cannot adapt to the role of a deacon in their parish and feel uncomfortable with the idea, because it is something that was not part of their own training. Fortunately, the priests who have difficulty with deacons are in the minority, and for the most part the permanent diaconate is thriving.

RELIGIOUS ORDERS AND CONGREGATIONS

Religious orders and congregations, such as the Dominicans, Franciscans, and Jesuits, are communities who live under a religious rule and publicly profess the vows of poverty, chastity, and obedience. They are recognized by Church authority and subject to Canon Law. Each group has a central authority structure. There are also some religious communities, such as the Benedictines, who belong to associations of autonomous monasteries and follow a common rule. The distinction between "orders" and "congregations" is outdated and was based on technical differences concerning the status of one's vows.

Religious orders and congregations are composed of those ordained to the priesthood and brothers who take the vows of poverty, chastity, and obedience but who choose not to present themselves for ordination. This is the brothers' way of responding to a call to live the Gospel in a religious community. Since Vatican II many brothers have moved from the more traditional ministries such as education and health care to a wide variety of other ministries, such as those pertaining to peace and justice. Religious brothers are often members of the older monastic orders, such as the Benedictines and Trappists, and of the more active clerical orders that arose beginning in the thirteenth century, including the Franciscans, Dominicans, Jesuits, and others. There are religious brothers who do not belong to clerical orders or congregations, such as the Christian Brothers, known formally as De La Salle Christian Brothers, who were founded in 1680 by Jean Baptiste de La Salle in Rheims, France, for the education of poor children. Christian Brothers are members of a religious congregation of laymen who do not aspire to be priests but who serve the Church in a variety of ways, including teaching young people, especially poor individuals. They are also involved in ministries such as family counseling, refugee work, writing and publishing, retreats, and campus ministry.

Religious life began toward the end of the third century in Egypt, and its development has been of great importance to the Catholic Church. At Vatican II one of the 16 documents issued was the *Decree on the Appropriate Renewal of the Religious Life*. Such renewal depends on two principles: first, a continuous return to the sources of all Christian life and to the original inspiration behind a particular community; and second, an adjustment of the community to the changed conditions of the times.[55] Each community must always see itself as part of the Church and as participants in its mission, and make adjustments according to the spirit of the Gospel. However, some religious communities have freely decided to preserve the traditional forms of religious life, such as wearing traditional religious clothing (habits), maintaining traditional places of residence (convents and other religious houses), and observing traditional modes of exercising authority (more directive than collegial).

The decline in the number of priests (which includes both diocesan and religious priests) has previously been discussed. The same kind of decline is found among women religious in the United States, despite the important adjustments and contributions being made by the sisters who remain in religious life. In the three-year period of 1963 to 1966, an estimated 4,332 left the convent. Yet new members continued to join the various communities during those years. As a result the total number of women religious in the United States peaked in 1966 at 181,421.[56] In 1993, there were only 94,022 nuns, of whom only 3 percent were 40 years of age or younger, 37 percent were older than 70 years of age, and 12 percent were older than 80. The median age for nuns today is between the ages of 65 and 70 and for priests between 55 and 60. Sociologists have analyzed why there has been such an exodus from religious life during the past 30 years and have arrived at fairly consistent answers. According to research, the primary reason priests leave is that they find difficulties with the structure of the Church and the work they are called on to do, and because many of them wish to get married. With regard to women religious, the desire for greater self-fulfillment, aside from marriage, is the primary personal reason they give for leaving religious life. Other reasons relate to the religious life itself; some women see no value in it, and others feel their communities were not following the teachings of Vatican II and as a result were not changing fast enough, if at all.

Most sisters who are active members of their communities today are very well-educated and committed individuals, and they are making great contributions in many areas, including theological and biblical scholarship. In addition, many religious sisters have left their traditional work of teaching and have entered a variety of new ministries. It is not uncommon to see sisters directing public service agencies, working as hospital and prison chaplains, and serving as campus ministers and as community organizers. In the future some communities will cease to exist and others will flourish, depending on their faithfulness to the Gospel and their ability to adjust to the conditions of the day.

THE LAITY

Initially, after Jesus's Resurrection, his followers called themselves the "brethren" (Acts 1:16), "disciples" (Acts 11:26), "believers" (Acts 2:44), and members of "the Way" (Acts 9:2). But early in Church history the name "Christian" was applied to the disciples of Jesus by those who were not members of the new community. The use of this name apparently began in Antioch, Syria, in approximately 40 A.D. (Acts 11:26). Others spoke of "Christians" as those loyal to Christ, just as they spoke of "Caesareans" as those who were loyal to Caesar. By the beginning of Nero's persecution of the Christian community in 64 A.D., "Christian" was the Roman Empire's official name for Jesus's followers, or so it would seem from the *Annals of Tacitus* (15:44).

"Laity" comes from the Greek *laos,* which means "people" and originally referred to the entire early Christian community, the members of whom believed they were the new "chosen people." In the early Church there was no hard and fast distinction between clergy and laity. All the baptized were members of Christ's body. Some of the baptized were "set apart," which is the meaning of the word "clergy" *(cleros)*. They were "set apart" for service to the entire community. As was discussed earlier, a division between laity and clergy began to develop with the establishment of Christianity as the state religion in the fourth century and, as Richard McBrien points out, was fostered "with the transformation of the clergy into a kind of civil service, with all the political and economic privileges of rank and status."[57]

The division between clergy and laity widened during the Middle Ages when theologians and canonists divided the Church into two separate states: the *ordo clericorum* and the *ordo laicorum*. As McBrien writes,

> The latter (the laity) was composed of men of the world, given to the flesh. The former was composed of those devoted to the spiritual realm (the clergy), responsible for the governance of the Church. The division was influenced also by a Neoplatonist view of the world, which defined reality as gradational and hierarchical, consisting of lower and higher forms. The clergy were at the higher end, with the pope at the very top, and the laity were at the bottom.[58]

The subordination of laity in the Church continued until Vatican II, when the laity came to be regarded more positively than it had since the time of Constantine. The council emphasized that all Christians, laity and clergy alike, are called to be active and responsible members of the Church. All have a role to play in the building up of the Church and in the salvation of the world. By baptism all Christians belong to the priesthood of Jesus Christ. *The Dogmatic Constitution on the Church* states,

> For their part, the faithful join in the offering of the Eucharist by virtue of their royal priesthood. They likewise exercise that priesthood by receiving the sacraments, by prayer and thanksgiving, by the witness of a holy life, and by self-denial and active charity.[59]

The council made clear that an *essential* distinction exists between the ordained priesthood and the priesthood of the faithful. Ordination is not simply an intensification of the common priesthood. The common and ordained priesthoods are not different in terms of their Christian calling because all are called to holiness. Rather, the distinction lies in the ministries. Preaching and teaching, service and sacraments, for the sake of the entire community, belong in a distinct way to the ordained priesthood. However, the apostolate of the laity "is a participation in the saving mission of the Church."[60] The idea of the lay apostolate as a participation in the apostolate of the hierarchy is explicitly abandoned. The apostolate does not belong exclusively to the ordained members of the community. The Holy Spirit is not the private preserve of any special group in the Church. In fact, the council reminds pastors that they have a duty of "acknowledging with joy and fostering with diligence the various humble and exalted charisms of the laity."[61]

There are a number of positive ideas concerning the laity found in the documents of Vatican II. Most important of all is the teaching that the laity, as part of the people of God, have the fullness of Christian life, dignity, and mission. They are not second-class citizens but full members of the Church. Before the council the so-called lay apostolate was understood in terms of "Catholic action." Whatever lay persons did in the Church was always in terms of assisting the hierarchy with *their* ministry. The hierarchy decided when and under what circumstances the laity would be asked to share in that ministry. Vatican II changed this by teaching that the lay apostolate has a *direct sharing* in the mission of the Church and are participants in this mission not by reason of delegation by the hierarchy but because of their baptism and confirmation, which empower all believers to share in some form of the ministry. *The Dogmatic Constitution on the Church* states, "The lay apostolate is a participation in the saving mission of the Church itself. Through their baptism and confirmation, all are commissioned to that apostolate by the Lord himself."[62]

Clergy and laity alike are partners in the life and mission of the Church. The clergy, especially including the bishops, deal primarily with the ecclesial realm and the laity with the temporal. However, both clergy and laity have a role to play in all areas of life. Concerning the clergy, the *Pastoral Constitution on the Church in the Modern World* makes clear that they have an important role to play in the so-called temporal order. The *Constitution* says they have "the right to pass moral judgment, even on matters touching the political order, whenever basic personal rights or the salvation of souls make such judgments necessary."[63] Conversely, the laity have an important role to play in the internal life of the Church as we learn from *The Dogmatic Constitution on the Church*. The internal life of the Church, we are told, pertains to liturgy, religious education, ministry to needy individuals, and even to matters of governance.[64] The internal life of the Church is every Catholic's business. So, too, is the Church's external mission to the world at large. The two are not mutually opposed.

Christian service in the world is represented in a preeminent way by the laity, who make up more than 98 percent of the people of God. Such service includes civic and public activity, peace and justice concerns, and social, political, and economic involvement. It is the laity who are called on to portray Christian values in the areas of business ethics, economics, cultural development, and family life. Also, many laypersons, male and female, now perform professional ministries within the Church, and this represents a new development, at least in relation to the more recent past. Many dioceses have inaugurated training programs for lay ministers. Religious education has become an especially popular field for the laity, a result in great measure to the dearth of religious sisters and priests in the Church today.

Other areas in which laity have become strongly involved ministerially are liturgical music, youth programs, social justice activities, counseling, and visiting sick and elderly individuals. The expansion of the concept of ministry to include the nonordained is not without its problems, such as the low salaries often paid to full-time lay ministers. Another difficulty is the lack of authority and decision-making authority such people have in a clerically controlled Church. As time passes, these problems, it is hoped, will be rectified. Authority of almost any kind has difficulty sharing its power, but such sharing must eventually take place. This is especially true because in the twenty-first century even more of the Church's members, women and men alike, will be involved ministerially, though not ordained.

It is of great importance to recall that Vatican II did away with the differentiation of the various "states of life," which place the laity in the most subordinate position. The council clearly proclaimed the universal call to holiness of all Christians, clergy and laity alike. *The Dogmatic Constitution on the Church* states,

> Thus it is evident to everyone that all the faithful of Christ of whatever rank or status are called to the fullness of the Christian life and to the perfection of charity. By this holiness a more human way of life is promoted even in this earthly society.[65]

Not only are lay people included in God's call to holiness but theirs is a unique calling requiring a unique response, which itself is a gift of the Holy Spirit. They receive this call in their daily lives, in and through the events of the world and the complex decisions and conflicting values with which they have to struggle. The response of the laity to their call promises to contribute much to the spiritual heritage of the Church. Everyone has special charisms that can and should contribute to the total life of the Church. Many of these gifts were simply not evoked or heeded in the preconciliar Church, and this presents a challenge to the local parish and the pastor, because, for the most part, the spiritual needs of the laity must be met in the parish.

THE LOCAL PARISH

The word "church" can be understood in a variety of ways, but there are three usages most commonly applied. First, *church* may refer to all Christ-

ian believers throughout the world, whatever their denominational preference. Second, *church* for Catholics can refer to the hierarchy—the pope and
the bishops. When one speaks of the teaching of the Church on a particular
issue, the official stance of the magisterium concerning a question of doctrine or morality is often the point of reference. Finally, *church* may mean
the local church, which represents a particular geographical place such as
a diocese. The cultural ethos of the local church, whether in Africa or Latin
America, for example, contributes to the uniqueness of that community and
helps determine its role in the universal church. The three ways of describing the "church" are obviously interrelated. One of the achievements of Vatican II was the rediscovery of the relative autonomy of the local church in
relation to the primacy of the Church of Rome. This marks a dramatic
change because, following the Council of Trent and especially during the
past two centuries, emphasis was placed by Catholic theologians on a uni-
versalist ecclesiology that stressed papal authority and left little room for a
theology of the local church.

Vatican II affirmed the presence of the universal church in the local
church. At times the word "particular" is used rather than "local" in desig-
nating the local community. The words are interchangeable in the documents of the council. The local church may be defined in two ways. In the
strictest sense, the local church is primarily a diocese, though it can also
mean several dioceses in the same nation or region. In a broader sense, the
local church is the parish. The local church, both the diocese and the individual parish, *is* the church, because they have Christ totally present. *The
Dogmatic Constitution on the Church* states, "This church of Christ is truly
present in all legitimate congregations of the faithful."[66] The universal
church is the communion of local churches. The local church represents the
universal church, but obviously is not the whole church. The local and universal church are mutually dependent. As Granfield writes, "Local churches are not self-sufficient nor isolated; they do not stand alone but always in
communion with other local churches. Otherwise the unity of both the universal and the local church is endangered."[67]

It is clear that the local church is the Church of Christ, but nevertheless remains only partially autonomous and must always be in contact with
the shared faith of the universal church and with the Church of Rome.

The parish must meet the spiritual needs of its people. It must be a
place in which parishioners can come together with their leaders for mutual spiritual enrichment, much as in the early Church. Spirituality depends
on *community*. This is true theologically and sociologically. Research makes
clear that living one's faith depends on the support of the community. The
work of the priest–sociologist Father Andrew Greeley and others indicates
that support of one's spouse and family of origin, or of some other important
community, is critically important for the development of an active faith.[68]
Greeley points out that the most important influences are local—the religious behavior of one's spouse and the quality of preaching in the parish

church. He goes on to say that there are four important religious socialization experiences, four sets of influences that shape a person's religious life: parents, spouse, parish priest, and children. Parents are most important of all, but one's spouse will powerfully reinforce or perhaps even reverse parental influence. The parish priest, though not as important as either parent or spouse, still plays an important role, because it is in the parish in which people do their living and dying, their mourning and rejoicing, their meditating and praying. It is in the parish where Christ's presence is most visibly represented.[69]

A vital parish has a real sense of church community. This is found to a high degree in some parishes, but is lacking in others. In recent years there has been an erosion of community, both within the Church and in society at large. Evidence indicates that American Catholicism has acquired a less communal cast than it once had. Most obviously, a good number of American Catholics no longer regularly attend Sunday Mass. Also, many of the shared factors that fostered an intense community life have dwindled, including immigrant status, low income, and discrimination. As Philip J. Murnion observes,

> Now American Catholics have become part of other communities that have acquired significance for them, communities associated with their middle-class status and income level, with the neighborhoods in which they live, or with their vocational or avocational interests. The church is no longer needed as an enclosed, protective, and exclusive community.[70]

Murnion argues that presently in the United States there are five basic approaches to restoring church community. Another way of saying this is that there are five approaches currently being used to revitalize the life of a given parish. These are traditionalism, sectarianism of the left and the right, intimacy, association, and solidarity.[71] It will be useful to briefly summarize and comment on these approaches.

The *traditionalist response* to revitalizing the parish community is a return to the past and may entail the use of the Baltimore Catechism, the Tridentine (Latin) Mass, pious devotions of the past, and even earlier forms of church discipline. Traditionalists want religious women, for example, to wear their habits and perform the kind of ministry that they did so well before Vatican II. As Murnion observes, this view canonizes a particular period and endows it with a special authority that no other period in Church history ever enjoyed. In this approach ministry again becomes a clerical preserve and the participative structures, such as parish councils, are greatly reduced in importance, if not totally eliminated.

The *sectarian response,* whether of the left or of the right, to revitalizing parish life inevitably reduces true discipleship to an elitism that sees the true Church in rather narrow focus. Those on the left see themselves as a prophetic and religious remnant. They are pacifists who engage in fasts and demonstrations or risk their freedom to preserve life and promote justice. This is certainly a powerful position but one that will never include the whole community. The sectarian of the right is given to testimony of praise rather than of prophecy. This is the community of the Spirit, the spirituality of the charismatic renewal. For them, interior renewal is the key to community revitalization. The point is to live as much as possible the new life of the spirit rather then to try and change the world. Murnion correctly observes that no parish will completely embody either of these types of sectarian community, but some parishioners will operate with their approach as the ultimate model of community. Though both groups, the prophetic and charismatic, have much to offer, they are communities of the special movement and not the model of renewal to which all members of the parish will be called.

The third response to the problem of community comes from those who would try to restore relationships within the Church on *intimate terms*. Murnion refers to this response as the community of the encounter weekend, groups that foster marriage encounter, teenage encounter, and renewal programs that focus on emotional relationships among the participants. The intimacy proposed is certainly valuable because it pertains to family, forgiveness, and other important needs. Some priestly renewal programs belong in this category. Although they do not specifically propose intimacy, they put a premium on fraternal relationships among priests and with the bishop. Such intimacy responds well to the fragmentation of our time and the anonymity of urban culture and can be very helpful to a parish. But it can be but one aspect of parish life, because true intimacy can be achieved only with a few others.

A fourth approach, described by Murnion, is to give up the attempt to create community altogether and to settle for the parish as an *association*. A parish is a good association if it offers a variety of useful activities for its diverse members without trying to bind them together in a common faith, a common understanding, or a common action. Delivery of services becomes prominent, and multiplicity of activity is necessary. Many of these activities and services are undertaken not only with religious conviction but within a religious context. The association model, according to Murnion, "offers efficient services and is impatient with all the passions of the traditionalists or sectarians, and all the personal involvement required for intimacy. This is the 'civilized' religion."[72] The association model forsakes the attempt to bind people together in a community and to maintain the connections among its members while respecting their diversity of interests.

The fifth position, and the one endorsed by Murnion, is what he refers to as the *community of solidarity*. Such a congregation moves beyond the circle of intimacy and speaks to the inclusiveness of community. Jesus did not come to bind us together with those with whom we are already intimate or with whom we already share close ties. He came to bind us together with strangers. Hence Jesus's constant positioning of the Samaritan, of the stranger, in the center of the community's concern and interest.

A community of solidarity is not only an inclusive community but is also one that sees its faith as a basis of action. This community always links its beliefs and actions. Thus the Sunday liturgy becomes its central action. All are met with hospitality and joy. A community of solidarity puts a high premium on the action of God in the human community—action that sanctifies one's daily actions and makes it possible to transcend his or her limitations. Such a community places high value on respecting tradition, on linking the past with the future, on building structures for participation and action, on presenting strong theological foundations for the positions it adopts, and on recognizing the importance of authority for any enduring and authentic community. Obviously, the achievement of solidarity depends on the quality of ministry. A strong parish team is needed, as is excellent preaching. The challenge is to remain open to all while representing commitment to Christian discipleship. Paternalism, or clericalism, would mark the death knell of such a parish community. Such a community of solidarity must also foster smaller, more homogenous groups throughout the parish to meet the needs of all. Finally, a community of solidarity calls for a church in which everyone in every situation is treated with respect.

DEMOCRATIZATION OF STRUCTURES

The Catholic Church is not in any formal sense a democracy, as has been discussed previously. As Pope Paul VI wrote in his first major encyclical, *Ecclesiam Suam:* "The Church is not a democratic association, established by human will."[73] In the Church, authority is not derived through constitutional structure from the sovereignty of the people but from the authority of Jesus Christ. In a democracy legitimate government rests on the consensus of the ruled, and citizens always retain their basic power to serve as the ultimate source of legitimate authority. The notion of the inalienable sovereignty of the people further distinguishes Church structure from democracy. However, it is important to distinguish between authority as a formal system of governance and an ethos of democracy. As John Coleman writes,

> [N]othing, in principle, impedes its [the Church] adapting democratic forms of governance that it then tailors and transmutes to fit its own unique theological self-understanding. That theological understanding

is the constitution of the church as a hierarchical communion institut-
ed by the will of Christ and governed by norms of *collegiality, subsidiarity,* and *justice* as participation.[74]

A program of reform ordered to improve participation of Church members meets no obstacle from Canon Law. The 1983 revised *Code of Canon
Law* either mandates or allows many new forms of participative governance in the Church. Yet a genuinely participative structure in the Church
remains an ideal rather than a reality. As Coleman observes, "Democratization, in forms of governance that are not democracies, envisions the formal enactment of norms of consultation, collaboration, accountability, and
due process, even in the absence of a mechanism of election."[75]

Churches in democratic societies such as exist in the United States
and elsewhere can expect to experience pressures toward democratization,
and this has taken place. The strongest demands of many American
Catholic laypersons is urging greater democratization of the structures of
Church governance. A representative sample of American Catholic laity
shows that a majority of those 55 years of age and younger favor the idea
that the Church should have more democratic decision making at the local
parish, diocesan and Vatican levels.[76] Moreover, as Granfield and others
persuasively argue, when the Church exists as a voluntary organization
within a democracy its very credibility as an authority depends on its responding to calls for democratization.[77] Without democratization the
Church suffers a crisis of legitimization. As Granfield notes,

> On a practical level, the bureaucratic system of the church diminishes its
> legitimization when it neglects consultation, collaboration, accountabil-
> ity and due process and when it assumes an adversarial and negative at-
> titude. An overly monarchical and centralized bureaucracy distances
> itself from the faithful and loses its contact with urgent pastoral needs.
> Administrative procedures and management styles have to be critically
> assessed, in order to avoid the undesirable aspects of bureaucracy such
> as inflexibility, cumbersomeness, inefficiency and unfairness.[78]

Even though the Church is not formally a democracy, its theological
self-understanding since Vatican II encourages a thorough application of
the democratic ethos to its structure and behavior, and this is rooted in the
notion of a universal priesthood of all believers. Added to this, *The Dogmatic
Constitution on the Church* states, "There is in Christ no inequality on the
basis of race or nationality, social condition or sex."[79] And Vatican II chose
an inclusive rather than a hierarchical metaphor, "the people of God," as its
primary model for understanding the Church. The major impetus for democratization in the Church derives from Vatican II's definition of the
Church as a collegial community. Collegiality is extended not only to the
bishops and priests but to the laity as well. As was seen earlier, the council

stated that laypersons have the right and often the duty to give their judgment on the Church's internal affairs.[80] The revised *Code of Canon Law* teaches that the laity also share in the governing office of Christ. The *Code* states that the Christian faithful "have become sharers in Christ's priestly, prophetic and royal office and are called to exercise the mission which God has entrusted to the church to fulfill in the world, in accord with the condition proper to each one."[81]

The Church must rethink its structures in more communal, diversified, and democratic ways. But it would be naive to advocate pluralism and decentralization in the reshaping of the Catholic Church without considering the dangers of fragmentation and factionalism. In this regard Eugene Bianchi and Rosemary Ruether, the editors of *A Democratic Catholic Church*, write,

> Yet these dangers are no more endemic to democratic than to totalitarian systems. Moreover, within democratic societies the tendencies to alienation and disintegration can be more favorably mitigated by the many networks of dialogue and representation that are lacking in authoritarian, vertical systems of control. If the centralized authority of the Vatican monarchy were structurally changed, the result could be an even greater sense of unity in the Church. Individuals and groups at various levels would feel responsible for the welfare of the Church. They would experience the unitive thrust of upholding an institution that maximized their freedoms. The polarity of resolving conflicts is necessary and beneficial. It pushes us to overcome barriers between persons and groups.[82]

At the beginning of the twenty-first century, a major task for the Catholic Church is inner reform toward democratic structures. The history of the Church from its inception offers many examples of participational movements. A truly renewed Church could be a catalyst for other great reforms in relation to social justice and true peace.

SUMMARY

An important question asked today by Catholics is how the Church can better express a shared authority. In other words, how can the concept of collegiality be put into practice in a realistic fashion. The clerically controlled institutionalization of the Church began in the fourth century and reached its zenith in the nineteenth century at Vatican I (1870) with the dogmatic definition of papal primacy and of papal infallibility. Vatican II emphasized the coresponsibility among the bishops of the world with the pope as expressed in ecumenical councils, synods, and episcopal conferences. It gave the Church new directions in its authoritative structures in calling on the pope to work more closely with the bishops.

Clergy and laity alike are partners in the life and mission of the Church. Both clergy and laity have a role to play in all areas of life. The concept of ministry has been expanded to include nonordained people. The response of the laity to their call promises to contribute much to the spiritual heritage of the Church. We all have special charisms that can and should contribute to the total life of the Church. Many of these gifts were simply not evoked or heeded in the preconciliar Church, and this fact presents a challenge to the local parish and the pastor, because the spiritual needs of the laity must be met in large part in the parish. The need for a collegial relationship between priests and people is evident.

We have seen that the need for collegiality at all levels of the Church's life is most important. Many American Catholic laypersons are urging greater democratization of the structure of Church governance. As Granfield and others have argued, because the Church exists as a voluntary organization its very credibility as an authority depends on its responding to calls for democratization. Even though the Church is not a democracy, its theological self-understanding since Vatican II encourages a thorough application of the democratic ethos to its structure and behavior, and this is rooted in the notion of a universal priesthood of all believers. The Church must rethink its structures in more communal, diversified, and democratic ways. A truly renewed Church could be a catalyst for other great reforms in relation to social justice and true peace for the world.

Study Questions

1. What does John A. Coleman mean by "progressive" Catholics; By "integralist" Catholics? Is this a valid distinction? Can two such diverse groups coexist within the same Church?

2. When did the beginning of a clerically controlled institutionalization of the Church take place? Why? Has this changed since Vatican II?

3. What is the importance of Gratian's *Decrees* (1140 A.D.) concerning celibacy? What do you think would happen if celibacy were made optional for priests?

4. What is the meaning of "collegiality"? How is this applied at the parish level?

5. Describe the function of the following: Synod of Bishops, Episcopal Conferences, Priests' Senates, Diocesan councils. Why do you think parish councils were not mandated?

6. What are some of the reasons for the decline of vocations to the priesthood? The sisterhood? How can this be remedied?

7. What is the primary role of a priest? Explain.

8. List some of the new roles being played by Catholic women in general and the sisterhood in particular? How have these changes influenced the Church?

9. Describe the three usages most commonly applied to the word "church." How do most people understand the word "church" today?

10. What is the role of a deacon?

11. What kind of parish does Philip Murnion advocate? Do you agree with his position?

12. What is meant by the term "apostolate of the laity"? How does the correct understanding of this term affect the ordinary Catholic?

CHAPTER 3

Catholicism as a Global Church: The Problem of Inculturation

Fr. Karl Rahner, the noted Jesuit theologian, proposed in several lectures he gave in the late 1970s that the most fundamental significance of Vatican II is that it was the first historical manifestation of a truly world Church that acts through the mutual influence of its various parts. For centuries preceding Vatican II the Church had been characteristically Western. But Catholicism is moving from a long period of being centered culturally in Europe and North America to a period in which its life unfolds in the world as a whole. Most consequences of this development have yet to be realized, but it seems clear that they will have major implications for the missionary movement, for variety in liturgical celebrations, and for real pluralism in Church law and practice.

Questions about the de-Europeanizing of the Church raise theoretical problems whose answers are not clear, and it is also evident that leadership in Rome still has the mentality of a centralized and Western bureaucracy. Further complicating matters is the fact that individual cultures, often emerging from centuries of European colonization, are in a process of change. As a consequence it is impossible at the moment to say what values many individual cultures can offer to the Church. Nevertheless, it is incontestable that at Vatican II, for the first time, a worldwide council with a worldwide episcopate came into existence. Representatives of the episcopate, including many native African and Asian bishops, actively participated. Something like a qualitative leap took place, even though many of the characteristics of the old Western Church continue to predominate.

Rahner believed that theologically speaking there are three great epochs in Church history. He says the third period began at Vatican II:

First, the short period of Jewish Christianity. Second, the period of the Church in a distinct cultural region, namely, that of Hellenism and of European culture and civilization. Third, the period in which the sphere of the Church's life is in fact the entire world. These three periods signify three essential and different basic situations for Christianity and its preaching. Within them, of course, there can be very important subdivisions: for example, in the second period, through the caesuras or breaks which occur with the transition from antiquity to the Middle Ages and with the transition from medieval culture to European colonialism and the Enlightenment. In all this one would have to clarify the causes of these multiple and yet interrelated breaks.[1]

Transitions from one epoch to another take place unreflectively. They are not first planned theologically and then put into effect. Rather, the process of change occurs and is later recognized. Presently, together with the recognition of Catholicism as a world Church with indigenous leadership, there is the equally important realization that the Church must be rooted in the various cultures of the world. In becoming Christians the peoples of the world are expected to be fully themselves in their respective historical contexts and to enrich the universal Christian community with their particular cultural heritage. There is a growing tendency to designate such a process by the term "inculturation," which deals with the interaction of faith on the one hand and culture on the other.

The term "culture" denotes the set of customs, rules, institutions, and values inherent in the life of a community, which express the aspirations of the society and the norms for the interactions of people and groups in that society. "Inculturation" is defined by Aylward Shorter as "the creative and dynamic relationship between the Christian message and a culture or cultures."[2] Fr. Pedro Arrupe, S.J., as general of the Jesuits, in 1978 in a *Letter to the Whole Society on Inculturation*, defines the word as follows:

> Inculturation is the incarnation of the Christian life and of the Christian message in a particular cultural context, in such a way that this experience not only finds expression through elements proper to the culture in question (this alone would be no more than a superficial adaptation) but becomes a principle that animates, directs and unifies the culture, transforming it and remaking it so as to bring about a "new creation."[3]

Shorter lists three notable traits of inculturation. First, it is an ongoing process and is relevant to every country or region in which seeds of the faith have been sown. Second, Christian faith cannot exist except in a cultural form. Third, between Christian faith and culture there should be interaction and reciprocal assimilation.[4] Inculturation differs from a mere external adaptation. It signifies an interior transformation of authentic cultural values through their integration into Christianity and the rooting of Christianity in various cultures found throughout the world.

The Church has always expressed its faith through cultural forms. Inculturation implies that the Christian message transforms a culture and in turn is transformed *by* culture. This mutual transformation occurs, according to Shorter, "not in a way that falsifies the Christian message, but in the way by which the message is formulated and interpreted anew."[5] The inculturation of Christianity into different cultures is a duty of the Church. This is certainly true of the teachings of Vatican II and of Pope Paul VI and Pope John Paul II. However, because inculturation raises hard questions and involves unprecedented challenges, it is often not seriously applied. Because the Church is accustomed to its Euro-American domination, alternative expressions of the Christian faith are discomforting. And yet positive action must be taken.

Today, at the beginning of the twenty-first century, we are conscious of how long the Church has been concentrated in the West. In modern written histories of the Church more than 90 percent of the material deals with the Western Church. Statistically, at the beginning of this century, approximately 85 percent of all Christians lived in the West. European hegemony over both the world at large and the Church in particular reached both its peak and the beginning of its decline during World War II. Africans and Asians were still under European domination at the end of the war. Since that time, however, more than 100 developing nations have won their independence in the demise of colonialism.

In 1900, 70 percent of Roman Catholics lived in the Northern hemisphere and only 30 percent in the Southern hemisphere. However, those numbers are now reversed, with approximately 70 percent of the Roman Catholic population living in the Southern hemisphere and 30 percent in the Northern hemisphere. Numerically, Roman Catholicism has become a church of developing nations. And developing-nations' communities are more youthful, with more than 40 percent of the population age 15 or younger. It seems clear that in the third millennium important Church leadership will come from the southern hemisphere. The various cultures found therein must be respected and inculturation must be permitted.

Roman Catholicism is in a period of transition. Just as the transition from the Jewish to the gentile Christian church took place under tension, so also the transition from a Western to a truly world Church, from unity to pluriformity, will take place under tension. As Walter Buhlmann writes,

> One pole in the church, central power, concentrates on unity. This is its right and duty. All the more, however, must the other pole, the bishops and the episcopal conferences, enter into dialogue defending their interests and their complementary viewpoints so that genuine parity and balance can come between the two poles. Unity certainly, but within pluriformity.[6]

Until Vatican II complete uniformity reigned in the Catholic Church for more than 16 centuries. The same Latin liturgy was used everywhere and there was the same centrally controlled Church discipline. As long as the Church lived in a European cultural setting such a modality was workable and acceptable for most people. But today the Church exists on six continents (North America, South America, Africa, Asia, Australia, and Europe), each having its own political, cultural, and ecclesial histories. The Church must be radically incarnated into these cultures. Because of this, Vatican II in a cautious fashion, and later more boldly by Pope Paul VI in *Evangelii Nuntiandi* (Preaching the Gospel or On Evangelization in the Modern World), spoke of the incarnation (inculturation) of the Church in diverse cultures, and with it legitimate pluriformity, not as a threat to unity but as an enrichment of Church life, a true expression of unity in diversity.[7]

HISTORICAL EXAMPLES OF INCULTURATION

A review of some of the most dramatic attempts of what is presently referred to as "inculturation" will help to illustrate the difficulties of the transition from a single (European) cultural framework to a recognition and acceptance of diverse cultures in relationship to the Church. Two examples germane to this problem are the efforts of Saints Cyril and Methodius in Moravia in the ninth century and of the Jesuit missionary Matteo Ricci in the sixteenth century.

Saints Cyril and Methodius

Constantine, later renamed Cyril, and his brother Methodius were born in Thessalonica, Greece, in 825 A.D. and 826 A.D., respectively. Because their father's business in trade and commerce brought them into contact with the Slavic peoples, they learned the Slavonic language as children. Cyril studied in Constantinople and became the librarian at the cathedral Hagia Sophia. Methodius became a monk on Mount Olympus in Bithynia and later was elected abbot of the monastery of Polychronion in the Hellespont. Cyril eventually followed Methodius by entering the monastic life, where he became a professor at the Patriarchal Academy of the Holy Apostles in Constantinople.

In 862 A.D. Ratislav, duke of greater Moravia (now part of the Czech Republic), asked the emperor of Constantinople if he would send as missionaries to the Slavic people men who would respect their language and culture. Cyril and Methodius were chosen. The Slavic people had originally been evangelized by Irish and Scottish missionaries, and before the arrival of Cyril and Methodius they were being served by German missionaries from Bavaria. It seems clear that the Germans had little interest in adapting their efforts to the language and culture of the Slavs. Rather, as was commonly the case among the Western clergy of the day, they were committed to "trilingualism," the notion that only three languages, Latin, Greek, and Hebrew, were legitimate languages for the study and presentation of the Bible and for use in the liturgy. Cyril and Methodius created a unified, literate, Slavonic culture. They translated the Greek and Roman liturgies into Slavonic. To do so they first created the Glagolitic (predecessor of the Cyrillic) alphabet and used this to commit a particular dialect of Slavonic to writing. They went on to produce codes of civil and Church law in that language, and after Cyril's death in 869, Methodius translated the entire Bible into Slavonic. The Slavonic language created by Saints Cyril and Methodius is to this day the liturgical language of Serbs, Ukrainians, Bulgarians, and Russians.

In producing a vernacular Church in Moravia, Cyril and Methodius clashed with the Bavarian missionaries who had preceded them into Moravia and for whom the Latin language in particular was inseparable from evangelization. The Bavarians did not perceive, as did Cyril and Methodius, that the Slavonic language and the Slavonic way of life could be related to the Gospel without adopting Western culture and the Latin language.[8] Yet the attitude of the German clergy is understandable. They had been raised in the Latin tradition, in a liturgy that through the centuries had become intimately associated with their whole way of life. The Germans reported the brothers to Rome on suspicion of heresy because of their actions. Pope St. Nicholas I summoned Cyril and Methodius to Rome to answer the charges against them, but the pope died before their arrival and so they presented themselves to his successor, Pope Adrian II. This meeting took place in 867. The pope responded very favorably to their efforts. He solemnly approved the Slavonic Rites and also ordained them both as bishops. Not long thereafter, Cyril died in Rome, on February 14, 869, at the age of 42. Methodius returned to Moravia to continue his work, but the controversy continued, and in 879 he was summoned to appear before Pope John VIII. As a result of this meeting the pope issued the bull *Industriae Tuae* (Your Work, 880), which approved Methodius's work. In 881 he issued another bull, *Pastoralis Solicitudinis* (Pastoral Solicitude), further clarifying Methodius's authority. Methodius died on April 6, 885, and was succeeded by bishops who remained in union with Rome. However, following the schism of 1054 the great majority of the Slavic peoples affiliated with Constantinople rather than with Rome. It is important to note that those Slavs who sided with Rome never questioned their union with the papacy and were allowed to keep the liturgy in their own tongue.

Matteo Ricci and the Chinese Rites

One of the most creative and daring examples of inculturation of Catholic belief and practice occurred in the development of what has come to be known as the Chinese Rites—the reordering of Catholic belief and practice to the language and culture of the Chinese people during the fifteenth and sixteenth centuries. This effort was made by a group of Jesuit priests. The leader of this movement was an Italian Jesuit, Matteo Ricci. Ricci arrived in China in 1583 when he was 31 years old, and he remained in China until his death in 1610. Ricci and his fellow Jesuits faced a completely different situation from what was encountered by Saints Cyril and Methodius in Europe. Chinese civilization possessed an ancient and sophisticated culture that had avoided foreign influences of any kind and knew little or nothing of the West, including any knowledge of Christianity. Rather than impose European culture and values on the Chinese, Ricci, as had Saints Cyril and Methodius with the Slavs, tried to adapt Catholicism to the life and culture of the Chinese so that their way of life would not be radically disrupted but rather would receive a more creative fulfillment in the context of Christian belief and practice.

Ricci spent six years preparing himself for his work with the Chinese people. He mastered the Chinese language and became a mandarin by passing all the examinations required of such Chinese scholars. Ricci and his fellow Jesuits, on the advice of Chinese friends, adapted the dress of Chinese mandarins. They shaved their beards, let their hair grow long, and wore the scholar's hat always, even while celebrating Mass. Ricci also assembled a large collection of scientific books, instruments, and maps from Europe and invited Chinese scholars to learn from him as he did from them. His proficiency in astronomy, mathematics, and physics was greatly appreciated, especially in connection with the establishment of an accurate calendar around which the whole of Chinese social and religious life revolved.

Ricci mastered not only the Chinese language but the literature and history as well, including the teachings of Confucius. He became convinced that the original writings of Confucius did not contain anything that was clearly anti-Christian. However, he believed that some pantheistic and atheistic interpretations of Confucius's ideas had penetrated Chinese belief and thus had to be eliminated. When Chinese scholars complained that his ideas were opposed to the principles of Chinese society, Ricci responded by saying that Christianity perfected and developed the truths that formed the original traditions of Chinese life. He argued that the missionaries, as representatives of Catholicism, did not wish to destroy Chinese ideals but rather to restore them and purify them of the corruptions that had crept in. As Joseph J. Fitzpatrick observes,

> He [Ricci] was passionately convinced Chinese traditions were an admirable preparation for Christianity and that, if they could be freed from the pantheistic and materialistic interpretations given them they would render the Chinese most willing to accept Christianity.[9]

Ricci and his fellow Jesuits engaged in a meaningful dialogue with the religious culture of the Chinese. Their aim was inculturation in the true sense of the word. They hoped to achieve a Christian reinterpretation of Chinese culture, which in turn would result in a Chinese interpretation of Christianity that would emerge from the sympathetic Chinese form. As Shorter remarks, "It is, perhaps, a measure of the success of this policy that three thousand [Chinese] people had been baptized by the time of Ricci's death in 1610."[10]

The controversy of the so-caed Chinese Rites resulted from the arrival in China of Catholic missionaries from other religious orders. This occurred in 1620, about 10 years after Ricci's death. When these newcomers observed the practices that were tolerated by the Jesuits they were deeply troubled and complained to Rome. Rome had previously approved the methodology used by the Jesuits, but this did not placate the new arrivals, whose objections were persistent and often based on a lack of knowledge of Chinese culture and religion. Basically the concern was over the use of three "Chinese Rites," which Riccci had accepted as compatible with Christian faith and morals. These rites are clearly summarized by Shorter:

> Firstly, there was his approval of the application of the traditional Chinese title "Lord of heaven" to the God of Christianity. Secondly, there was the honour paid to the founding philosopher, Confucius, through periodic rituals; and finally there was the cult of the familial dead which was characterized by prostrations, the burning of incense and the offering of food at graves. Ricci authorized the cult of Confucius and of the familial dead in 1603, as probably not superstitious. At least, in his view, there was no evidence of superstition.[11]

Concerning the title "Lord of heaven," Ricci's intensive studies of Chinese literature led him to conclude that the term could legitimately be applied to the Christian God. He also believed the honors and rituals used to honor Confucius were not idolatrous but simply cultural recognition of the greatness and importance of his teachings. And more clearly than many of his successors, he recognized that funeral rites were more a social instrument than a religious rite. As Nicholas Trigault observes,

Indeed it is asserted by many that this particular rite was first insti-
tuted for the benefit of the living rather than for that of the dead. In this
way it was hoped that children and unlearned adults as well, might
learn how to support their parents who were living, when they saw that
parents departed were so highly honored by those who were educated
and prominent.[12]

Charles Maigrot, the Vicar Apostolic of Fukien, China, began the in-
dictment against the Chinese Rites in 1693, following years of controversy.
Eleven years later, in 1704, on the recommendation of a committee of car-
dinals, Pope Clement IX issued a decree condemning the Chinese Rites.
This condemnation was finalized by Pope Benedict XIV, who closed the discussion with his decree *Ex Quo Singulari* in 1742. In 1935, almost 200
years later, this condemnation was overturned when Pope Pius IX accepted
the cult of Confucius as essentially nonreligious and therefore not opposed
to Catholic doctrine. Then, in 1939, Pope Pius XI issued his *Instructio Circa
Quasdam Caeremonias Super Ritibus Sinensibus* (**Instruction on Certain Ceremonies Concerning the Chinese Rites**), which accepted traditional Chinese funeral rites and the cult of the familial dead.

Perhaps the most significant statement from the Catholic hierarchy
was given by Pope John Paul II in 1982 at a conference in Rome commem-
orating the 400th anniversary of Matteo Ricci's arrival in China:

Father Matteo Ricci . . . adapted the style of life of the scholars caught
up as he was with the social life of that community. In this way, he intended to show that his religious faith would not lead to any withdraw-
al from that society, but rather to an involvement in the world in view
of the perfection of social life up to an opening to redemption in Christ
and participation in grace through the Church.[13]

He went on to say,

It was thanks to this kind of an effort of inculturation that Father Matteo
Ricci with the assistance of his Chinese collaborators, achieved a task
that seemed impossible to work out, that is, a Chinese terminology of
Catholic theology and liturgy and, in this way, to create the conditions
to make Christ known and to incarnate his evangelical message of the
Church within the context of Chinese culture.

Toward the end of his address the Pope seems clearly to endorse the
missionary methods of Ricci in a remarkably emphatic manner:

In the light of the spirit of dialogue and of the openness which was characteristic of the Second Vatican Council, the missionary method of Fa-

ther Ricci appears so much more alive and contemporary. The Decree of the Council, *Ad Gentes (On the Church's Missionary Activity)* seems to be alluding to this when it describes the attitudes which Christians should have: "That they may be able to give this witness to Christ fruitfully, let them be joined to those men by esteem and love, and acknowledge themselves to be members of the group of men among whom they live. Let them share in the cultural and social life by the various exchanges of human living. Let them be familiar with their national and religious traditions, gladly and reverently laying bare the seeds of the word which lie hidden in them."

INCULTURATION AND RECENT CHURCH TEACHINGS

The interpenetration of a culture by a religious faith is referred to as "inculturation." Beginning with Pope Pius XII and continuing to the present, the papacy has addressed this question as it pertains to Catholicism in a very open manner.

Pope Pius XII

An address given by Pope Pius XII in 1944 to the Pontifical Mission Aid Societies marks an important step in the Church's understanding of inculturation.[14] In this address the pope presents the first official recognition of the plurality of cultures in that he calls for the preservation and development of local usages and customs. However, the same pope, on other occasions, spoke in terms of a monolithic culture. There was clearly an ambivalence on his part regarding the plurality of cultures. Nevertheless, his 1944 address did introduce the concept of cultural pluralism into the life of the Church and made clear the distinction between European culture and the Gospel.

Pope John XXIII

Pope John XXIII's encyclical *Princeps Pastorum* (Prince of Pastors), published in 1959, represents movement in the direction of a multicultural Church and of equality among the various cultures:

> Whenever authentic values of art and thought can enrich the culture of the human family, the "Church is ready to encourage and give her patronage to these products of the spirit. As you know, she does not identify herself with any one culture to the exclusion of the rest—not even

with European and Western culture, with which her history is so closely linked. True, her divinely appointed task is not directly concerned
with these things, but with religion and man's eternal salvation. Nevertheless, the Church in her unfailing youth, continually renewed by the
breath of the Holy Spirit, is ever ready to recognize and acknowledge—
and indeed to sponsor wholeheartedly—everything that can be set to
the credit of the human mind and spirit. And it is a matter of no consequence that these things may not always spring from Mediterranean
lands, which in God's providence formed the cradle of her infancy.[15]

Pope John XXIII did not develop a full ecclesiology of a multicultural
Church, but he certainly recognized the Church's cultural pluralism. He
was not denying the importance of the cultures represented in the Bible but
he was emphatic about cultural equality in the contemporary Church.

Vatican II

The great breakthrough in official statements about the relationship of the
Catholic Church to the various cultures of the world took place at Vatican
II and appears in several Church documents, including the *Pastoral Con-
stitution on the Church in the Modern World*. The council addressed the
issue of culture as it is presently understood in the social sciences, stated its
own definition of the term, and formally discussed the relation of the
Church to cultures. Part II, Chapter 2, of the *Constitution* is, "The Proper
Development of Culture":

> The word "culture" in the general sense refers to all those things which
> go to the refining and developing of man's diverse mental and physical
> endowments. He strives to subdue the earth by his knowledge and his
> labor; he humanizes social life both in the family and in the whole civic
> community through the improvement of customs and institutions; he
> expresses through his works the great spiritual experiences and aspi-
> rations of men throughout the ages; he communicates and preserves
> them to be an inspiration for the progress of many, even of all mankind.
>   Hence it follows that culture necessarily has historical and social
> overtones, and the word "culture" often carries with it sociological and
> ethnological connotations; in this sense one can speak about a plurality
> of cultures.[1]

The *Constitution* goes on to say,

> There are many links between the message of salvation and culture. In
> his self-revelation to his people culminating in the fullness of manifes-
> tation of his incarnate Son, God spoke according to the culture proper to
> each age. Similarly the Church has existed through the centuries in

varying circumstances and has utilized the resources of different cultures in its preaching to spread and explain the message of Christ, to examine and understand it more deeply, and to express it more perfectly in the liturgy and in various aspects of the life of the faithful.

Nevertheless, the Church has been sent to all ages and nations and, therefore, is not tied exclusively and indissolubly to any race or nation, to any one particular way of life, or to any customary practices, ancient or modern. The Church is faithful to its traditions and is at the same time conscious of its universal mission; it can, then, enter into communion with different forms of culture, thereby enriching both itself and the cultures themselves.[17]

The *Constitution* also states that when the Gospel "enters into communion" with a given culture it continually renews, connects, purifies, completes, and restores the culture in question. The document then speaks of the human right to culture but maintains that this is not an absolute right. Rather culture must be subordinated to a person's human development in every area of life, including an individual's spiritual and religious needs.

Apart from Vatican II's *Constitution on the Sacred Liturgy*, other council documents, such as *The Dogmatic Constitution on the Church*, represent a decisive starting point for the development of a theology of inculturation. As was discussed in Chapter 2, *The Dogmatic Constitution on the Church*, in one of the most important insights of the council, located the primary reality of the Church in the "particular church." In regard to the particular (or local) churches, we are told, "It is in these and formed out of them that the one and unique Catholic church exists."[18] The Catholic Church is a communion of the particular churches. Within this communion of churches the particular Church of Rome and its bishop, the pope, exercise a ministry of unity. Concerning the role of the pope and the particular Church of Rome, Shorter writes,

> This does not mean that the particular Church of Rome should be universalized and a cultural uniformity imposed on other churches by Rome. But it does mean that the successor of Peter enjoys an effective primacy over all the churches, effective because it is a primacy of jurisdiction, as well as of honour.[19]

The Decree on the Church's Missionary Activity, Ad Gentes, was one of the final four documents to be approved by the council in December 1965. Because it came at the end of the council's deliberations, the decree benefited from earlier discussions. From the very beginning of this document, stress is placed on human communities and their sociocultural traditions as the focus of missionary interest. The *Decree* states,

If the Church is to be in a position to offer all men the mystery of salvation and the life brought by God, then it must implant itself among these groups in the same way that Christ by his incarnation committed himself to the particular social and cultural circumstance of the men among whom he lived.[20]

In order to bear witness to Christ fruitfully, they [Christians] should establish relationships of respect and love with those men, they should acknowledge themselves as members of the group in which they live, and through the various undertakings and affairs of human life they should share in their cultural and social life. They should be familiar with their national and religious traditions and uncover with gladness and respect those seeds of the Word which lie hidden among them.[21]

This *Decree*, in referring to the Church's presence among various peoples, envisaged a transformation of cultures as an "incarnation" and as a commitment to the social and cultural traditions of the peoples of the Church. However, in this document, and throughout the teachings of Vatican II, the notion of inculturation is not fully explicit. In fact, language is frequently obscured, which can leave one with the impression that the concept of a monolithic and monocultural Church is being retained. A careful reading of the texts, however, shows this not to be the case. The documents opened the door to the importance of inculturation as is seen in the writings of Pope Paul VI and Pope John Paul II, which will be examined in the next section.

A key example of the impression that a monolithic church will be retained can be found in the *Constitution on the Sacred Liturgy,* which was the first conciliar document to be approved and promulgated. In this document the importance of maintaining the Roman rite was upheld. This took place in 1963 and preceded the document that describes the nature of the Church—in other words, *The Dogmatic Constitution on the Church* and other conciliar statements concerning the nature and mission of the Church. This explains why Rome has been able to appeal to this constitution in its decision to inhibit liturgical experimentation and diversification. The key passage of the liturgical constitution provides for a single, reformed Roman rite, with the possibility of "legitimate variations and adaptations."[22] The Latin of the Roman rite could be translated into the local vernacular according to the policy and approval of the local episcopal conference.[23] The revision of the Mass was to be made for the benefit of different "groups, regions and peoples," but the Conciliar fathers did not foresee the creation of new rites. In fact, the preservation of the "substantial unity of the Roman rite" was the underlying condition of all liturgical renewal, even though "adaptation" to this rite was allowed.[24] Notable liturgists, such as Anscar Chapungco, argue that liturgical inculturation demands the creation of new rites.[25] And as Shorter observes, hopeful signs toward liturgical pluriformity were given at the Congress of Presidents and Secretaries of National

Liturgical Commissions held in Rome in 1984. The congress stated that the Roman rite should be the starting place for initiatives taken primarily by the particular churches themselves. Shorter writes,

> The members of the Congress were asked to use the existing possibility for renewal more fully before passing on to creativity. There was also a request for liturgically trained personnel to assist the particular churches in their task. The Congress appeared to assume that creativity and pluriformity in liturgy were the eventual goals of liturgical renewal.[26]

Inculturation was not considered in the *Constitution on the Sacred Liturgy*. The present proposals for liturgical inculturation stem from other conciliar documents concerning the nature and purpose of the Church and from the use of the vernacular in the Roman rite, which has produced for many an increased desire for a more creative liturgy and new rites in the various Catholic communities worldwide. Approval for such measures has not yet come from Rome but pressure for such change is being felt in many quarters.

Pope Paul VI

The thrust and direction of Vatican II concerning inculturation was continued by Pope Paul VI, who succeeded Pope John XXIII. He was elected to the papacy on June 21, 1963, and held that office until his death on August 6, 1978. He continued Vatican II, which was interrupted by Pope John XXIII's death. The need to adapt theological reflection to local circumstances and cultures was stressed by him even before Vatican II ended. In subsequent years he developed his stance on what is now termed inculturation. This is seen in his missionary theology, most notably in his apostolic exhortation *Evangelii Nuntiandi (On Evangelization in the Modern World)* in 1975. The latter not only continued his own thought but grew out of what he had heard and formulated in the Synod of Bishops in 1974, which was devoted to the question of the mission of the Church.

In his address to the African bishops assembled in Kampala, Uganda, in 1969 Pope Paul VI stated,

> The expression, that is, the language and mode of manifesting this one Faith, may be manifold; hence, it may be original, suited to the tongue, the style, the genius, and the culture, of the one who professes this one Faith. From this point of view, a certain pluralism is not only legitimate, but desirable. An adaptation of the Christian life in the fields of pastoral, ritual, didactic, and spiritual activities is not only possible, it is even favored by the Church. The liturgical renewal is a living example

of this. And in this sense you may, and you must, have an African Christianity. Indeed, you possess human values and characteristic forms of culture which can rise up to perfection such as to find in Christianity, and for Christianity, a true superior fullness, and prove to be capable of a richness of expression all its own, and genuinely African. This may take time. It will require that your African soul become imbued to its depths with the secret charisms of Christianity, so that these charisms may then overflow freely, in beauty and wisdom, in the true African manner.[27]

The pope went on to encourage the African bishops to set up centers of pastoral training. He then reminded them of the following dangers: religious pluralism, turning Christianity into a folklore, racialism, and egoistic tribalism. Their task was to formulate Catholicism in terms congenial to their indigenous culture. He also made clear that he expected African culture to make a positive contribution to Christianity.

The 1974 Synod of Bishops asked Paul VI to draw up a document of his own reflecting the ideas they had discussed. The resulting document, *On Evangelization in the Modern World*, presents a theology of a multicultural Church. Unequaled by any other official statement in this regard, the document paved the way for theological reflection on inculturation, which continues to the present. Among many salient points concerning the Gospel and culture the Pope wrote,

> The Gospel, and therefore evangelization, are certainly not identical with culture, and they are independent in regard to all cultures. Nevertheless, the Kingdom which the Gospel proclaims is lived by men who are profoundly linked to a culture, and the building up of the Kingdom cannot avoid borrowing the elements of human culture or cultures. Though independent of cultures, the Gospel and evangelization are not necessarily incompatible with them; rather they are capable of permeating them all without becoming subject to any one of them.
>
> The split between the Gospel and culture is without a doubt the drama of our time, just as it was of other times. Therefore, every effort must be made to ensure a full evangelization of culture, or more correctly, of cultures. But this encounter will not take place if the Gospel is not proclaimed.[28]

In this section of his exhortation, Pope Paul is making a concerted effort to safeguard the autonomy of the Gospel in relation to the various cultures found worldwide. In addition, and most important, he makes clear that the Gospel is not exclusively tied to any one culture and that evangelization consists of penetrating the very heart of a given culture. Nor should the Gospel be *subjected to* culture but rather it should permeate and elevate that culture. Later on, the pope warns against what has come to be called "culturalism"—in other words, sacrificing the content of the Gospel to incompatible cultural values.[29] He also introduced the idea of the mutual enrichment of particular Catholic churches in various regions of the world by their interchange with one another.[30]

The idea of inculturation received its fullest theoretical expression in the writings of Pope Paul VI. The need to implement his teaching in practice has never been felt so acutely by theologians and Church leaders as it is today. This is particularly true in the developing world.

Pope John Paul II

Pope John Paul II has an intense interest in the question of inculturation. His enunciation of the principles involved is presented in his writing both theologically and sociologically. In fact, in his Apostolic Exhortation *Catechesi Tradendae (Catechesis in Our Time),* issued in October 1979, the pope quoted a statement he made to the Pontifical Biblical Commission earlier that same year. The statement contained, for the first time in a papal document, the word "inculturation." However, throughout his writings he manifests a certain reserve, at least at the practical level, concerning the outcome of the dialogue that the emerging Catholic churches of the developing world wish to undertake with their own non-Christian traditions. Pope John Paul seldom directly expresses this reserve but conveys it by the tone or phrasing of passages. For example, he does not spontaneously refer to the cultural values of the developing world, and he conveys a certain skepticism by pointing out the dangers of inculturation rather than highlighting its advantages. His attitude helps one to understand the discrepancy between his brilliant teaching on the subject of inculturation and actual Church practice. There are problems with the notion of inculturation, which will be discussed later in this chapter, that undoubtedly inhibit the pope from permitting full-scale inculturation at the level of practice.

Pope John Paul has emphasized, in an almost apocalyptic tone, the urgent need to relate faith and culture. In a letter to Agostino Cardinal Casaroli, on the occasion of the creation of the Pontifical Council for Culture in 1982, the pope wrote, "I have considered the Church's dialogue with the cultures of our time to be a vital area, one in which the destiny of the world at the end of the twentieth century is at stake."[31] The Pontifical Council for Culture was charged with the defense of the cultural inheritance of humankind, which is being threatened by materialistic and dehumanizing values. The ongoing dialogue between the Christian faith and the Western cultures was at the forefront of the pope's mind in this letter, but there is much in the letter that is relevant to inculturation in the developing world. For example, the letter states,

> [T]he synthesis between culture and faith is not just a demand of cul-
> ture, but also of faith. A faith which does not become a culture is a faith
> which has not been fully reviewed, not thoroughly thought through, not
> fully lined out.[32]

This passage contains perhaps the clearest official Church statement
on the relationship of faith and culture. However, in this letter and in his
other writings on the subject, Pope John Paul gives the impression that he
highly values the synthesis in the historic cultures of Christian Europe and
fears for their future, and at the same time hesitates to risk the deposit of
faith in dialogue with the cultures of the non-Christian developing world. It
is possible that the pope shares the attitude of Cardinal Joseph Ratzinger
regarding developing-world cultures. In Cardinal Ratzinger's case, this derives from the cardinal's belief that European thought has spread to the
whole world, and from what he calls "the *universal* significance of Christian
thought as it has evolved in the West."[33] This is a position not dissimilar to
monoculturalism.

PROBLEMS RELATING TO INCULTURATION

Cultural Relativism

Recognition of the diversity of cultures immediately raises the question of
cultural relativism and the possible relativizing of Catholic teaching. However, any local theology that is truly Catholic has to be engaged with the
Christian tradition, which includes the Bible, the great conciliar and con-
fessional statements, and the magisterium of the Church. Without such an
engagement there is no guarantee of being part of the Catholic tradition.
The Christian message originates in the revelation of divine mystery. It is
not simply human truth. It is in the light of this divinely revealed truth that
all human cultures are judged—and not by their own criteria. If evangelization, for instance, is properly carried out, it will help individuals fulfill
their culture's promise. They will not be taught to despise their culture but
rather to reappraise it in the light of Gospel values. The work of the Church
should be carried out without detriment to any particular culture and without the loss of any element that is essential to it. In becoming Christian,
people are not invited to abandon their cultural identity. Rather, that identity is challenged and enhanced. Aspects of a particular culture that contradict Gospel values are evaluated, challenged, and overcome, and the
Christian values of a particular culture are enhanced.

Christian living supposes a critical attitude of discernment. Unjust
laws, immoral practices, racist, sexist, and ideological discrimination, as

well as unjust domination of economic structures are to be opposed. Christians will try to discuss what is contrary in their culture to full human living and will act against whatever they consider to be countervalues or obstacles to true cultural progress. Bringing Christian values to a culture presupposes an attitude of dialogue and cooperation. The Gospel acts as a ferment in the world, and it is through their personal and social commitments that Christians manifest the fundamental link between the Gospel and the enrichment of humanity. Dialogue must be practiced in a spirit of cooperation with all men and women of goodwill. As John Paul II stated in an address to the Pontifical Council for Culture:

> the Church does not stand outside culture but inside it, as a leaven, on account of the organic and constitutive link which joins them closely together. The Council will pursue its ends in an ecumenical and brotherly spirit, promoting also dialogue with non-Christian religions, and with individuals or groups who do not profess any religion, in a joint search for cultural communication with all men of goodwill.[34]

Through inculturation the Gospel acquires a new cultural language, and this enriches the Church. Every sector of Christian life is affected: Theology is reformulated; religious education opens the door to dialogue between the Gospel and the local culture; the liturgy gives cultural expression to the people's faith; and the universal, hierarchical structures of the Church are not replaced but rather put in the service of the community even as they acquire new tasks in dialogue with a particular culture. In all of this, the meaning of authoritative faith statements cannot be contradicted or diluted. But such teachings can only be understood in a cultural context, which may need subsequent reformulation to be understood by people of another culture.

There are numerous problems that arise in the dialogue between the Gospel and particular cultures. For example, the problem of polygamous marriages occurs in rural Africa. Must a man send away all of his wives except his first wife to receive baptism? This is a very complicated issue but one that must be dealt with. All the aspects of this question cannot be discussed in this chapter, however. Eugene Hillman in *Polygamy Reconsidered* provides excellent insights into this question, which Westerners often do not understand.[35] It is obvious that monogamy has been the constant teaching of the Catholic Church. The question remains, how is this problem going to be satisfactorily resolved? The celibacy of the clergy is also problematic in many cultures outside of the Western tradition. In addition it is also difficult for many African cultures to understand the doctrine of original sin, because they do not have a story of the fall in their own origin stories. These and many other issues will be resolved over time by means of honest dialogue between representatives of particular cultures and the magisterium of the Church. A great deal will be learned in the process on both sides. Robert Schreiter in *Constructing Local Theologies* presents excellent reflections that lay the groundwork for dealing with such issues.[36] Schreiter notes that his ideas are provisional and incomplete, because many of these problems have rarely been the object of direct reflection in Christian history. Nevertheless, the book is excellent and has become an important part of the dialogue that is attempting to establish a complete theological methodology for the meaning of inculturation and its impact on the Catholic Church.

Canon Law

There is a problem of translating the insights concerning inculturation and multiculturalism produced by Vatican II, Pope Paul VI, and Pope John Paul II into pastoral practice. This raises the question of universal norms and, in particular, concerns the 1983 *Code of Canon Law*. The problem is that the *Code of Canon Law* is culturally Western and is intrinsically unable to express the concerns of non-Western cultures. Although Vatican II did not sufficiently deal with this problem, it did encourage the prospect of further research into this matter.[37] As early as 1978 the Symposium of Bishops of Africa and Madagascar proposed that there should be an African Canon Law that should flow from African theology just as the new *Code* emanates from Western theology.[38] Nothing has come of this proposal, but it seems clear that a code of universal church law can never do justice to the various cultural realities found throughout the world. The 1983 *Code of Canon Law* is likely to be revised much sooner than was the 1917 code. And it seems that a general law is needed. However, such a law must be complemented by particular laws in a world Church to deal effectively with such questions as marriage, family life, and medicine. A more flexible approach to law in the Church is an essential condition for a multicultural Church. This constitutes a challenge to authoritarianism and exaggerated centralism in the Church because local churches would thus enjoy relative autonomy. In an age of instant communication and rapid travel, this should not be a threatening prospect for Rome.

LIBERATION THEOLOGY AND INCULTURATION

In the past it was almost taken for granted that the theology of the Western churches was supraregional and universal in its Western form, and thus directly accessible to all cultures. But, as we have seen, the need to adapt theological reflection to local circumstances began receiving official support at Vatican II. Pope Paul VI developed this approach in his address to the bishops of Africa in 1969 and in his apostolic exhortation *On Evangelization in the Modern World* in 1975. Pope John Paul II has continued in this vein in many of his addresses and in his establishment of the Pontifical Council for Culture. The issue was forced when local churches began to ask new questions that the traditional framework of theology could not answer to their satisfaction, such as how to understand Church–state conflicts in various Latin American countries that had repressive regimes. Old answers that did not fit were often given to new questions. As a result, many local churches felt they were being dealt with in a paternalistic fashion. This was also a problem in North Atlantic churches, especially among women and African Americans. A deepening dissatisfaction with existing approaches to theology began to be seen in a more widespread fashion following the decade of the 1960s, as seen in the writings of liberation theologians, such as Gustavo Gutiérrez, Leonardo Boff, and Juan Luis Seamdo.

Rather than beginning to apply traditional theology to the local context, a contextual theology arose and began its efforts with an analysis of the context itself. The awareness of how context shapes reflection has led to a greater awareness of procedure. Although the professionally trained theologian's role is to relate the experience of other Christian communities and of the Christian tradition to the experience of a local church, the community itself takes greater responsibility in shaping its theological response. Theology since the thirteenth century in Western Christianity has been dominated by an approach that emphasizes clarity and precision. Today other ways of engaging in theological reflections are taking place. The role of the community is stressed, which is giving shape to how Christians understand themselves and their faith in a more personal and existential manner. A local theology begins with the needs of the people and from there moves to the traditions of the faith. It asks questions such as, How is a Haitian refugee to be Catholic in Miami; or a Vietnamese person in Houston? The particular strength of a local theology is that it begins with the questions the people have themselves and not those posed by perennial theology.

Liberation theologies are chiefly concerned with salvation and are perhaps the major force in contextual models of theology today. They analyze the lived experience of a people to uncover the forces of oppression, struggle, violence, and power that affect them. Local theology based, for example, on liberation theology is the dynamic interaction between the Gospel, the church in question, and culture. The experience of renewal following Vatican II presented a point at which many local churches found themselves situated between a theology that had given them identity for centuries (since the Council of Trent that was held from 1545 to 1563) and the challenge from the council to understand that identity in light of today's situation. The ability of liberation models to speak the language of Christian communities attests to their power and importance.

The community itself is the primary author of theology in local contexts. The Holy Spirit, working in and through the believing community, gives shape and expression to Christian experience. Some of the communities have taught the larger Church to read the Scriptures in a fresh way and have led others to a greater fidelity to the prophetic Word of God. However, not everything a particular community says can be called theology. The professional theologian, persons such as Gustavo Gutiérrez and Jon Sobrino, serves as important resources. Their writings help a community clarify its own experience and relate it to the experience of other communities, past and present. The theologian thus helps to create the bonds of mutual accountability between the local and world Church. Without the presence of such outside experience, a local church runs the risk of turning in on itself and becoming self-satisfied with its own achievements.

In an ideal situation, for a genuine contextual theology the theological process should begin with the opening of a culture, that long and careful listening to a culture to discover its principal values, needs, interests, directions, and symbols. Listening to culture calls for what American anthropologist Clifford Geertz has described as the "thick description" of culture.[39] Not only the major themes but also the forms of theology can be profoundly affected by cultural patterns. It is important not only to know how meaning is organized in a culture but how it is to be communicated. In much of Christian history, East or West, the written text has been the most common medium for the communication of theology. This presumes the primacy of literacy, and because for centuries theology was the preserve of an educated clergy, this was a legitimate presumption. But as Robert Schreiter notes, "We cannot presume written texts—with all they in turn assume about argumentation—as the sole form for communicating cultural meaning, and therefore theology."[40] He points out that perhaps in line with oral tradition African theology is more often communicated by means of proverbs just as the use of spirituals and blues is the medium of black theology in the United States.[41] The opening up of culture makes clear that the mode of communicating theology, oral as well as written, is critical to a clear understanding of a local theology.

Parallel to the opening up of culture a similar movement is taking place in Church tradition, which is the beginning point of a local theology. Too often this has been done through the Eurocentric lenses of missionary leadership, without due reflection on how they were attempting to westernize a people as they Christianized them. For those Roman Catholics whose knowledge extends only to the uniformities presented at the Council of Trent, and the past two centuries of strong centralized Church authority, tradition seems to be monolithic. But modern studies show that this is not so. This has to be taken into account in constructing a local theology. Christian tradition, in all of its aspects, can make a vital contribution to local theology by urging the local community to reflect on issues that have not occurred to them, or by pointing to implications that have not yet been fore-seen. On the other hand, local theologies are vital for the development of the tradition. By raising questions as they do, local theologies can remind the larger community of parts of the tradition that have been neglected or for-gotten. For example, the contributions of feminist communities in attempt-ing to reconstruct and rehabilitate the Church is making the Church as a whole aware of how parts of the tradition were forgotten, skewed, or even suppressed.

For Roman Catholics the stress on universality has been such that it has become difficult to think about how to find the intersection between lo-cality and universality. There is no simple answer to the question of local theology and the Church as a whole. In this regard Schreiter writes, "Ener-gies and resources will probably limit theologies being fully constructed on the level of a small community."[42] In fact, local theology is not new to Chris-tianity, but a direct awareness of it is relatively recent. In Roman Catholic circles the need to adapt theological reflection to local circumstances began receiving official support at Vatican II, especially in *The Dogmatic Consti-tution on the Church* and in the *Decree on the Church's Missionary Activity*. *The Dogmatic Constitution on the Church* states,

> This church of Christ is truly present in all legitimately organized local assemblies of believers, which in union with their pastors are them-selves also called churches in the New Testament. For these assemblies are in their own localities the new People called by God, in the power of the Holy Spirit and in full conviction (cf. 1 Thess. 1:5). In them believers are gathered together by the preaching of the Gospel of Christ and the mystery of the Lord's Supper is celebrated. . . . In each altar-communi-ty, under the bishop's sacred ministry, a manifest symbol is displayed of that charity and "unity of the mystical Body. . . . ." In these communities, although they are often small and poor or scattered, Christ is present through whose power the one holy, Catholic, and apostolic Church is brought together.[43]

These small communities are called churches because in them Christ is at work, gathering his one and Catholic Church. Pope John Paul II in an address to the Roman Curia in 1984 presented the special role of the papa-cy as a service of Catholic unity in that it sees to it that the gifts of the var-ious local churches flow toward the center of the Church and that these same gifts, enriched by this mutual encounter in turn flow out to the vari-ous members of the Mystical Body of Christ, "bringing them new impulses of fervor and of life."[44] The role of the pope is best conceived as mediator be-tween one local church and other local churches to ensure that the special Christian experiences that derive from their socio-cultural particularities do not contradict one another but are harmonized with and enriched by one another so that they may constitute a genuine communion. The achievement of catholicity requires the symphonic harmony of all these special, local, ecclesiastical experiences. Local particularity, multiculturalism, is a necessary element of concrete catholicity. But this catholicity is more than diversity and particularity. It is an integration of this cultural diversity into a fullness, into a wholeness, around Jesus Christ and in the Spirit. Such catholicity must take place at every level of Church existence: in small communities, in parishes, in dioceses, in the papacy. As a result, catholicity is not an attribute external to local communities of faith, found only when they assemble in a universal community. Rather, as Joseph Komonchak writes, such catholicity

> must characterize every assembly of Christians of which it must be true that here there is no Jew and Greek, no male and female, no slave and freeman, but all are one in Christ. A community in which such integration of all is not accomplished falls short of being a realization of the one and Catholic Church. Catholicity, in that sense, is a constant challenge for every assembly of believers. . . .[45]

Basic Christian Communities and Inculturation

Basic Christian Communities

The most obvious example of the reawakening of the role of the community at the pastoral level since Vatican II is the grassroots development of "basic Christian communities," which began in Latin America in the 1960s. This in turn led to a new formulation of theology known as "liberation theology." Liberation theology was created by Latin American theologians and has had an unprecedented impact in the Christian world. It is an excellent example of a local theology that offers new possibilities, challenges, and hopes not only to those situations in which it is lived and formulated but also to the universal church. It demonstrates how a theology can emerge from a local context and then through dialogue with the larger Church become a leaven, a source of renewal, for all theology and all churches. The Church in Latin America is a powerful paradigm of a Church coming to grips with its own particular context and culture. Many Christian communities throughout Latin America have set the Gospel and the Christian tradition over against their contemporary religious, political, and social situations. Their contemplation has led them to affirm the good in the Church and in their culture and to attempt to eradicate the evil in both. This in turn has moved them more closely to a vision of the Kingdom of God. The theology of liberation that has resulted offers a challenging model for the inculturation of the Gospel in every context.

Vatican II, especially in the *Pastoral Constitution on the Church in the Modern World*, encouraged the Church to reach out in a special way to the poor, the suffering, the weak, and the marginalized. The bishops of Latin America took up this challenge both individually and as a group in CELAM (The General Conference of Latin American Bishops). The Second General Conference of Latin American Bishops (CELAM II) was held at Medellín, Colombia, in 1968. The objective of the conference was to examine the implications of Vatican II for Latin America. Pope Paul VI in his first visit outside of Rome inaugurated the conference, called "The Church in the Present-Day Transformation of Latin America in the Light of the Council." Sixteen documents were produced at Medellín (the same number produced at Vatican II). The bishops attempted to define the role of the Church in confronting the social and political problems of their people. The documents dealt with subjects such as the poverty of the Church, justice, the mass media, peace movements, and lay movements. The essence of the Medellín documents is epitomized in two of its passages: "By its own vocation Latin America will undertake its liberation at the cost of whatever sacrifice."[46] Also,

> The Lord's distant commandment to "evangelize the poor" ought to bring us to a distribution of resources and apostolic personnel that effectively gives preference to the poorest and most needy sectors.[47]

The conference presented an unambiguous statement that the Church should exercise a "preferential option for the poor." It committed the Church to a change of social, political, and economic institutions to correct the injustice and violence that were "structured" into society. The Church was no longer to identify itself with the wealthy and powerful but with the cause of the poor in their demand for a just and human society. The documents, a call for liberation, encouraged the establishment of basic Christian communities in which reflection on the Bible and Catholic teaching, as well as on local conditions and injustices, would occur. The groundwork for such liberation had been prepared at the local level with the emergence of basic Christian communities throughout the decade of the 1960s. They at that time received the official sanction of the Church. Such communities had already begun to analyze their situations and to articulate liberating Christian responses.

"Basic Christian communities" are found mostly in rural areas and on the outer edges of cities. They are formed by simple Christians who come together to worship God, study the Bible, and attempt to live in such a way as to make Christ real in their lives. Such communities are local, small-scale (20 or so members), grassroots, and are grounded in the realities of the daily lives of the people. As Edward Cleary writes,

> Basic Christian communities are like living cells in an organism newly coming to life. Generally twelve to twenty persons make up a community. They usually come together in their neighborhood or village once a week. They read sacred scripture, pray together, and sing hymns. They reflect on what the scriptures mean in their daily lives. That reflection frequently leads them to courses of political action to improve the living conditions in the barrio.[48]

Because such communities are grassroots innovations, they tend to vary from place to place. But there is enough similarity to describe them in common terms. Lay leaders are the key to the continuity and dynamism of the communities. They assemble the community at least once each week in a set place, usually a family home, in a chapel, or simply in the shade of a tree. The community prays, listens to the Word of God, and discusses problems affecting the life of the community. The leader moves the group along. Members are called on to perform certain tasks, depending on the need of the moment. Jeanne Gallo notes that such communities

> are communities whose purpose includes action. This action will vary depending on the level of commitment of the members to their local community and to the society at large. The action may be in the religious domain: catechesis, Bible Study, planning a prayer week. It may also be in the social arena: improvements in the neighborhood, collective works, teaching the illiterate to read, doing political and legal education, creating and strengthening trade unions, participation in political activities.[49]

The type and degree of commitment in these areas depends on the social character of the community and the degree of development it has reached. In describing the developmental process of basic Christian communities Leonardo Boff writes,

> This generally began with the reading of the Bible and proceeded to the creation of small base or basic ecclesial communities. Initially such a community serves to deepen the faith of its members, to prepare the liturgy, the sacraments, the life of prayer. At a more advanced stage these members begin to help each other. As they become better organized and reflect more deeply, they come to the realization that the problems they encounter have a structural character. . . . Thus the question of politics arises and the desire for liberation is set in a concrete and historical context.[50]

Whatever action such communities undertake, whether religious or social, it comes from the reality of the community, and its needs are perceived through the dynamic of analysis, reflection, dialogue, and prayer. The basic Christian community is a new and original way of living the Christian faith. It is a renewed way of organizing Christians around the Word of God, around the sacraments, and around lay ministries (of both men and women). A new distribution of power is evident; such groups are participatory and avoid all centralization and domination. Nor do members of such communities see themselves as separate from other Catholics. They understand that they are linked to other basic Christian communities and to all other members of the institutional Church. They are "cells of the body." The center of life for members of the basic Christian communities is the person of Jesus Christ, whose life is seen as an expression of fidelity to God and of commitment to humanity within a specific historical context. Jesus as liberator is seen as present with and among the poor. There are several hundred thousand such communities in Latin America today, communities that signal the beginning of a change in the medieval structure of the Catholic Church from a hierarchical mode of being to one that is communal. The change has not been finalized but the process has begun. A whole new model of Church is being born whose building blocks are the basic Christian communities.

Liberation Theology and Inculturation

What basic Christian communities represent in the area of pastoral developments, liberation theology represents for theology, presenting a model of inculturation of the faith based on the social reality of Latin America. It examines the meaning of the Gospel in relationship to the religious, social, political, cultural, and economic conditions of the people. One of the most obvious implications of the Gospel is that everyone must be liberated from the injustice and oppression that prevent them from living a fully Christian life. Whatever the problems associated with liberation theology, it is clear that liberation theologians have responded creatively in an effort toward a new inculturation of the faith and that they have made a profound impact on the Church in Latin America and elsewhere.

Pope Paul VI in his 1975 encyclical letter *Evangelii Nuntiandi* (On Evangelization in the Modern World) used the language of liberation. He made clear that liberation is not only political and economic but, above all, a spiritual liberation from sin and the effects of sin. In a passage that has been cited frequently in subsequent papal writings and speeches, Pope Paul VI wrote,

> The Church, as the bishops (of the synod [a reference to the Roman synod of 1974]) repeated, has the duty to proclaim the liberation of millions of human beings, many of whom are its own children—the duty of assisting the birth of this liberation, of giving witness to it, of ensuring that it is complete.[51]

The encyclical also made the first official reference to the basic Christian communities and gave guidelines for their growth. It called such communities a hope for the universal Church provided they remain centered on the Word of God, attached to the local church, maintain sincere communion with their pastors and the magisterium, and show themselves to be universal in all things and never sectarian.[52] This is an example of a local theology, one incarnated in the soil of Latin America, becoming a proposal and an opportunity for all Christian churches through a papal document.

In 1979 the Third General Conference of Latin American Bishops (CELAM III) took place in Pueblo, Mexico, with Pope John Paul II in attendance. There was some concern that the bishops might withdraw or pull back from the forward momentum of liberation theology. This did not happen. Rather, the bishops again affirmed and deepened the commitment of Latin American Catholics to work for justice. The strategies of the basic Christian communities and the options for the poor were reaffirmed.

This commitment to a theology of peace and justice for all had tragic consequences, as witnessed in the assassination of Archbishop Oscar Romero in San Salvador on March 24, 1989, as he was celebrating Mass. Romero had witnessed the murder of one of his own priests, who was advocating justice for the poor, and as a result he began to speak out strongly against certain government policies. He paid for this with his life.[53] In fact, many laypersons, priests, sisters, and religious have been persecuted, imprisoned, tortured, and killed by various political factions in Latin America for living and preaching the liberating message of the Gospel. A notable example of this was the murder of six Jesuits and two Catholic women in El Salvador on November 16, 1989.

Father Gustavo Gutiérrez of Peru is considered by most observers to be the preeminent Latin American liberation theologian. His *Teología de la Liberación*, published in 1971 (the English translation, *A Theology of Liberation*, was published in 1973) is still seen as the cornerstone of liberation theology. Gutiérrez and the other liberation theologians believe that the primary task of theology is not to convince the nonbeliever of the "truths" of the Christian faith but rather to help free the oppressed from their inhuman living conditions. In this way the "truth" of theology becomes the "liberation" of the oppressed. Gutiérrez uses the term *liberation* in three senses. First, *liberation* refers to freedom from oppressive economic, social, and political systems. Second, it means that human beings should take control of their own destiny. Third, it means persons being emancipated from sin and accepting a new life in Christ. The use of the term *liberation* encompasses all three meanings in Gutiérrez's work—not only the first meaning, as some of his critics indicate. Nevertheless, liberation theology primarily develops the social dimension of faith. Still, it must be emphasized that the point of departure of the theology of liberation is the theological virtue of faith. In fact, it is because of the transcendent dimension of faith that a liberation theology is possible at all.[54]

In 1984 and 1986 Cardinal Joseph Ratzinger, prefect of the Roman Congregation for the Doctrine of the Faith, issued two documents specifically on liberation theology. The first, *Instruction on Certain Aspects of the Theology of Liberation*, does not impugn the theology of liberation at its root, but it does show extreme severity concerning its performance.[55] The most critical point of *Instruction* is an expression of fear that Marxism will cause Christians to deviate from the faith and betray the poor. Such a characterization was seen as a caricature and vehemently denied by the liberationists. Leonardo and Clodovis Boff responded that "Marxism is a secondary, peripheral issue. When Marxism is used at all, it is used only *partially* and *instrumentally.*" Liberation theologians often distinguish Marx's social analysis from his atheism. Marx's analysis of class conflict and the effects of capitalism are accepted as basically correct. Most of the liberation theologians attempt to distinguish the idea of class conflict from the militant Marxists by setting it in a context of love, not hatred, a love that reaches out even to one's enemies. In the same paragraph the Boffs go on to say,

> It is the faith that assimilates or subsumes elements of Marxism, then, and not the other way about. And the assimilation is effected from a point of departure in the community of the poor, so that the elements assimilated are profoundly transformed in the very assimilation, in such a way that the result is no longer Marxism, but simply a critical understanding of reality.[56]

Boff admits that when liberation theologians have incorporated Marxist philosophy, they have not always done so with "adequate lucidity, perspicacity, and maturity. But we are improving along the way."[57] It is very difficult to find a liberation theologian who would completely accept Marxism. Deane William Ferm, who has studied extensively the writings of liberation theologians, expresses surprise in discovering how few references there are to Karl Marx in the writings of liberation theologians because the liberation theologians are often linked with Marxism. He also observes that references to Marx are laced with a "heavy dose of emendation."[58] Because liberation theologians are diverse in their analyses, one has to say that the 1984 document issued by Cardinal Ratzinger in effect affirms the validity of the Church's commitment to work for liberation at all levels. In 1986 the Congregation for the Doctrine of the Faith issued a lengthier document, *On Christian Freedom and Liberation*, which affirms and ensures that the insights and the basic direction of liberation theology now have a significant role to play in the formulation of all Christian theology for all its contexts.[59]

As we explore, read, and learn from liberation theology, we see that it touches the Christian faith wherever that faith is found. Essays have been written and conferences have been held on the theology of liberation and its implications for every continent. Hispanic and African American theologians as well as feminist theologians in the United States have learned much from the struggle of the Latin American churches. In the next section the use of liberation theology by Hispanic Americans will be discussed. Instead of slavishly imitating what is occurring with Latin American liberation theologians, Christians in other regions of the world are called to accomplish within their own context what the Latin Americans have done in theirs—namely, gather in small groups, analyze their own unique cultural context or situation in light of the Gospel, and then synthesize it with the Gospel and the Christian tradition in a manner that leads to transformation. Liberation theology, in other words, furnishes one with a concrete example of inculturation and a method for truly inculturating Gospel values into one's particular cultural milieu.

INCULTURATION IN THE UNITED STATES

The history of the United States presents one of the most amazing examples of the intermingling of people from many different nations and cultures into one politically unified society. We are people from many different religious backgrounds, most of us Christian. Americans have molded a common nation and a common society out of an extraordinary array of differences. While melding into one nation, Americans had to overcome many prejudices. As William Cenkner writes,

> The early tragic years of the American experiment gave witness to the cultural imperialism against the indigenous first peoples of this continent, soon followed by the black slave markets, and continued against the immigrants from the suffering and suppressed communities of Europe.[60]

As far as Catholicism's inculturation into American society is concerned, there is a consensus among historians and sociologists that the American Catholic Church has gone through four phases following the colonial period (1492–1790.)[61] The first phase was *the republican era* (1790–1852). Catholics had been a small, rather elite group of colonists in the period preceding the American Revolution (1775–1781). A few of them played prominent roles in the founding of the new nation. For example, Charles Carroll, a prominent Catholic from Maryland, signed the Declaration of Independence. Another member of the Carroll family, John Carroll, became the first American bishop. It is interesting to note that John Carroll was elected as bishop by his fellow priests; in addition, he helped establish Georgetown University, the first Catholic University in the United States. When John Carroll became bishop in 1789 there were approximately 90,000 Catholics in the colonies. However, by the end of the republican era there were approximately a million and a half Catholics in the United States.

The second stage of American Catholicism's history was *the immigrant phase* (1850–1924). The early migrations (1780–1860) came mainly from northern and western Europe—from Great Britain, Ireland, Germany, and France. Many of the French and Germans were Catholic, but the greatest number of Catholic immigrants during this period came from Ireland. Oppressed by the English, the Irish began to emigrate in the late eighteenth century. Their migration continued in the nineteenth century and was dramatically increased when survivors fled the potato famine (1846), which left millions dead. The immigrants from Ireland were mainly poor and uneducated, but they brought with them extraordinary skills in political organization, which helped them, despite persecution and discrimination, to rise to political power in the cities in which they settled. Irish bishops also came to dominate American Catholicism. The Irish and the Germans were very prominent among the rapidly growing number of Catholics in the United States.

The so-called *new immigration* (1860–1920) brought large numbers of people from eastern and southern Europe: Italians, Poles, natives of Austria–Hungary, Russia, and Greece. Immigrants continued to arrive from Great Britain, Ireland, France, and Germany. Millions of Roman Catholics arrived during this period. For example, in the 20 years from 1880 to 1900 the number of Roman Catholics increased from approximately 6 to 12 million. In 1924 the predominantly Protestant, Anglo Saxon U.S. Congress passed a very restrictive immigration law that limited the number of immigrants entering the country. All Asians were excluded. The law allowed 165,000 visas each year, granted on the basis of national origin. Two percent of the number of immigrants from a particular country who were already in the United States were allowed visas. The law was designed to favor immigrants from Great Britain, Ireland, and Germany and to restrict immigration from central and southern Europe. This quota system was not discontinued until 1965.

The third stage of American Catholicism's history, *the maturing phase* (1924–1960), is characterized by the upward mobility and gradual penetration of Catholics into the middle-class and their success in every sector of society, culminating with the election of John F. Kennedy as president of the United States. As citizens Catholics now participated as equals in the political process of the new world. They became "middle-class Americans" and brought the Catholic Church with them into the middle-class style of American life.

The fourth stage, *the Post-Vatican II stage* of American Catholicism (1960–present) is marked by an identity crisis, as Catholics are being challenged to confront culture by witnessing to Christian values in all walks of life. However, as part of the American experience, the grandchildren of the immigrants for the most part have lost the language of their forebears, have become involved in the political, economic, and social activities of American society, have intermarried with persons of other ethnic or religious backgrounds. As Fitzpatrick writes,

> The use of holidays, food, heroes, and national achievements of the old country are interwoven in celebration of the ethnic background. But the living substance of the old culture is gone. The basic values which guide human life, the social customs and lifestyle represent, in all their variety, the expression of a common culture which is accurately called the "American Way of Life." The recollection of the "ethnic identity" is largely what Herbert Gans calls "symbolic ethnicity."[62]

The great fear at present, as Fitzpatrick notes, is that "in their adjustment to middle-class society, Catholics have simply accepted the dominant values of American life."[63] These values involve the unrestrained competition for upward social and economic status and a spirit of consumerism that is characteristic of a capitalist society, which often leads to a contradiction of Christian values. As far back as 1955, Will Herberg, the noted sociologist, wrote that the Catholic Church had accommodated itself to the dominant values of the United States. Instead of calling God to witness to the activities of American life, it lost its prophetic emphasis and conformed to the "world" as it was unfolding in the American experience. Herberg goes on to say that the Catholic Church faces the challenge of finding a new cultural expression of Catholic life, a pattern of ideas and behavior that reflect in the contemporary world the vital presence of the Church, the spirit of Jesus in the midst of American culture.[64] More than 40 years later, and in light of the teachings of Vatican II, it is clear to most that the challenge Herberg speaks of has yet to be met.

Recent Inculturation in the United States

The pastoral letters of the American bishops on peace, written in 1983, and on the U.S. economy, written in 1985, represent efforts on the institutional level to inculturate Gospel values into American culture. For the first time, these letters attempt to influence the values of American culture. The Church has given up its status as a ministry to a minority, immigrant population and instead is asserting itself as a cultural factor in a country that purports to be multicultural. These letters have opened a new chapter in American Catholicism's effort to bring about social justice. At the same time, the letters startled the average American, including many Catholics, who were not cognizant of the great range of social issues addressed by the bishops since the close of Vatican II in 1965. The bishops' pastoral letter on war and peace in the nuclear age, *The Challenge of Peace; God's Promise and Our Response* (1983), for example, was a significant event in American Catholicism. It represented for the first time an official statement of the Catholic Church challenging, on moral grounds, the policies of war and peace of the U.S. government. And the letter on the U.S. economy, *On Catholic Social Teaching and the U.S. Economy* (1985), challenged the accepted economic norms on the basis of religious and moral principles. Previous statements of the Church, such as the papal encyclicals, have challenged the capitalist economy in general, but this is the first time that the American bishops have challenged the functioning of the U.S. economy on moral grounds.

The Challenge of Peace is a model of how religion and politics can interact in a pluralistic society.[65] In producing this pastoral letter the bishops went through a long process of consultation with a variety of groups, as was mentioned in Chapter 2: biblical scholars, moralists, arms-control experts, top officials in the Reagan administration, two former secretaries of defense, military leaders, peace activists, and others. The hearings process ended with a full day of discussion with representatives of the Reagan administration. As Richard McBrien points out in *Caesar's Coin*, the bishops were trying to be faithful to a principle enunciated by Vatican II: "[N]amely, that the church must interpret the Gospel only after 'scrutinizing the signs of the times,' that is, it must make a concrete examination of the moral questions to be addressed before moving to a theological reflection on them."[66] The letter was addressed not only to Catholics, but "to the whole of humanity."

In *The Challenge of Peace* the bishops point out that although the Church has sanctioned war as a last resort throughout most of its history on the basis of the "just war" theory, times have changed. We now live in a nuclear age. Because of the threat of nuclear annihilation, we are forced to make a fresh appraisal of war. As a result, the bishops arrive at several conclusions, which I list in *Roman Catholicism, Yesterday and Today*:

> First, they oppose the use of all nuclear weapons directed at population centers, including retaliatory action that would "strike enemy cities after our own have already been struck." They also rule out a first strike as morally unjustifiable, and they base their decision on their "extreme skepticism about the prospects of controlling a nuclear exchange." The bishops do feel it is morally justified to maintain nuclear weapons as a

deterrent until alternative methods of defense can be found. However, they argue that to possess nuclear weapons is permissible only if limited to a "sufficiency" to deter; thus the quest for nuclear superiority is not legitimate. Finally, deterrence must be considered as only a step in the path to nuclear disarmament.[67]

The bishops recognize that sincere Catholics may disagree with their conclusions and they make clear such disagreement is acceptable. From the tenor of the letter it is evident that any disagreement should be based on moral and not simply on pragmatic grounds.

The other landmark pastoral letter of the American bishops, *On Catholic Social Teaching and the U.S. Economy*, is also a challenge to all American citizens, regardless of their religious affiliation.[68] The bishops again consulted with experts in writing this letter. Symposia and conferences were held at various Catholic and non-Catholic institutions of learning throughout the United States. Among those consulted were business persons, labor leaders, economists, politicians, social scientists, government officials, theologians, scripture scholars, and others. Drafts of the pastoral letter were circulated publicly, and criticism was welcomed from all quarters. The letter considers four specific areas: employment, poverty, the distribution of food and agriculture, and the relationship between the United States and the world economy. Among other items, the bishops call the current level of poverty and unemployment in this country "a social and moral scandal." They ask for a renewal of the war on poverty and call for a reduction of unemployment to 3 to 4 percent, which in fact has been reached in the early twenty-first century. The bishops also suggest a restructuring of the tax system to eliminate taxation of the poor. The most striking aspect of the entire letter is its strong critique of current American cultural and economic values.

As with the pastoral letter on peace, the letter on the U.S. economy recognizes that sincere Catholics may disagree with the conclusions reached in this document. The bishops point out that when they present concrete moral judgments, they do not intend these norms to be binding in conscience, because it is impossible to attain the same degree of certitude about specific moral judgments as is possible in the case of universal moral principles. They also state that the Church's teaching authority simply does not have the same binding power in dealing with technical solutions involving particular means as it does when speaking of principles or ends. What the bishops are trying to do, then, is to awaken Americans to the problems of social justice. They are encouraging Catholics and others to become involved in the struggle for peace and human rights. The bishops have made considerable efforts to present the issues to the public. It is hoped that out of this process the Church will emerge as a force for peace and justice in a manner that respects and heightens the true dignity of all human beings.

The *process* of writing these letters is very important. As Charles Curran writes in regard to the letter on the U.S. economy,

> The very process itself has been a great teaching tool in terms of awakening consciousness both within the Church and society in general to the moral issues involved in the U.S. economy. The dialogical and collegial style of writing this document contrasts with the approach still used in most Catholic documents, especially those emanating from Rome. An increasing difficulty will be experienced in the future for Church authorities to propose documents that have not been prepared with this same wide-ranging and public dialogue.[69]

Other examples of attempts at inculturation are found in many other letters of the United States's bishops or groups of bishops that deal with more particular questions relating to Hispanics, black Americans, and the Native American population. We see in these instances the importance of national and regional conferences of bishops in dealing with the particular problems facing their regions. An outstanding example of an attempt at inculturation by bishops of a particular region is "Strangers and Guests: A Regional Catholic Bishops' Statement on Land Issues," which was produced by 72 Midwestern bishops from 44 dioceses after two years of consultation with a variety of groups. The document deals with stewardship of the land and with rural development. Individual and corporate responsibilities are discussed, including fair wages and proper working conditions. The rights of Native Americans are also delineated. Many agencies and institutes throughout the United States are involved in the process of inculturation, which means, as has been indicated, being fully and truly Christian in a particular cultural context or situation. Washington, D.C., for example, is the locus for a number of agencies and institutes involved in reflecting on the Church in the United States. Among them are the Center for Concern, the Woodstock Center, and the Quixote Center. Each of them in its own way fosters dialogue between American culture and the Gospel.

Those involved with the question of inculturation generally proceed with a two-fold methodology: first, sociological analysis, which seeks to identify with the help of the social sciences the structure and functioning of American society; and second, theological reflection, which seeks with the help of scripture and religious traditions to arrive at a judgment about American society and culture in light of the Gospels. The pastoral letters on war and peace and on the U.S. economy used such a methodology. Sociology has become very important to the process of inculturation. Scholars such as Father Andrew Greeley use sophisticated research methods to provide an accurate description of the Catholic people in the United States. His data provide an interesting portrayal of "middle-class" Catholics, who although still identifying themselves as Catholic are often in disagreement with the

Church's teaching and yet in many cases manifest a deep spiritual life with new perceptions of God and religion.[70] An interesting summary of the development of Greeley's research and analysis is found in his *Confessions of a Parish Priest*.[71]

Many other sociologists of religion such as John A. Coleman, Robert Bellah, and Peter Berger are also seeking to identify the relationship of religious values to American society. Coleman's *An American Strategic Theology* provides a helpful analysis.[72] He uses not only sociological data but includes an impressive range of historical and theological information. His description of the crisis of American Catholicism is similar to what has been presented in this chapter. This includes the loss of the symbols, practices, and solidarity of the immigrant communities and parishes and the general rise of Catholics to middle-class status. He observes that no new symbols, practices, and solidarities have been created to take their place. Catholics have generally accepted the middle-class way of life, including supporting its values and ideals, and many are beginning to recognize that these are often not in line with authentic Christian values. Coleman also thinks that because of their capitulation to the middle-class American lifestyle, many Catholics have lost the sense of mysticism and contemplation and have accepted a religious style oriented to action and pragmatic achievement. For example, to be involved with projects such as Habitat for Humanity is admirable and worthwhile, but if this is not accompanied by a life of prayer and meditation, much is lost. Much is missing as well when a person works constantly to achieve success in business but spends little time on contemplation and other spiritual practices. He argues that American Catholics must come to a realistic understanding of the strengths and limitations of American culture and ground their lives in the Gospels. He also insists that Catholic involvement in any society, including the United States, must be committed to justice as an essential manifestation of faith.

Sociological studies and the theological reflection of scholars and religious leaders are all part of the widespread effort to create a meaningful cultural expression of the Catholic faith in the United States. This is a new challenge and is very different from that which the Church faced in its immigrant experience. (Because so many Catholics belong to the middle class, they belong to the very culture they seek to change.) If Catholics face this challenge successfully, a new and creative inculturation will result, representing a revolutionary relationship between the Church and American society. The Church in Latin America is a powerful paradigm of a church coming to grips with its own particular context and culture. Many Christian communities throughout Latin America have placed the Gospel and the Christian tradition over their contemporary political, religious, and social situations. Their efforts have allowed them to confirm the good in their culture and in the Church and to lessen the evil in both their culture and the Church. This presents a challenging model of great significance for the inculturation of the Gospel in the United States. It is probably not too much to say that inculturation is the most important challenge for the American Catholic Church today. In areas dominated by Western culture, such as the United States, Church growth has leveled off or, as in Western Europe, is shrinking. On the other hand, in many areas of the developing world, which are only modestly influenced by Western culture, the Church is growing steadily or even spectacularly. Perhaps Lesslie Newbigin is correct in arguing that modern Western culture, more than almost any other, is proving resistant to the Gospel.[73] If so, the process of inculturation will experience an abundance of obstacles. Yet it is a primary task for all Christians.

The Question of the Other: Multiculturalism in the Local Church

Multiculturalism, as used here, is understood as communion across cultures, or communion among communities living their faith out of a diversity of culture, without trying to reduce each other to a common fusion of cultural faith experiences. The issue being considered pertains to a local church that is dealing with its own inner cultural pluralism. The Christian faith came to the United States in a variety of European cultural expressions, yet throughout the history of the immigrant churches a certain Roman identity was maintained. However, in recent years there have been pastoral letters and pastoral programs inaugurated by Catholic leadership for various cultural groups such as Hispanics, black Americans, Native Americans, and Asian Americans, suggesting efforts to maintain their own cultural identities.

Several histories have been written in the past few decades that show the part that ethnicity has played in the development of Roman Catholicism. Ethnicity is defined by Greeley and David Tracy as "religious, racial, national, linguistic, and geographic diversity."[74] These authors and others argue that ethnic experience is a legitimate source of theological reflection. In analyzing the life of the community, one has to ponder over patterns and experiences that are proper to its members' particular heritage. As for the place of ethnicity in the present life of the Church, Philip Gleason says that it may not have the fervor of the late nineteenth or early twentieth century, but its importance is made more urgent because of the waves of new immigrants from all continents.[75] Gleason notes that in the past there were real differences of viewpoint and policy preference between different ethnic groups, and from the past we can learn the danger of dismissing either the importance of the ethnocentric or the importance of looking for convergence. In this regard David Power writes,

> As we profit from a more critical awareness of the nature of ethnicity, we see that there can be no melting down into a uniform culture. Rather,

what is required is a communion in the recognition of the other, and in the ways of communication which allows partners in communion to share the diversity, and indeed to come to communion out of diversity.[76]

For Catholics, reflection on popular devotion is vital in gaining an understanding of the variety of cultures in the United States. Such reflection is useful in understanding how such devotions relate various ethnicities to their own reality as well as to the surrounding community. The fact that ethnic traditions vary so greatly is the basic reason for different liturgies, which are celebrated in varieties of aesthetic cultural forms that best embody the hopes and memories of each ethnic group. Power writes,

> Within such communion in diversity, to prevent isolation and encourage communion with othernessess, there need to be periodic (not, however, weekly) celebrations of diversity. These are intercultural rituals that are designed as such, when the church celebrates its manifold richness and its liberating eschatological hope. Such celebration, for example, might very well mark the feast of Pentecost or the common celebration of saints who have become popular across cultures.[77]

And finally Power writes,

> The witness of a life of faith and charity, the exercise of charisms, that telling of stories, mutual rendering of services, a variety of ritual activities, devotional appeals to God, Christ, Mary or the saints, all exist in some measure prior to and beneath, or within the cracks of, canonical language, doctrines, rites and institutions. Too often the canonical has suppressed them, or even styled them heterodox. Their retrieval counts for much in the recognition of the other, in the sounding of cultural voices, and in the commerce of polycentric communion, as also in the forging of different canonical boundaries and institutions, which can serve this polycentric model of being church.[78]

In allowing others to be "other" and in responding to one another lovingly, a new solidarity and richness in Christian community will be shaped.

Hispanics in the United States

One of the most obvious efforts at inculturation in the United States pertains to Hispanics. The American hierarchy is conscious of the rising importance of the Hispanic population, who are projected to constitute the largest percentage of U.S. Catholics in the next two decades. The word *Hispanic* is used in this book to cover a variety of Spanish-speaking national groups, including Mexican Americans, Puerto Ricans, Cubans, Dominicans, and Central and South Americans. Currently the Hispanic population in the United States is estimated at 20 million, of which the largest group is of Mexican origin, followed by Puerto Ricans and Cubans. Anywhere from a low of 75 percent to a high of 95 percent of the Hispanic population is estimated to be baptized Catholics.

In an effort to make better known the life of Hispanic Catholics, Moises Sandoval has written an excellent book, *On the Move: A History of the Hispanic Church in the United States.*[79] The Hispanic population, because of its number, may well give a particular character to the Catholic Church in the United States in the twenty-first century, just as European immigrants gave their particular character to the Church during the nineteenth and twentieth centuries.

The definitive statement of the policy of the Church in relation to Hispanics and their inculturation was published by the American bishops in a pastoral letter in 1983, *The Hispanic Presence: Challenge and Commitment,* followed in 1987 by another pastoral letter, *National Plan for Hispanic Ministry.*[80] I will concentrate on the 1983 letter, which is the basis of the bishops' policy. The letter describes the social, cultural, and religious situation of Hispanics in the United States. The bishops are well aware that Hispanics come from a culture that has been penetrated by the Catholic faith, but in a very different way from that of European Catholics. They are also cognizant that Hispanics are among the poorest people in the United States, whereas Catholics in general are middle class. It is difficult to bridge the gap across cultures and even more difficult to bridge the gap across social class. This complicates the problem of inculturation, as does the fact that, unlike Europeans in the past, Hispanics have come to the United States largely without their own clergy.

In *The Hispanic Presence* the bishops outline the challenge to the Church in terms of ministry and response to the social, economic, and political needs of the Hispanics and make a commitment to provide whatever resources are needed to help them realize their full potential as vital contributors of the Catholic experience in the United States. An important feature of the letter is the firm commitment to a policy of cultural pluralism in the United States and of religious pluralism within the Catholic Church. The letter also discusses the poverty of Hispanics, and though it is not presented as a problem of difference of social class, the letter calls for a "preferential option for the poor" and asks that the Church be a strong advocate of the poor. The bishops describe Hispanic culture as an experience in which "faith and life are inseparable." The Spanish colonial experience brought about a distinct culture penetrated by the Catholic faith, which in turn became the cultural support of the faith. This is different from the religious experience of life in the United States, which generally is lived in a secular culture:

As with many nationalities with strong Catholic traditions, religion, and culture, faith and life are inseparable for Hispanics. Hispanic Catholicism is an outstanding example of how the Gospel can permeate a culture even to its roots.[81]

In coming to the United States Hispanics face, on the level of everyday living, a clash of cultures that can be upsetting and even traumatic. In great measure this occurs because of the conflict between the highly individualistic and competitive culture of the United States and the personalistic and family-oriented culture of Hispanic countries. Tension also occurs between the Hispanic style of Catholic life and practice and the style practiced by the Church in the United States. These differences of style can lead to misunderstanding and tension. Central to this issue is the fact that Hispanics are calling for a cultural pluralism that would permit the continuation of Hispanic language and culture in the process of their adjustment to the United States. In response to this problem, the bishops wrote,

> The pastoral needs of Hispanic Catholics are indeed great; although their faith is deep and strong, it is being challenged and eroded by steady social pressures to assimilate.
> Respect for culture is rooted in the dignity of people made in God's image. The Church shows its esteem for their dignity by working to ensure that pluralism, not assimilation and uniformity, is the guiding principle in the life of communities in both ecclesial and secular societies.[82]

One of the problems Hispanics face when they emigrate to the United States results from the fact that in their homelands their faith was supported by their culture, even in the absence of clergy and religious instruction. Because of this the change of religious environment is a profound shock to them, and the adjustment to a new culture is difficult. This problem is compounded by the fact that Hispanics are the first Catholic immigrants to come to the United States in large numbers without a native clergy to accompany them. Earlier immigrants had many of their own clergy and religious priests and nuns with them, and this allowed for a perpetuation of their culture. The Hispanic clergy are not sufficient in number, generally speaking, to allow them to accompany their countrypeople to the United States.

The lack of Hispanic clergy has presented a great challenge to the clergy of the United States. Thousands of American priests and religious personnel have learned to speak Spanish and to understand the Hispanic culture to prepare themselves to minister to the newly arriving Hispanics. This response has been admirable though inadequate. Centers have been established to prepare Americans for Hispanic ministry. The Mexican American Cultural Center established by Father Virgil Elizondo in San Antonio, Texas, has made a remarkable contribution in this regard.

One of the serious concerns of the Church is the small number of Hispanics aspiring to the priesthood and the religious life in the United States. Because vocations to the priesthood were never numerous in Latin America, there is no tradition on which to build. Added to this is the drop in vocations worldwide, which was discussed earlier. Most dioceses in which Hispanics are numerous have established an Office of Hispanic Ministry. And many Hispanics have been active in their response to life in the Church in the United States. The Cursillo Movement is very popular, for example. It is a brief retreat designed to bring about a deep conversion of the individual, which is followed up by regular meetings to keep the experience alive. The charismatic movement and the Christian Family Movement are also widespread.

One of the most difficult questions facing the contemporary Catholic Church in America is the assimilation of Hispanics into American society. An important study of this issue was done in 1980 by A. J. Jaffe, Ruth M. Cullen, and Thomas D. Boswell, *The Changing Demography of Spanish Americans.*[83] They found among Hispanics a consistent pattern of assimilation similar to that of earlier ethnic groups. Using the indicators of language, socioeconomic levels, fertility, and intermarriage of Hispanics with other ethnic groups, Jaffe and his group found evidence of a trend toward adopting the dominant cultural patterns of the United States: English becomes the language of common usage; socioeconomic advancement improves in the second and third generations and with the number of years in the United States; fertility declines with education. The pace at which this convergence is taking place differs for each Hispanic group and differs within each group, of course. But the evidence of a trend toward convergence is consistent. The Jaffe group concludes their study in this way:

> The Spanish-American groups in the United States ... have changed and will continue to change in a manner paralleling the general society. ... With each passing decade, they are being brought closer to the mainstream of social change and economic development of the larger society until eventually there will be a merging ... in another generation or two they will be almost indistinguishable from the general U.S. population.[84]

The standard sociological indicators, therefore, lead to the conclusion that the experience of the Hispanics will be similar to that of previous immigrant groups. However, there are some notable differences today that may result in a retention of Hispanic culture. Hispanics come from "next door," from Cuba, the Dominican Republic, Puerto Rico, Mexico, and Central and South America. Mexico borders the United States, and Central America can be reached by land. Both the proximity and the ease of travel back and forth reinforces an already deeply rooted culture. At the same time, the increasing emphasis on cultural pluralism in the United States has created a climate much more favorable to the retention of a native culture than was the case with earlier immigrants. Added to this, the strong emphasis by Hispanics on bilingual and bicultural programs in the public schools reflect their strong sense of culture and a determination to perpetuate it.

Hispanics are not alone in attempting to retain their culture. This is certainly true of African Americans as well as others who celebrate their ethnicity in festivals, neighborhood parties, and in literature and dance. There are many reasons given for this recapturing of cultural roots, one of the most prominent of which is an effort to retain supports for self-identity in a world marked by uncertainty and rapid change. Among the Hispanics, cultural adaptation to the United States is taking place as it has for all previous ethnic groups within the second and subsequent generations that achieve a new cultural understanding, one that hopefully is a dynamic blend of Hispanic and American influence. As a consequence the twenty-first century may witness a new life radiating from the Hispanic community, which will have a significant impact on the Church, liturgically and theologically, and in many areas pertaining to social justice.

Hispanic American Theology

Peter C. Phan, in his essay "Contemporary Theology and Inculturation," gives an excellent overview of the development of Hispanic theology, which I will summarize.[85] One important event in the development of Hispanic theology was the founding of the Academy of Catholic Hispanic Theologians of the United States (ACHTUS) in 1988. The Academy includes male and female theologians. It has deliberately differentiated U.S. Hispanic theology from Latin American liberation theology, even though they have much in common, because the purpose of the Academy is to concentrate on problems unique to the United States. The Academy also endorses ecumenical dialogue with Hispanic Protestant theologians. This is being done with a Protestant group, La Communidad, and *Apuntes*, until recently the only journal of Hispanic theology in the United States. In October 1993, the Academy began publishing its own quarterly journal, *Journal of Hispanic / Latino Theology*.

Fr. Virgil Elizando, a priest of the Archdiocese of San Antonio, Texas, is seen as the first contemporary U.S. Hispanic theologian. From the late 1960s to the late 1980s he was the sole, highly visible U.S. Hispanic theologian. He is a prolific and internationally known theologian, and he is now followed by a new generation of well-trained and well-published theologians who are dedicated to developing a distinctive Hispanic theology that is contextualized into the cultural situation of the United States.

Hispanic theology begins with a cultural and social analysis of the Hispanic community in the United States. Elizando, both in *The Galilean Journey* and in his article "Mestizaje as a Locus of Theological Reflection," writes that U.S. Hispanics are characterized by what he terms *Mestizaje*.[86] Mestizaje does not simply refer to the physiological fact that Hispanics, like many other peoples, are a mixed race composed of many bloods. Rather, it refers to the violent forging of a new people from the sexual intercourse that occurred between the Spanish Conquistadores and the vanquished Amerindian women. *Mestizaje* also refers to the subjugation of the Amerindian religion by medieval Roman Catholicism. Because of this double conquest, the *mestizos* are forced to live as foreigners in their own land. As Elizando puts it, Mexican Americans suffer from an unfinished or undefined identity. Their Spanish is too Anglicized for the Mexicans, and their English is too Mexicanized for the Anglo Americans. For Mexicans, Hispanics are too close to the United States, and for Anglo Americans they are too close to Mexico. The *mestizo* reality is feared and rejected by both racial groups that produce it because it blurs the identity-constituting boundaries between them. This is the peculiar situation of U.S. Hispanics, which Elizando describes with the term *el rechazo* (rejection). The combined character of "Mexican American" cannot be adequately understood by an analysis of either group. Elizando maintains that *mestizaje* is a symbol of biological–cultural oppression, exploitation, and alienation. However, and this is most important, this symbol contains a seed for creating a new reality and a new culture, provided it is not reabsorbed into either of the cultures that produced it. Thus *mestizaje* is a starting point for U.S. Hispanic theology.

Hispanic theology is deeply rooted in the Hispanic experience of Church rather than from a somewhat removed academic mindset. It is a Church experience that is strongly sacramental but steeped in popular devotions. It also tends to be nonclerical. As Phan writes,

> Indeed, one of the distinctive features of the Hispanic church is that since its beginnings it developed in spite of the scarcity of priests. The laity has always exercised a key role in the life of the Church: *sacristans* who functioned as parish administrators, *rezadores* [prayer leaders] who led funeral prayers, *mayordomos* [stewards] who were in charge of parish finances, and *catechists* responsible for religious instruction.[87]

Because Hispanic theology is rooted in the Hispanics' experience of *mestizaje* and *rechazo* and is in solidarity with them, it must begin with the existential option for the poor. This means that central to its methodology is the relation between theory and practice. Robert Goizueto, who has written extensively on this issue, warns U.S. Hispanic theologians not to yield to the antiintellectual temptation of renouncing theory in favor of practice. He also cautions them not to follow postmodernity's premature rejection of the Enlightenment's demand for rationality. This might lead to the marginalization of Hispanic theology by Anglo theologians as no more than

"Hispanic advocacy theology," which could perhaps be judged as devoid of intellectual rigor and therefore irrelevant to the theological enterprise.[88]

From its very beginning the Academy of Catholic Hispanic Theologians of the United States has sought to recognize the work of Hispanic female theologians. Approximately 25 percent of U.S. Hispanic theologians are women. They are in the process of developing a *mujerista* theology—a theology that has as its point of departure the experience of Hispanic American women in the dominant Anglo Saxon culture, facing oppression and discrimination from both a sexist world as women and a racist world as Hispanics.[89]

The current production of Hispanic theology is quantitatively nowhere near that of Latin American theology or black theology. But U.S. Hispanic theology has had an auspicious beginning. It has made, and undoubtedly will continue to make, original and lasting contributions to theological inculturation in the United States. African American theology and feminist theology already have made important contributions to the American theological enterprise. Contextual theologies such as these are very important: However, concomitant with the rise of ethnic consciousness, there is also the phenomenon of globalization, which has numerous causes, including the growth of economic unions (e.g., the European Community), the rise of economic power in Asia, the end of the East–West determination of geopolitics, high-speed global travel, electronic communications, and the emergence of a new global capitalism. This global culture undermines the importance of ethnic groups and nation states. The reconciliation of the demands of a particular inculturated theology with those of a global or universal theology and the discovery of new symbols of hope for this emerging global culture certainly constitutes one of the most difficult and yet exciting challenges for theology. To do so demands respect and cooperation among the world's religions and theologians.

SUMMARY

Rahner proposed that the most fundamental significance of Vatican II is that it was, at least in an initial way, the first historical manifestation of a truly world church that acts through the mutual influence of its various parts. Catholicism is moving from a long period of being culturally grounded in Europe and North America to a period in which its life unfolds in the world as a whole. Most consequences of this development are as yet unseen, but it seems likely that they will have major implications for the Church. It is incontestable that at Vatican II, for the first time, a worldwide council with a worldwide episcopate came into existence. Together with the recognition of Catholicism as a world church with indigenous leadership, there is the equally important realization that the Church must be rooted in the various cultures of the world. In becoming Christians the peoples of the world are expected to be fully themselves in their respective historical contexts and to enrich the universal Christian community with their particular cultural heritage. There is a growing tendency to designate such a process by the term "inculturation," which deals with the interaction of faith on the one hand and culture on the other.

Historical examples of inculturation are seen in the lives of Saints Cyril and Methodius and in the work of Father Matteo Ricci. Recent Church teachings support the efforts of these extraordinary men.

The Church has always expressed its faith through cultural forms. Inculturation implies that the Christian message transforms a culture and in turn is transformed *by* that culture. This mutual transformation occurs, according to Shorter, "not in a way that falsifies the Christian message, but in the way by which the message is formulated and interpreted anew."[90] The inculturation of Christianity into different cultures is acknowledged as a duty of the Church by all leaders of the Church.

The great breakthrough in official statements about the relationship of the Catholic Church to the various cultures of the world took place at Vatican II and appears in several official documents, including the *Constitution on the Church in the Modern World, The Dogmatic Constitution on the Church*, and the *Decree on the Church's Missionary Activity*. Pope Paul VI and Pope John XXIII have expanded and deepened the Church's commitment to the notion of inculturation. Pope John Paul II has also emphasized the urgent need to relate faith and culture. Nonetheless, the Church is aware of some of the problems that arise from the interaction of faith and culture and strongly opposes all cultural relativism. A critical attitude of discernment must be used in this regard.

Many Christian communities throughout Latin America have put the Gospel and the Christian tradition above their contemporary religious, political, and social situations. Their contemplation has led them to affirm the good in their Church and in their culture and to attempt to eradicate the evil in both. The theology of liberation that has resulted offers a challenging model for the inculturation of the Gospel in every context.

Inculturation in the United States is already taking place. Several histories have been written in the past few decades that show the role that ethnicity has played in the development of Roman Catholicism in this country. The Christian faith came to the United States in a variety of European expressions, yet throughout the history of the immigrant churches a certain Roman identity was maintained. However, in recent years there have been pastoral letters and pastoral programs inaugurated by Catholic leadership for various groups such as Hispanics, African Americans, Native Americans, and Asian Americans, suggesting their efforts to maintain a cultural identity, and the promotion of inculturation.

Study Questions

1. What is meant by the term "inculturation"? Is the idea of inculturation supported by the Vatican in practice as well as in theory?

2. Describe the accomplishments of Saints Cyril and Methodius. How can their accomplishments be imitated in today's Church?

3. Who was Matteo Ricci? What was the Chinese Rites controversy? Did this event negatively affect the missionary movement?

4. What is the importance of Pope John XXIII's encyclical *Princeps Pastorum*?

5. What is "cultural relativism"? Why is it unacceptable?

6. What is the "theology of liberation"? Does it have any application in the United States?

7. Gustavo Gutiérrez uses the term "liberation" in three senses. Name them. Which of the three areas is most important?

8. What is "ethnicity"? What role has it played in the development of Roman Catholicism in the United States? Does it play the same role for recent immigrants?

9. Explain the importance of the writing of Virgil Elizando.

10. Has the Church reached out to Hispanics, Asian Americans, and other recent immigrants to help them assimilate to American culture? Explain.

11. What is the meaning and importance of the word "*mestizaje?*"

CHAPTER 4

Catholicism and the World Religions

The validity of other religions has emerged as an important question in contemporary Christian theology. Especially since Vatican II, Catholics have begun to ask what the God who revealed Himself in Jesus as the Christ is doing in the human family beyond the boundaries of the Church. This question emerges with a certain urgency, because the theological evaluation of the truth as found in other religions will determine the Church of the twenty-first century and beyond. For Catholics to make a determination of their relationship to the other world religions, it is necessary first to clearly and accurately understand Catholicism's claim that final revelation has occurred in Jesus as the Christ.

In relation to the non-Christian religions, the concept of "religion" is understood in a broad sense. Included are not only the Western religions such as Judaism and Islam but Asian religions as well, such as Buddhism and Hinduism. Before discussing the present situation, it will be helpful to survey briefly the history of past Roman Catholic attitudes toward other religions by examining sacred Scripture and tradition.

EARLIER ATTITUDES TOWARD OTHER RELIGIONS

Sacred Scripture

The early Christians looked to the Old Testament for clues concerning their relationship to members of other religions. Most of the Old Testament references are purely negative in this regard and abound in condemnations of the polytheistic and idolatrous cults surrounding Israel. The earlier prophets have nothing positive to say about the religion of other nations. The pagan gods are at first treated as real in the Old Testament but inferior to the God of Israel in power and righteousness. In the later prophets, however, the gods of the nations are declared to be false. In Isaiah we read, "I am the first and I am the last; besides me there is no god. Who is like me? Let him proclaim it" (Isa. 44:6).

But there are other strands in the Old Testament tradition that indicate a more tolerant and positive attitude toward other nations and their religions. The Old Testament affirms that all human beings are created by God. Moreover, they are created "in the image of God"—that is, in a special relationship of responsibility to God. All stand in a solidarity of sin, of having turned away from God in rebellion and disobedience. And this applies to Israel as well as to the other nations. Thus all nations stand under the grace and judgment of God, who is the sovereign Lord of all humankind (Amos 9:7). The pagan nations and their rulers often appear as fulfilling the divine will in the judgment of Israel (Isa. 10:5).

Another element of the tradition sees Israel and the nations standing in a special relationship to God, known as the Covenant. In the ninth chapter of Genesis it is asserted that God enters into a covenant with Noah and his descendants—that is, with all humankind—one involving the promise of God's favor as manifest in the order of nature. Then within this universal covenant God establishes a special covenant with Israel as God's chosen people. But this covenant, which begins with Abraham, does not involve simply a favored position for Israel but rather a special responsibility— namely, to bring God's blessing to all humankind (Gen. 12:1–3; Isa. 49:6). *Thus the whole of human history becomes a history of salvation,* a history of God's seeking out all His or Her children to bring them to their fulfillment. Because of this every human being lives in a relationship to God, and there are a few suggestions in the Old Testament that even non-Jewish religions can be a proper response to God (Mal. 1:11). We implicitly have the idea of a salvation history on two levels: the special salvation history of Israel leading up to the messianic fulfillment and a general or universal salvation history, including all peoples, the purpose and destiny of which is not clearly recognized by them. Thus outside of Israel there is not simply darkness and divine judgment but rather even there God reigns and is graciously at work. As a matter of fact, the Old Testament discusses individuals who were close to God even though they did not belong to Israel. Jean Daniélou has written a brief study of these biblical figures, such as Melchizadek, the pagan king and priest of Salem, in his book *The Holy Pagans of the Old Testament.*[1]

In the New Testament Jesus presents Himself and is presented as the fulfillment of the Covenant between God and Israel intended for all humankind. He is a Jew who is sent to announce the judgment and fulfillment of Judaism. Though He knows little or nothing of pagan religion, He continually rejects the nationalistic and exclusivistic attitude toward the Gentiles, which He finds among some of His Jewish contemporaries. The Gentiles will share in the salvation of the Kingdom of God and will be judged on the same basis as the Jews. Jesus even threatens the Jews that their place in the Kingdom will be taken by the Gentiles if they do not repent. He often points to the faith and love of Gentiles as putting the Jews to shame (Luke 10:29–37, 17:11–19; also Matt. 8:5–13). St. Paul is directly concerned with the religions of the Gentiles. He addresses this question in the first chapter of his Letter to the Romans, which has always been cited as a classic passage in the Christian attitude toward other religions. In it he condemns pagan religion as idolatry, the worship of the creature instead of the creator. His point, however, is that the Gentiles are responsible, because they should have known better. St. Paul writes, "For what can be known about God is plain to them, because God has shown it to them. Ever since the creation of the world his invisible nature, namely, his eternal power and deity, has been clearly perceived in the things that have been made" (Rom. 1:18–19). The Gentiles should have known God through His or Her revelation in the Creation, but they refused to do so and instead worshiped images of human beings and animals. God's judgment on the Gentiles is to "deliver" them into all kinds of immorality. But the Jews are no better off, because they, too, are under the power of sin. So St. Paul's purpose is to demonstrate that all have fallen short and are saved only by God's grace.

A passage in the New Testament that bears only indirectly on the attitude toward other religions but that was to play a larger part in later discussions is the prologue to the Gospel of John (John 1:1–14). In it the active "word" or "reason" *(Logos)* of God that was His or Her agent in the creation of the world is seen as the "light of man," which "enlightens every man." And this word of God has become human in Jesus Christ and has shown forth the glory and grace of God. Thus every human life is related to God through its creation and illumination by the word of God. In the next section, which deals with tradition, we will see how this idea of the *Logos* was used to interpret pagan religion.

In summary, the attitude of the Scriptural authors toward other religions is on the surface strongly negative, but there are many passages in the Bible that indicate on a deeper level an approach that is more tolerant and universal. God is the Lord of all who has not left Him- or Herself without witness in any nation and who wills to bring all to salvation (1 Tim. 1:15).

Tradition

Among the Christian apologists who were second- and third-century Christian writers who defended the faith against those who were attacking it, the common interpretation of polytheism held that it was the work of demons who were understood to be spiritual beings who were created by God but who had rebelled against Him and now attempted to disrupt His creation.[2] This completely negative attitude meant that the proper Christian approach was to destroy these idols and persuade people to give them up.

But the most common theory of the apologists was based on the idea of the *Logos*. As God's agent in the creation, the *Logos* is the pervasive divine principle of reality. Human beings who are created in the image of God participate in the *Logos* in the form of their rationality. But this participation is a matter of degree, and is always in some measure distorted by sin. All of humankind's cultural creations, including religion, are understood to be informed in part by the *Logos*. The Christian gospel teaches that the *Logos* of God is perfectly manifest in Jesus Christ. On this basis the apologists were able to recognize in some of the greater pagans and in the higher aspects of pagan religion prefigurations of the Christian faith and life. Thus Justin Martyr wrote,

> We have been taught that Christ is the First-begotten of God, and have previously testified that he is the Reason of which every race of man partakes. Those who lived in accordance with Reason are Christians, even though they were called godless, such as, among the Greeks, Socrates and Heraclitus and others like them; among the barbarians, Abraham, Ananiah, Azariah, and Mishael, and Elijah, and many others, whose deeds and names I forbear to list, knowing that this would be lengthy.[3]

The *Logos* doctrine as an interpretation and attitude toward other religions occurs again and again in various forms throughout Christian history. It is an approach that enables Christians to perceive positive elements as well as distortions in other religions, to see other religions as preparations for the Christian gospel, and to present the Christian faith as the fulfillment of other faiths.

Perhaps the most perplexing aspect of the history of the relationship of Christianity to non-Christian religions is found in the axiom "No salvation outside the Church." The roots of this ecclesiocentric statement go back to the Fathers of the Church, namely to Ignatius of Antioch,[4] Iranaeus,[5] Clement of Alexandria,[6] and others. Its first complete formulation is the negative one found in Origen: "Let no one persuade or deceive himself: outside this house, that is, outside the Church, no one will be saved; for if someone leaves, he himself is guilty of death."[7] Cyprian was the first to apply the axiom—using the ark as an illustration—with juridical exclusiveness and with all the consequences thereof:

> Anyone who separates himself from the Church and unites with an adulteress (schism), shuts himself off from the promises of the church, and anyone who leaves the church of Christ, will not deserve Christ's re-

wards. He is an outcast, unholy, an enemy. God is not his Father, if the Church is not his mother. If anyone outside Noah's ark had been able to escape, then so might a man outside the Church. [8]

It is important to recall that Cyprian wrote during the time of the great Roman persecutions of the Church. Because of this an "introvert" ecclesiology took shape, of which Bishop Cyprian was a typical representative. "Outside the Church there is no salvation" was to become the slogan of an embattled Christianity. It is very probable that the clear-sighted circumspection of St. Augustine had much to do with the propagation of this axiom, contrary to his own intention. Then as now, fine shades of meaning are apt to be missed. It is easier to popularize clear-cut slogans than subtle distinctions. Augustine had great respect for Cyprian, whom he revered as a saint.[9] Nonetheless, he did not share all his opinions. Augustine could not of course say this bluntly.[10] He preferred to make use of more prudent formulations. Thus Augustine writes,

There is no salvation outside the Church, says Cyprian. Who would want to deny this? Hence it is true that all that one receives from the Church does not count for salvation outside the Church. But it is one thing not to have something, and another to have it fruitlessly. [11]

Augustine could hardly have expressed more gently his opposition to Cyprian. A few pages later he allows himself to speak even more clearly when he says,

Some of those who are baptized outside the Church, are really counted by God's foreknowledge among those who are baptized within the Church, because the water of baptism begins to work their salvation even there [outside the Church]. [12]

A century later Fulgentius of Ruspe thought he was rendering Augustine's own thoughts exactly when he declared,

It is absolutely certain that not only all pagans but also all Jews and heretics and schismatics who die outside the Church will go into the eternal fire which is prepared for the devil and his angels. [13]

The interpretation of Augustine became definitive, according to Boniface Willems, when the work of Fulgentius was attributed to Augustine by later copyists.[14] Thus the principle "Outside the Church there is no salvation" acquired an authority in the Middle Ages that was almost unquestionable. Alcuin, Ratramnus, Ivo of Chartres, Abelard, Peter Lombard, and Thomas Aquinas all attributed the authorship of the axiom to St. Augustine. However, it is important to recall that at the time when this axiom took root the *ecclesia catholica* (the Catholic Church) extended more or less throughout the known world. It even seemed for a period that the whole world was Christian. Given these limited geographical perspectives, it is rather understandable that the axiom won acceptance.

NEW INSIGHTS INTO NON-CHRISTIAN RELIGIONS

New insights into non-Christian religions began to develop as a result of the tremendous historical experience of the discovery of new continents with civilized and morally good people. Now Christians did not just know that there were countries and races outside the Church, but they were forced to take a positive interest in them. There was a growing awareness of what it meant to belong to a world that did not begin and end with Europe and the countries immediately surrounding the Mediterranean basin. With new perspectives of this kind theology inevitably began to move gradually away from the axiom "Outside the Church there is no salvation." In the sixteenth century, the great age of discoveries, theologians such as Bellarmine and Suarez and the Council of Trent taught that baptism could be received not only *in re* (in fact) as Christians received it, but also *in voto* (by desire).[15] The *in voto* concept was later applied directly to membership in the Church. Thus in the eighteenth century, faced with the extreme views of the Jansenists, which was a seventeenth- and eighteenth-century movement in Europe, especially France, which stressed moral austerity and taught a very restrictive concept of grace, which they believed was limited to members of the Catholic Church alone, the Catholic Church refuted the proposition "No grace is granted outside the Church."[16] Finally, by the nineteenth century, not only because of the unbaptized but also because of the Protestant Christians who had been separated from the Roman Catholic Church for several centuries, the "outside" was interpreted by Pope Pius IX in such a way that it could be stated,

> [E]qually it is our firm belief that those who live in ignorance of the true religion incur no guilt in the eyes of the Lord, if this ignorance is invincible. Who, however, would dare to take it upon himself to determine the limits of this ignorance according to the type and variety of peoples, regions, natural dispositions and so many other things?[17]

THE TWENTIETH CENTURY AND THE EARLY TWENTY-FIRST CENTURY

In the twentieth century the encyclical *Mystici Corporis* (Mystical Body, 1943) repeated the original axiom, "Outside the Church there is no salvation," in a rather limited form, and the Jesuit Fr. Leonard Feeney, with a group of Catholics in Boston, tried to take the words of the encyclical literally and to maintain the damnation of all who lived outside the visible Catholic Church. As a result, Rome was forced to intervene, protesting against this interpretation and finally declaring all those to be excommunicated and *extra ecclesiam* (outside the Church) who maintained that *extra ecclesiam* no one could be saved.[18]

The development of theology in Roman Catholicism was thus a lengthy process, culminating in Vatican II's emphatic affirmation that salvation is open to all, not just to schismatics, heretics, and Jews—including atheists if they are in good conscience.[19]

It is important for our consideration of the Catholic understanding of the meaning of the "non-Christian religions" that we keep in mind that the previously discussed interpretations clearly stated that there *is* salvation outside the Church, and this was so even when the axiom "There is no salvation outside the Church" was nominally retained. Nevertheless, it cannot be denied that the ambiguity of the expression misled many Catholics and non-Catholics alike. An effort to give a positive explanation of this negative axiom has been attempted by many modern theologians. Perhaps the most famous of the modern responses is the concept of the "anonymous Christian" developed by Karl Rahner. We will analyze Rahner's solution later in this chapter, as well as the strenuous objections made by various theologians to Rahner's theory. Before doing so, I will present a Hindu response to the Christian claim of the finality of revelation in Christ. Following this I will examine briefly the meaning of salvation history and of revelation as an introduction to Rahner's theory.

A NON-CHRISTIAN OBJECTION

The most frequent protest on the part of non-Christians regarding the teaching of Christianity is in regard to the Christian claim to exclusivity. For example, Ananda Coomaraswany, a Hindu, writes,

> The one outstanding, and perhaps the only real heresy of modern Christianity in the eyes of other believers is its claim to exclusive truth; for this is treason against Him who "never left himself without witness," and can only be paralleled by Peter's denial of Christ; and whoever says to his pagan friends that "the light that is in you is darkness," in offending these is offending the Father of lights. In view of St. Ambrose's well known gloss on 1 Corinthians 12:2, "all that is true, by whomsoever it has been said, is from the Holy Ghost" (a dictum endorsed by St. Thomas Aquinas), you may be asked, "On what grounds do you propose to distinguish between your own 'revealed' religion and our 'natural' religion for which, in fact, we also claim a supernatural origin?"[20]

Such quotations could be given at length from members of other religions, but Coomaraswamy's statement is at the heart of the objection and can serve as a symbol of the non-Christian protest against Christianity's exclusivistic claims, or what appears to them to be so.

SALVATION HISTORY

Salvation history refers to the pattern of events in human history that realize God's salvific activity. The notion of salvation history as a theological category was originally formulated in the nineteenth century to express the biblical teaching that God acted in the Jewish community's Covenant with God and later in the person of Jesus Christ, whose life, death, and Resurrection constitute God's definitive act of redemption. In its understanding of salvation history the contemporary Catholic community contends that all history is the arena of God's salvific action, even if unrecognized.

The Church's attitude toward other religions insofar as it is set within the framework of salvation history is based on the belief that God is the Lord of history, and in all human history God is working out a plan of salvation for all humankind. The importance of a theological conception of redemptive history for the understanding of faith and revelation has become increasingly apparent in recent Roman Catholic theology. Vatican II used the language of salvation history. This was true of Roman Catholic theology even before Vatican II gave its official sanction to the concept. Although the interpretation varies, the writings of Hans Urs von Balthasar, Daniélou, Heinrich Fries, Henri de Lubac, Rahner, Heinz Robert Schlette, and Johannes Metz, among others, reflect an acceptance of the notion of salvation history.[21]

To grasp the full significance of salvation history, it is necessary to be aware of the philosophical analysis of humanity's historical character as presented, for example, by the philosopher Martin Heidegger, who argues that humanity never exists except suspended, in a manner difficult to define, between past and future. The past is never totally past but always present and future as well, and the future is never totally future but always adumbrated in the past, thereby contributing to the determination of the present. Actual existence purely and exclusively in the now of the present, without past or future, is never found in life. Concerning this analysis of humanity's historical character Schlette writes,

> Men therefore always find themselves in a situation in which what they are at present is a mode of anticipation, itself performed by the past. This constitutive feature of man, which we term his temporal character, always points the way to true correspondence to the reality of what is.[22]

If we take this analysis of humanity's historical character as the starting point, and if this character is also understood to be the condition of the factual sacred history recorded in Scripture and coextensive with sacred history, it is possible to say, according to Schlette, that a theology of salvation history can be described as a "transcendental theology" to the extent that the universal history of salvation, grounded in human beings' historical nature, represents not only the setting but also "the most general fundamental *condition* of revelation, faith, theology and religion as such."[23] At the same time, such a theology of sacred history has itself also been historically mediated. The process or occurrence of the coming to consciousness or reflective self-awareness of sacred history is the result of the history of revelation having actually occurred in world history. In other words, a mediation takes place through history, and sacred history, in this sense a revelation, was needed for the theology of redemptive history to become explicitly aware of itself as transcendent theology. Rahner points out that secular history as such is always ambiguous and of itself cannot cause sacred history to be distinguished from it and become clear.[24] In fact, according to Rahner, secular history itself cannot be understood distinctly as secular history but can only be recognized as such in a demythologized way from the standpoint of salvation history. Rahner writes,

> Salvation-history explains profane history . . . because, in the form of general salvation-history, it represents the most profound character and basis of profane history, and because, in the form of official and special salvation-history, it manifests this ultimate character of all history in the revelation in which salvation takes place and at the same time shows itself historically.[25]

Catholic theologians generally argue that only in Jesus Christ is saving history clearly and permanently distinguished from secular history. Everything, such as the Church, the sacraments, and the Scriptures, which follows from this Christ-event and which participates essentially, although fragmentarily, in the unsurpassable finality of Christ's redeeming action participates also in the distinction from secular history. In Christ, and in the Church, saving history reaches its clearest and absolutely permanent distinction from secular history and becomes an unequivocally distinct manifestation within the history of the world, thus bringing general salvation history to self-realization and to its historical reality in word and social structures within the history of this world. By this very fact, this distinct salvation history of an explicitly verbal, social, and sacramental kind is also destined for all persons of every future age. It intends to gather into itself the whole general salvation history and to represent it historically within itself. It *strives* therefore to coincide with general salvation history and also with secular history, although adherents to this theory know quite well that these two can never be fully identified in history but that this will occur only with the Second Coming of Christ at the end of history.

Secular history, thus demythologized and stripped of its numinous quality by the judgment of sacred history, is itself always sacred history. As Schlette points out, the sacred history (i.e., Judaism, Christianity) that is in a position to recognize secular history itself as sacred history is a *special* sacred history and has become aware of itself in an essentially different way from that "other" sacred history wherein God touches the lives of all in some way, which is then referred to as *general* sacred history and which has only been recognized and interpreted as such in the light of sacred history in the special sense. Thus sacred history, taken as a whole, presents itself to theological reflection with a three-fold distinction, at least as viewed from a Christian perspective. Besides general sacred history there is, at a date that cannot be precisely determined, a special history, that of Israel, and this is followed by a mode of sacred history different from both general sacred history and the special sacred history of Israel, namely the history of Christianity.[26]

A closer inquiry into general sacred history is needed. To accomplish this, the present understanding of revelation must be clearly understood. After examining the traditional and contemporary understanding of revelation, I will present Vatican II's teaching on the relationship of Catholicism to the world religions. I will follow with Rahner's basic methodology concerning this question, which includes his theory of the "anonymous Christian," together with objections raised by several scholars to Rahner's position. I will include a discussion of the Church's attitude concerning the need for dialogue with the world religions. I will present the dialogue with Judaism as a case in point. Finally, I will conclude the chapter with an examination of Catholicism's teaching concerning other Christians together with a discussion of the need for a true dialogue with those religions and with other Christians.

THE MEANING OF REVELATION

Revelation is the self-communication of God. Revelation, or the "unveiling" of God, occurs in nature itself, in historical events, through the words and activities of special individuals (prophets, apostles, evangelists), of special communities (the Christian Church), and especially in and through Jesus Christ. All of history is oriented toward Jesus's saving power, which is understood as history's center by all Christians. The manner by which revelation has been understood has a history that we will examine next.

The Traditional Understanding of Revelation

Before beginning our analysis of Rahner we must say something about the understanding of divine revelation as it is commonly held today. The traditional view of revelation, which has been supported, generally speaking, by Catholics and Protestants alike, was formulated with great clarity by St. Thomas Aquinas. The major division of Christianity's knowledge of God was between natural and revealed knowledge.[27] The "natural knowledge" of God was seen as knowledge that the human mind could attain without any kind of outside help. All the world religions under this scheme would have a "natural" knowledge of God. But however lofty such knowledge might be, it would still not be of saving benefit. At best, so both Catholic and Reformation theologians maintained, it was the knowledge that made humankind "without excuse" in the eyes of God.[28] But God did not leave the human race in this condition. In addition to the natural knowledge of God there is also revealed knowledge. The term "revelation" was denied to natural knowledge, because no supernatural aid is required. Revealed knowledge is the truth that is supernaturally communicated to humankind—the truth of the Trinity or of the Incarnation, for instance. Three points in particular about the traditional notion of revelation should be recalled.

1. Revelation, in general, was thought of as propositional, and this fitted well with the Western propensity for exact definition.

2. It was felt, particularly in scholastic periods, that revelation was contained in the Scriptures, and therefore was "possessed." The proof that a revelation had occurred was as external as the proposition itself—namely, miracle and fulfilled prophecy.

3. Finally, the line between natural and revealed knowledge merely separated two kinds of intellectual knowledge. Revealed knowledge was an act of God's grace to humankind. Every person was understood as an *ens incompletum* (an incomplete being). But nothing in natural knowledge was contradicted by what God freely added on. This notion allowed Roman Catholic missionaries, particularly, to seek points of contact with other faiths, in the assurance that the path to saving knowledge was an unbroken one.

At the turn of the twentieth century the traditional view of revelation began to break down irreparably. The effects of nineteenth-century theology—biblical criticism, modern science, the comparative study of religion—all played a part in this break. As long as the distinction between revealed and natural knowledge, as described earlier, was allowed to stand, the religions of the world were easily placed by Christian theologians beneath the apex of Christianity.[29] These religions were denied the concept of revelation, as well as the salvation that was the accompaniment of revelation. Bereft of revelation they hardly had the nature of religion at all. That Christians in fact assumed this attitude of superiority to other religions is easily documented, as has already been seen. For example, it was only by a theory of invincible ignorance that the salvation of persons outside the Christian fold could be intellectually provided for.[30]

The Modern View of Revelation

Today the distinction between revealed knowledge and natural knowledge has given way to the distinction mentioned earlier between special revelations and general revelation.[31] What has traditionally been called natural theology is left with such fields as psychology, anthropology, sociology of religion, and philosophy of religion. The world religions are now understood as possessing revealed knowledge. For example, we find the following statement in *The Declaration on the Relationship of the Church to Non-Christian Religions*:

Men look to the various religions for answers to those profound mysteries of the human condition which, today even as in olden times, deeply stir the human heart: What is a man? What is the meaning and the purpose of our life? What is goodness and what is sin? What gives rise to our sorrows and to what intent? Where lies the path to true happiness? What is the truth about death, judgment, and retribution beyond the grave? What, finally, is that ultimate and unutterable mystery which engulfs our being, and whence we take our rise, and whither our journey leads us?

From ancient times down to the present, there has existed among diverse peoples a certain perception of that hidden power which hovers over the course of things and over the events of human life; at times, indeed, recognition can be found of a Supreme Divinity and of a Supreme Father too. Such a perception and such a recognition instill the lives of these peoples with a profound religious sense. Religions bound up with cultural advancement have struggled to reply to these same questions with more refined concepts and in more highly developed language.

The Catholic church rejects nothing which is true and holy in these religions. She looks with sincere respect upon those ways of conduct and of life, those rules and teachings which, though differing in many particulars from what she holds and sets forth, nevertheless often reflect a ray of that Truth which enlightens all men. Indeed, she proclaims and must ever proclaim Christ, "the way, the truth, and the life" (John 14:6), in whom men find the fullness of religious life, and in whom God has reconciled all things to Himself (cf. 2 Cor. 5:18, 19).

The Church therefore has this exhortation for her sons: prudently and lovingly, through dialogue and collaboration with the followers of other religions, and in witness of Christian faith and life, acknowledge, preserve, and promote the spiritual and moral goods found among these men, as well as the values in their society and culture.[32]

This statement marks an authoritative change in the approach of Roman Catholicism to non-Christian religions.[33] As long as the world religions were denied the reception of revelation by Christians, dialogue was not seen as profitable, because all the legitimate claims of the other participants were denied before the conversation began. Now there seems to be an increasing recognition of other religions as entities with which the Church can and should enter into dialogue.

Thus Catholic theologians no longer equate divine revelation solely with Holy Scripture or divine doctrine. The highly conceptual understanding of divine revelation has been superseded, and revelation is now understood as more than propositional truth.[34] From the standpoint of the Christian faith, revelation is understood as a divine self-disclosure. God does not merely reveal truths about Him- or Herself: God reveals Him- or Herself. In Christ God communicates Him- or Herself to humankind. The Church bears witness to, and mediates, this divine self-communication.

Although it is still necessary to say that the revelation of Christ is final, it is now possible to add that, from another point of view, divine revelation is an ongoing reality among human beings. God continues to communicate Him- or Herself to the human race. At the same time, God continues to utter in the Church the Word said once and for all in Jesus Christ. God's present Word evokes the faith of believers now. It is God's continuing self-revelation that creates the Church as the community of believers. Although theological discourse about continuing revelation frightened many theologians of the nineteenth century, today it is quite generally acknowledged that the affirmation of an ongoing revelation in no way weakens the once-for-all character of the revelation in Jesus Christ.[35] This shift in the understanding of divine revelation has been acknowledged and accepted by Vatican II in the *Dogmatic Constitution on Divine Revelation* and in other conciliar documents, such as *The Dogmatic Constitution on the Church,* to which we now turn.

VATICAN II: THE CHURCH AND THE WORLD RELIGIONS

The Dogmatic Constitution on the Church states, "Those who have not yet received the Gospel are related to the People of God in various ways."[36] Because the "People of God" in the documents of Vatican II is synonymous with "the Church," this means that all are called to belong to the Church. The same document teaches,

All men are called to be part of this catholic unity of the People of God, a unity which is harbinger of the universal peace it promotes. And there belong to it, or are related to it in various ways, the Catholic faithful as well as all who believe in Christ, and indeed the whole of mankind. For all men are called to salvation by the grace of God.[37]

Thus not only are all called to belong to the Church but the last sentence of the previous paragraph is an expression of belief in the universal salvific will of God, by whose grace all are called to salvation. The "call to the Church" certainly does not imply that it expected that every person will actually belong to the Church by baptism. However, the grace through which salvation is given does make it possible for everyone to be saved. One belongs to the Church of Christ through baptism. But how does the document explain the "various ways" others are related to the People of God? The answer depends on the kind of knowledge of God that is characteristic of each religion. These religions are presented in an order that goes from those whose knowledge of God is closest to the Christian faith to those who have not yet arrived at an explicit knowledge of God.

The first mentioned by Vatican II are the Jewish people, who were "the first to hear the Word of God."[38] The Jewish faith, unlike other non-Christian religions, is based on divine revelation and to the Jews "belong the sonship, the glory, the covenants, the giving of the law, the worship, and the promises; to them belong the patriarchs, and of their people, according to the flesh, is the Christ" (Rom. 9:4–5). And "the gifts of God and the call of God are irrevocable" (Rom. 11:29).

Next to be mentioned are the Muslims, because the plan of salvation includes those who acknowledge the Creator. Muslims profess "to hold the faith of Abraham, along with us adore the one and merciful God who on the last day will judge mankind."[39]

Following the Islamic religion are "those who in the shadows and images seek the unknown God." Presumably the council is referring to other non-Christian religions such as Buddhism and Hinduism, even though no religion is specifically named. The Church considers all goodness and truth found in these religions as "a preparation for the Gospel and given by him who enlightens all men that they may at length have life."[40]

The next two groups are referred to in the *Dogmatic Constitution on the Church* in the following way:

Those also can attain to everlasting salvation who through no fault of their own do not know the Gospel of Christ or his Church, yet sincerely seek God, and, moved by grace, strive by their deeds to do his will as it is known to them through the dictates of conscience. Nor does divine

Providence deny the help necessary for salvation to those who, without blame on their part, have not yet arrived at an explicit knowledge of God, but who strive to live a good life, thanks to His grace. Whatever goodness or truth is found among them is looked upon by the Church as a preparation for the Gospel. She regards such qualities as given by him who enlightens all men so that they may finally have life.[41]

The previous paragraph refers to two groups: One comprises "those who sincerely seek God"; the other comprises those who, "without blame on their part, have not yet arrived at an explicit knowledge of God." Concerning both groups it is stated that they strive with the help of grace to live a good life according to the dictates of their conscience. The grace in question is clearly the grace of Jesus Christ, who died to save all.

However, the question remains about how these various groups are said to be related to the Church. In regard to the Jews, there is a unique relationship to Christ and His Church from a Catholic point of view. As God's chosen people they are related to the people of the new Covenant because they are, as St. Paul writes, the good olive tree onto which the Gentiles, as branches of a wild olive, were grafted (cf. Rom. 11:17–21). The *Declaration on the Relationship of the Church to Non-Christian Religions* maintains that the covenant God made with the people of Israel, as recorded in their scriptures, is irrevocable. The statement also affirms that the Christian church is a partner in the Covenant with the God of Israel, although the exact relationship between what Christians refer to as the Old Israel and the New Israel, the Old Testament and the New Testament, remains a problem and an apt subject of the dialogue that has begun between the Jewish and Catholic communities.[42]

As for the other groups, the only common factors are their inclusion in God's plan of salvation, as well as the fact that they all receive the offer of grace. As Francis Sullivan writes, "It seems reasonable to conclude that it is because they are all recipients of God's offer of saving grace that they are also said to be related to the church."[43] Though this idea is not specifically stated in *The Dogmatic Constitution on the Church*, the theological commission that drafted the *Constitution* states in its commentary, "All grace has a certain communitarian quality, and looks toward the Church."[44] Sullivan gives several reasons for saying that every offer of grace directs the recipient toward the Church. One reason is that the ultimate goal of all grace is that the person might be numbered among those who "from Abel, the just one, to the last of the elect, will be gathered together with the Father in the universal Church."[45] Another reason is that the grace of salvation includes the gift of supernatural love of God and neighbor, and this is intrinsically ordered toward the communion in charity that is the inner life of the Church. Sullivan writes,

If I am not mistaken it was for reasons such as these that the theological commission said: "All grace has a communitarian quality and looks toward the church." In other words, there is an ecclesial character, an orientation toward the church, in every offer of grace, and since the offer of grace is made to all, all are, by that fact, "related to the Church."[46]

THE NON-CHRISTIAN RELIGIONS: MEANS OF SALVATION

One of the most serious questions in Catholic theology since the close of Vatican II centers on the means by which non-Christians can be saved. The council certainly taught that people who never become Christians can be saved. Can the Church, then, recognize a salvific role for the non-Christian religions? Another question concerns the salvation of those who belong to no organized religion. The problem is not whether they can be saved, because Vatican II teaches that they can—but how? And finally, how are these people truly related to the Church?

Fundamentalist Christians believe salvation can be had exclusively through faith in Jesus Christ. For example, following the teaching of Karl Barth, Hendrick Kraemer sees all the non-Christian religions as false and doomed to fail. Salvation is a gift of divine grace that comes only through Jesus Christ.[47]

At the other end of the Christian spectrum are those who see the Christian religion as but one of the various religions in which salvation can be found. John Hick is a leading exponent of this view. In effect Hick denies that Jesus is the unique Son of God who alone brings salvation to the world. He advocates a "theocentric pluralism." Hick not only denies the universal role of Christ in the plan of salvation but also the universal role of the Church. Jesus is but one of several individuals God sent to work out His or Her plan of salvation. Hick, and Paul Knitter, a Catholic writer, edited a book that basically upholds this view, *The Myth of Christian Uniqueness: Towards a Pluralistic Theology of Religions*.[48] Both Hick and Knitter continue to write extensively on this viewpoint. To adequately respond to their thesis goes beyond the scope of this book, but the task has been undertaken by several theologians, such as Jacque Dupuis in *Jesus Christ at the Encounter of World Religions*.[49] In light of the teachings of Vatican II it seems clear to me that the position of Knitter and Hicks is simply unacceptable. What is of importance is to understand the opinions of Catholics who accept the teaching of Vatican II about the possibility of salvation for non-Christians and the presence of positive elements in their religions but also insist that Jesus is the unique savior of the world and the Church of Christ is the sacramental sign of salvation. However, even those who accept the teaching of the council differ about whether non-Christian religions can be described as being means of salvation for their members. One of the most important Catholic responses to this question is undoubtedly that of Rahner, to which we now turn.

KARL RAHNER: THE "ANONYMOUS CHRISTIAN"

Rahner (1904–1984) was one of the most influential Catholic theologians of the twentieth century. A German, he was ordained a Jesuit priest in 1932. He developed his theology to meet contemporary challenges to Catholic thought, and he demonstrated that Catholic theology could be original and still remain true to the Catholic tradition. Among the topics he was most concerned with was the existence of grace in the world religions and among peoples who professed no organized religion. In this regard his theology is completely opposed to the fundamentalism of theologians such as Barth and Kraemer, as well as to the kind of religious pluralism advocated by Hick and Knitter. For Rahner, salvation comes only through the grace of Christ, and the Church of Christ is the historical, tangible presence of that grace in the world. This would seem to make salvation impossible for non-Christians. But Rahner insists that the salvific will of God embraces every human being without exception. He explains this in his theory of the "anonymous Christian." The term "anonymous Christian," however, raises this question: How can what is anonymous be called Christian, and if it deserves the name Christian, how can it be anonymous? Rahner interprets the Christian claim to absoluteness from within the limits of human nature and in light of a pluralism of religions as social and historical entities. (It is important to note that Rahner was not wedded to the term "anonymous Christian." He wished to be judged by the strength of his argument and not on the per se merits of this particular term.)

Rahner based his argument on the Catholic tradition that is grounded on the New Testament perspective of a Christocentric universe (1 Cor. 8:6, 15:24–38, 44–49; Rom. 8:19–23, 29, 30; Eph. 1:9–10, 19–23, 3:11; Col. 1:15–20, 3:4; Phil. 3:21; Heb. 1:2–3; John 1:3; 21:32). All creation is oriented toward the Covenant between God and the People of God, and the Covenant, in turn, toward the New Covenant grounded in the incarnation of the Son of God, in Jesus Christ. The human community and the entire world is oriented toward Christ and is sustained by Him. Although hypothetically it could have been otherwise, in fact it has not been.

From the Christian perspective, according to Rahner, human beings are, by their very humanity, conditionally open to God's revelation and self-communication in the God–man, Jesus Christ.[50] Because God's salvific will is universal (1 Tim. 1:15), God offers grace to all human beings at all times, and because there is no salvation without faith, which has to be a personal response to divine revelation, Rahner concludes that the universal offer of grace must include the revelation necessary to produce a response of faith. This involves the notion of grace as God's self-communication to human beings, and, secondarily, the effects of that self-communication. This divine self-communication is offered to human freedom, and before being accepted effects a change in the recipient's unreflexive consciousness and gives him or her the capacity of responding to the divine offer. This radical capacity is called, more technically, a "supernatural existential."[51]

This "supernatural existential" is a permanent modification of the human spirit, which transforms it from within and orients it toward the God of grace and glory. The "supernatural existential" is not grace itself but only God's offer of grace, which, by so modifying the human spirit, enables it freely to accept or to reject grace. Every human person has this radical capacity and many, perhaps most, have actualized it by receiving grace. This does not mean that they are conscious of grace *as* grace. On the contrary, as Rahner writes, "The possibility of experiencing grace and the possibility of experiencing grace *as* grace are not the same thing."[52] This supernatural capacity of responding to grace should be understood to mean that a person may have no explicit concept of God and know nothing about Christ; and yet God is revealing Godself to that individual in the very offer of grace, and one's free response to God revealing Godself has the nature of an act of faith.

Because offered grace and revelation are present in everyone, all can, in a personal way, realize and accept them. If grace and the revelation contained in it were wholly unconscious, they would be outside the range of a possible human choice or decision. This positive response to the divine self-communication takes place in a person's fundamental option to accept a demand of his or her conscience as absolutely binding, because in doing so she or he implicitly directs him- or herself toward God as the source of such an absolute demand and as the ultimate reason for submitting to it. The demand of conscience will require an individual to transcend egotism and to love others, and the love of neighbor is ultimately love of God. One's graced response to the divine self-communication will involve acts of faith and charity and thus the gift of supernatural friendship with God. Such an individual may know nothing about Jesus, but because He is the source of the grace one receives, such faith and love are objectively directed toward Him, even though the individual may never arrive at explicit Christian faith or membership in the Church. Rahner refers to such persons as "anonymous Christians." They are not members of the Church, but they are in spiritual communion with the Church.

Rahner envisions various possibilities of a non-Christian ordering his or her whole life to its due end. Everyday existence lived in the quiet honesty of patiently doing one's duty can be a form of "anonymous" Christian living. In fact, many people may grasp Christianity more genuinely in this way than in its more explicit forms.[53] The Christian sees anonymous Christianity at work in a person who is kind and loving and is faithful to his or her conscience, and no longer refers to such a person as having merely "natural virtues." As Rahner remarks, "Such virtues exist ultimately only in the abstract."[54] He objects to the idea of "natural virtues" because by assuming that purely natural moral acts actually occur, "the concrete order, instead of consisting of a situation of sin and supernatural salvation, is split into a threefold order of reality (and not only of possibility), and where moral decision is made, a neutral zone intrudes between salvation and perdition."[55]

A person may also decide for the God of eternal life in the act of dying. Because the affirmative interpretation of one's mortal life can only take place by the grace of Christ, then the act performed in virtue of the grace of Christ, whereby an individual positively accepts the comprehensive sense of his or her human existence in the face of the appearance of meaningless death, can and must necessarily be called an act of faith—the surrender of the whole person in the incalculability and impenetrability of human existence to the incomprehensible God. As Rahner observes,

> Whenever a man dies in this way, freely, believing and trusting, detached from all that is particular and concrete in the frank confidence that in this way he will obtain everything, at the point where he is apparently experiencing a collapse into emptiness, into the fathomless abyss, he is doing something that cannot be done except by the grace of Christ which celebrates its victory thereby. There a man is not dying the death of Adam, the death of the sinner. . . . Whether he knows it or not, a man is dying the death of Christ, for only Christ's death gained this grace for us and only his death freed our death into the life of God himself.[56]

All this does not mean that salvation is simply bestowed on anyone who has attained the use of freedom in a way that bypasses individual freedom and therefore without one's knowledge. Whenever a person arrives at a free decision about him- or herself, she or he is always capable of *fides virtualis* (virtual faith)—in other words, she or he is capable of an interior attitude toward God, which is morally of the same kind as Christian faith and which can thus become a saving act when elevated by an interior grace, if the grace is not rejected. The readiness to believe, to accept God's call that comes as yet inarticulately, if elevated by grace "becomes a supernatural moral act, virtually equivalent to actual faith in the Gospel sent by God."[57]

Anonymous Christians, then, share in the same grace and faith as one who is an explicit Christian. This grace is the grace of Christ, not only because of its origin but also on account of its inner reality. It really carries in itself the marks of Christ's salvific activity. *Because the Church is the extension of the mystery of Christ, the grace of Christ is always ecclesial in its nature, related to the Church and referring to the Church.* Thus the acceptance of grace in faith contains the source of an inner dynamism toward the Church. One who has existentially accepted grace, accordingly, possesses an implicit desire for membership in the Church.[58] This allows us to better understand the axiom "There is no salvation outside of the Church," which refers, of course, to the visible Church. The axiom implies a perceptible connection with the Church, which is not the same as perceived membership in it. In default of the adequate availability of revelation, sacraments, and the official Church, a person who personally says yes to his or her own supernaturally preconditioned nature has become a Christian in an anonymous manner.

It is most important to understand what Rahner means by an "implicit desire" for belonging to God's family. As we will see, many of the objections raised against his theory of anonymous Christianity are based on a misunderstanding of this term. Rahner does not mean by "implicit desire" that an individual has explicitly rejected the visible Church or has never heard of the Church but who nevertheless is somehow *made* a member of the Church against his or her will. By "implicit desire" he means that a person has "a serious general moral outlook and intention to do everything necessary for salvation."[59] Rahner frankly admits that one can have the intention to do everything necessary for salvation even when it is not explicitly known that membership of the Church is one of the objective factors necessary for salvation. Thus visible membership of the Church is necessary for salvation only as a conditional necessity rather than as an absolute necessity of means. The question remains, however, as to why Rahner feels obliged to refer to this *implicit desire.*

To answer this question, it is necessary to realize that Rahner agrees with tradition and the teaching of the Church that the Holy Spirit is the soul of the visible Church, as the encyclical *Mystici Corporis* (Mystical Body) reiterates.[60] Because of this, there cannot be a relation to the spirit of the Church by grace without at the same time implying that there is in some way or another a further reference, relation, and connection with the *visible* body of the Church for everyone who is touched by grace.

To explain what this relation to the Church is on the part of anonymous Christians, Rahner refers to the idea of the Church as the *proto-sacrament* of Christ. To say that the Church is the proto-sacrament means that the Church "is, in her whole, concrete, visible, and juridically verifiable appearance, a real sign and embodiment of the salvific will of God and of the grace of Christ."[61] Because the Church is a sacrament, a *desire for the Church* includes a quasi-sacramental visible aspect in the concrete, which can and must be included in the visible nature of the Church, because all grace comes through the Spirit of Christ. If we are to understand the profundity and universality of the sacramental structure of the Church in Rahner's thought *it is necessary to realize that he bases his thinking on the real unity of the human race.*[62] This unity of humankind is a natural dimension of an individual's personal decision and is determined by the Incarnation of the Word of God. Because God the Son became human, the one human race was called to share the life of God supernaturally. A person's ability to share the life of God, because it is a reality accomplished by the fact that the Word of God became *flesh*, belongs to the historical and visible dimension and as a factual determination of the human race as a whole, is also *a real ontological determination* of the nature of each human being.[63] By the very fact that the Word of God became human, "Humanity has already in advance become ontologically [essentially] the real sanctification of individual men by grace and also the people of the children of God."[64]

In other words, no one is simply "merely human" in the abstract sense of the Aristotelian–scholastic concept of the essence of humankind. In as far as the human race thus "consecrated" is a real unity from the very start, there already exists a "people of God," which includes all of humanity, even before any social and juridical organization of humankind as a supernatural unity in a church. This determination of the one humanity as the people of God, according to Rahner, is a real fact and not merely an abstract idea of what ought to be, because "it is based on the two coinciding facts of the natural unity of the human race and of the real Incarnation of the Word of God."[65]

This historical actuality of the people of God, which precedes the Church as a juridical and social body, is such that it can and, according to the will of God, had to be made more concrete on the social and juridical plane in what is called the Church. The Church is meant to be a further expression of the very fact that in Christ the human race is the people of God. Thus the people of God have a real relation to the Church as a social and juridical body, even though this relation came into being by a free decision of the God–man. Therefore, where there are the people of God, there radically also is the Church, *independently of the will of the individual person*. Whenever someone totally accepts his or her concrete nature by his or her own freely willed decision, that action is an expression of the supernatural salvific will of God.

According to Rahner, then—and this is a very important consideration —when the justifying act is thus understood as the *votum Ecclesiae* (i.e., a desire for the Church),

> It is not merely an act which aims in intention at the Church as its implicit object. It is, thus understood, a spiritual and personal act which, in fact and of necessity, already comprises something of the Church, since it is the ratification, in an ontologically real sense of the membership of the people of God.[66]

The *votum Ecclesiae* does not replace actual membership in the Church by expressing some kind of good will toward the Church. Rather, the *votum Ecclesiae* is the personal acceptance of membership in the people of God, which is already a fact on the historical and visible level and in which a real reference is given to membership in the Church as an established society. Rahner concludes his argumentation in the following manner:

[T]he proposition about the Church as necessary means for salvation suffers no exception through the possibility of justification by the *votum Ecclesiae*, in so far as that necessity of the Church for salvation always does and must mean—by "Church"—*at least* what we have called "people of God"—and, indeed, always can mean this. Because "people of God" has an objective reference to the Church in the proper sense (a reference which is not left to the discretion of the individual human being), the proposition of the necessity of belonging to the people of God for salvation does not impair the proposition of the necessity of the Church in the proper sense for salvation.[67]

According to Rahner, then, any question about belonging to the Church as a necessary means for salvation must distinguish between the two strata in the very being of the Church, the sacrament of salvation for all human beings—in other words, the Church as an established juridical organization —and the Church as humanity consecrated by the Incarnation. Rahner strongly insists that one cannot belong to the Church in a manner that is *merely* "invisible." The justified person who belongs to the Church without being a member of it belongs "invisibly" to the visible Church by grace *and* that individual also has a "visible" relationship to the Church, even when this relationship is not constituted by baptism or a verifiable profession of faith. In other words, according to Rahner, "There is a lowest limit, in a certain sense, below which man's state of grace and its quasi-sacramental tangibility can no longer be separated from each other, as if the former could exist without the latter."[68]

Christianity understands itself as the universal religion, intended for all of humankind. It is the "definitive eschatological manifestation of God's grace,"[69] the visible embodiment of what is already interiorly binding, the historical concrete form of what is universally taking place and of what has been occurring since the creation of humankind.[70] The Church does not regard itself as the exclusive community of those who have a claim to salvation but rather as "the historically tangible vanguard and the historically and socially constituted explicit expression of what the Christian hopes is present as a hidden reality even outside the visible Church."[71] The Church is the leaven, always and for every age, not only where it has made its presence visible, but especially also "where the flour has not (yet) changed into the leavened dough in a way tangible to us."[72]

What, then, is the status of the non-Christian religions? Rahner believes that until the moment when the Gospel really enters into the historical situation of an individual, a non-Christian religion does not merely contain elements of a natural knowledge of God, along with false elements, but

It also contains elements arising out of the grace which is given to men as a gratuitous gift on account of Christ. For this reason a non-

Christian religion can be recognized as a lawful religion (although in different degrees).[73]

A "lawful religion," according to Rahner, "means here an institutional religion whose 'use' by its membership can be regarded on the whole as a positive means of gaining the right relationship to God and thus for the attaining of salvation, a means which is therefore positively included in God's plan of salvation."[74] This opens the way for a loving understanding of non-Christian religions and for a true dialogue with others on the part of Christians.

It must be clearly understood that it does not follow from the notion of the anonymous Christian that it is a matter of indifference what religion a person belongs to. The innate human longing for truth implies a self-critical concern for the true way of finding God, and thus excludes indifferentism and relativism, and shows that one cannot suppress the question of truth at the precise point at which what is in question is the correct attitude to the transcendent mystery. Because of the historical character of their mode of existence, human beings remain always and necessarily capable of submitting their whole beings to the claim of the divine mystery when it reaches them. When on the basis of such a mode of life, which can find its expression in the forms of the various religions and quasi-religions, or even without participation in any form of organized religion, people actually do attain salvation, this nevertheless does not take place by self-redemption but through Jesus Christ and His Church and in a universal human solidarity.

RAHNER'S THEORY: OBJECTIONS AND A RESPONSE

The difficulty with Rahner's theory, despite its many positive features, comes from the fact that it *seems* to extend the concept of the Church to a community or individual who does not believe in or publicly acknowledge Jesus Christ. Vatican II was undoubtedly correct in disclaiming Roman Catholicism's monopoly on Christianity, even a truly ecclesial Christianity. No longer is the Church of Christ exhaustively identified with Roman Catholicism but is rather said to "subsist in" Roman Catholicism.[75] The concept of the Church can certainly be rightly applied to those who compose a community of baptized Christians united by belief in Jesus Christ, living according to the message of the New Testament, celebrating the sacraments of baptism and the Lord's Supper, and wishing to be regarded by the world as a Christian church. But to extend the meaning of the Church to include people who know nothing of Christ, or who have rejected Christianity, seems to many observers to be unjustified. They feel that the fact that all those outside the Church are included in Christ's grace and thus capable of salvation should not lead to the conclusion that such people can be regarded as members of a specific ecclesial community against their will.

Hans Küng, for example, advises that "it is simply not permissible for the theologian to re-interpret reality according to apparently profound speculative constructions."[76] Küng remarks of Rahner's theory,

> The non-Catholic Christian, who in fact belongs to the Church of Christ, but who has no "votum" or "desire," either explicit or implicit, either conscious or unconscious, to belong to the "Catholic Church," who has if anything rather the opposite *votum* or desire, can not simply be transferred to the secret list of members of the Catholic Church. Similarly, the non-Christian who has no desire either explicit or implicit, either conscious or unconscious, to belong to Christ's Church, who has if anything quite the opposite desire, cannot be silently adopted by Christianity. *Man's free will must be respected. The sole criterion for entertaining the community of believers should be a profession of faith* [emphasis mine].[77]

Küng believes that the concept of the Church presented in the notion of "anonymous Christianity" contradicts the concept of the Church as revealed in the New Testament and as found in the Christian tradition. Included in the fundamental concept of the Church of Christ is an *explicit* belief in Christ. Küng warns that the New Testament concept of the Church should not be adulterated for the sake of formal adherence to the axiom "no salvation outside the Church," which "in its negative and exclusive formulation was highly dubious right from the beginning, has resulted in more or less serious errors, and has proved open to misunderstanding in its application to non-Catholic Christians."[78] If one wishes to insist on the negative axiom, then, according to Küng,

> We must not use it to threaten or damn those outside the Church, but interpret it as a hope and promise for ourselves and our community: it is true for me, we are able to say with joy, there is no salvation outside the Church for me personally. As far as others are concerned, we do better to use a positive formulation: "Salvation inside the Church!" and so emphasize the positive truth at the heart of the easily misunderstood negative axiom.[79]

Rahner would likely agree with Küng that one's free will should be respected. And despite the confusion caused by the term "anonymous Christian," he would probably agree that the sole criterion for entering the Church should be a profession of faith. At the same time, he understands all grace to be mediated by Christ through His Church. Everyone who possesses grace is "Christian" in the sense that all grace comes through Christ and His Church, and they are ordained to the Church insofar as they are destined for the explicit understanding of the grace they already possess—either during this life or in eternity.

George Lindbeck, a Lutheran theologian who is a professor of religion at Yale University and attended Vatican II as an invited Protestant expert, is of the opinion that Rahner's concept of the anonymous Christian goes too far.

Lindbeck notes that many Catholics and Protestants agree with the emphasis on the universal action of Christ's grace but disagree with the ecclesiological interpretation of that grace offered by Rahner. Lindbeck tells us that in stressing the *gratia Christi* outside of the domain of the explicitly Christian is one thing, but to interpret this "as involving a hidden presence of the Church" is basically unacceptable.[80]

Rahner is realistic enough to admit that for the great majority grace does not become manifest tangibly within Christianity. Nevertheless, because grace is omnipresent, possessing a modality whereby it contains an inner dynamism toward explicitness in the Christian Church, insofar as the Church is the sacramental presence of Christ on earth, Rahner continued to speak of non-Christians who possess grace as anonymous Christians. But again, Rahner wished to be judged on the merits of his overall argument and not simply on the use of one term. Henri de Lubac also opposed Rahner's use of the term anonymous Christians. He sees difficulty in speaking of individuals as anonymous Christians, and he objects to the use of the term because it suggests that the non-Christian religions would constitute an "anonymous Christianity." de Lubac believes this would mean that the Christian revelation would simply make explicit what was "anonymously" already present in the non-Christian religions. This would ignore the newness of the revelation that Jesus brought. Certainly this is not what Rahner meant. For him the term indicates living in the grace of Christ without explicit Christian faith. But Rahner felt that because of this ambiguity he had no objection if others preferred not to use the term. de Lubac also objected to speaking of non-Christian religions as "ways of salvation." He argued this would mean that various religions that at times contradicted one another in essential matters would be means of salvation positively willed and given by God.[81] However, the legitimacy Rahner attributes to other religions as "ways of salvation" is provisional and relative to the situation of those who in good faith fail to recognize Christianity as the religion that they must embrace to be saved.

Despite these objections and others that have been raised by well-respected theologians, the fact is that, apart from questions of terminology such as anonymous Christianity and with differences of emphasis and detail, Rahner's position is undoubtedly the position of modern mainstream Catholic theology. The salvation optimism that Rahner has described is one of the most extraordinary developments in Catholic theology today. His interpretation helps to explain the fullness of God's relationship to humankind and encourages mutual respect and honest dialogue between Christians and members of other religions.

THE CHURCH AND THE WORLD RELIGIONS: THE NEED FOR DIALOGUE

Many Christians today are aware of the need for a changed and more constructive relationship between the Church and the world's other religions. The obvious beginning of a relationship of this kind is dialogue, and this involves a reciprocal process in which both parties stand on an equal level and are willing to receive as well as to present their own positions. In turn this means seeing the other religions as in some sense a revelation from God from which Christians can learn previously unknown truths. The deeply felt Christian hesitancy about a real commitment to Christ on the one hand and true dialogue with other religions on the other hand presents a dilemma for many. As Geoffrey Paninder notes, any attitude of acceptance of the validity of other religions to a Christian

> is liable to be challenged with biblical texts such as "there is no other name under heaven given among men by which we must be saved" (Acts 4:12) or "no one comes to the Father but by me" (John 14:6).[82]

The suggested dialogue is likely to be seen as conflicting with the absolute claims of Christianity. This reaction would be valid not only for fundamentalist Christians but for many Catholics as well. Be that as it may, Vatican II's *Declaration on the Relationship of the Church to Non-Christian Religions* is a breakthrough in Catholic thought, which I will examine in the next section. The change of direction, in fact, is radical and not simply a minor deviation. It opens the way to true dialogue with other religions and ideologies that never existed in the past.

What is necessary for today is a theology for dialogue, a theology that justifies such an endeavor. Rahner's purpose in this regard was to provide a reasoned and coherent theology that is responsive to new insights while at the same time honestly representing Catholic teaching. He says that all human beings are open to "self-transcendence" and have an "orientation toward mystery." This orientation toward mystery is implicit in all genuine human forms of experience. "God" is the name for that "absolute mystery" toward which the distinctively human style of reflection inevitably points, at least in the Western religions such as Judaism, Christianity, and Islam. Rahner says that corresponding to this universal "orientation toward mystery" is an equally universal offer of divine self-communication, which he refers to as a "supernatural existential."

Divine self-communication is found in the history of revelation, and traditionally Christians have identified this history with the Bible, both the Old and the New Testaments. Because for Rahner the offer of divine self-communication is universal, its history cannot be so limited in scope. The history of revelation is the history of the various ways, however imperfect, in which God's self-disclosure has been recognized and expressed in human language and in different religious communities, non-Christian as well as Christian. The biblical recording of the events climaxing in the death and Resurrection of Jesus becomes one development of salvation history, not the only one, even though for Christians Jesus represents the fullness of divine offering and human response. Rahner is thus able to maintain that non-Christian religions can be realities within a positive history of salvation and revelation even though these religions are not equally adequate.

Official Catholic Teaching Concerning Dialogue with Others

The official teaching of the Catholic Church on the question of the non-Christian religions has passed through various stages throughout its history. There are four historical periods in the development of this teaching. In the first stage the Church's attitude toward others was primarily negative. Because Jesus was understood as the only mediator between God and humankind, it was taken for granted that other religions were not salvational. In the second stage, during the medieval period following the First Crusade (1095 A.D.) the Church felt threatened by Muslim military aggressiveness and the continual presence of distinct Jewish communities. Official Church pronouncements for the first time stated that salvation could be found only in Jesus and the Christian community. In the third stage, which took place in the nineteenth century, the problem was not in regard to other religions but rather concerned liberalism with its egalitarian philosophy that one religion is as good (or as bad) as another. This led to the condemnation of indifferentism. In the fourth stage, which has only recently emerged after Vatican II, because the reality of religious pluralism struck the consciousness of the Church in a formal way at that council the official teachings of Catholicism regarding non-Christian religions was forced to greatly change. The most important of the council's documents in this regard was published in 1965, *The Declaration on the Relationship of the Church to Non-Christian Religions.*

To summarize the official teaching of the Church: All religions are related to Christianity insofar as salvation is concerned. Apart from this relationship non-Christian religions have no salvific power. It is through the power of Christ that all of humanity has been redeemed. This teaching is very much akin to that of Rahner's notion of anonymous Christianity. Other religions contain many authentic values, even though they also contain certain errors from a Christian perspective. And because they contain elements of supreme truth divine grace works in and through them. Hence Catholics must support true religious freedom, and their relationship with other religious traditions should be characterized by acceptance, collaboration, and dialogue. Christians can learn from the values of other religious bodies.

To be more specific, the teaching of Vatican II relating to non-Christian religions can be found not only in *The Declaration on the Relationship to non-Christian Religions* but also in *The Dogmatic Constitution on the Church* (1964), the *Decree on the Church's Missionary Activity* (1965), and the *Pastoral Constitution on the Church in the Modern World* (1965). Vatican II's teachings concerning other religions include many elements. In fact, the council stresses those areas that unite Catholics with others rather than concentrating on differences.[83] Other religions such as Buddhism, Hinduism, Judaism, Islam, as well as the other world religions are mentioned with great respect.[84] These religions represent goodness intrinsic to the human heart that find expression in their rites and symbols and are a true preparation for the Gospel.[85] These religions contain treasures of ascetical and contemplative life.[86] Indeed, the Holy Spirit was at work in the world even before the time of Christ.[87] Catholics must also learn to appreciate the riches of the gifts of God to all the peoples of the world.[88] The Church therefore, as was mentioned previously, must adopt a wholly new attitude toward non-Christian religions.[89] Catholics are to reject nothing of truth and holiness found in those religions.[90] And respect should be given even those doctrinal elements that differ from their own because they may also contain a ray of truth.[91]

The Importance of Dialogue

Although the right to freedom from coercion in civil society is inviolate, Catholicism obviously has a moral duty to uphold its own self-understanding. At the same time, the Church must be open to all forms of dialogue, be imbued with the spirit of justice and love, and must engage in a common search for moral and spiritual enrichment.[92] Dialogue requires discernment, but it is part of the Church's task and can be done without compromise of its faith in Christ.[93] Pope John Paul II's encyclical *Redemptoris Missio* (The Mission of Redemption, 1991), which stressed the continued urging of missionary evangelization, also commends the need for interreligious dialogue as "a part of the church's evangelizing mission."[94] Without abandoning its own principles or promoting false agreements, the Church must enter into dialogue with other religions for the mutual enrichment of the respective communities. Pope John Paul II writes, "Dialogue leads to inner purification and conversion, which, if pursued with docility to the Holy Spirit, will be spiritually fruitful."[95]

It is important to recall that in the past, dialogue with members of the non-Christian religions was even rarer than dialogue with fellow Christians. It was common for most human beings to live their lives in isolation from other major religious traditions, having only a faint interest or awareness in their existence. Often the descriptions of other religions came secondhand and without a true conceptualization. Today Catholics can no longer ignore other religions. A global religion such as Catholicism constantly meets and deals with members of other faith traditions. It would be wrong to close one's mind and heart to the "other." Without dialogue, fear and misunderstanding can occur, which can lead to hostility and even warfare. In the case of dialogue with members of other religious traditions, there is always the danger of false compromise, but this is certainly not inherent in dialogue. When dialogue is conducted honestly, with full awareness of critical differences, the results can be healthy and fulfilling for everyone involved. This is true even when dialogue involves situations in which one is confronted with what is perceived as genuine evil in the other's attitude or practice. In such an instance confrontation can lead to an attempt to change the dialogue partner rather than clarifying ideas.

Pope Paul VI in his first encyclical, *Ecclesiam Suam* (His Church), wrote,

Dialogue is demanded nowadays. . . . It is demanded by the dynamic course of action which is changing the face of modern society. It is demanded by the pluralism of society, and by the maturity man has reached in this day and age. Be he religious or not, his secular education has enabled him to think and speak, and to conduct a dialogue with dignity.[96]

Vatican II made it clear that dialogue should involve as many persons as possible. The bishops at Vatican II exhorted all the Catholic faithful to take an active part in dialogue, not only with the other Christian churches but also with members of other religious communities. This attitude is found throughout the documents of Vatican II and was given further standing by the establishment of a permanent Vatican Secretariate for Dialogue with Non-Christians and Non-Believers.

Leonard Swidler, in *Death or Dialogue: From the Age of Monologue to the Age of Dialogue,* gives a brief but excellent definition of dialogue: "Dialogue is a two-way communication between persons who hold significantly differing views on a subject with the purpose of learning more truth about the subject from the other."[97] Such dialogue can be held not only between members of different religious traditions, but should include "religion" in the broadest sense of the word, namely, any system that attempts to explain the ultimate meaning of life and how to live accordingly. Therefore, not only religious traditions in the classical sense, but other traditions could become dialogue partners even though they would usually not be called religions but rather "ideologies," such as atheistic humanism or Marxism. Thus it is more accurate "to speak of both interreligious and interdiological dialogue," as Swidler observes.[98]

A dialogue partner can become an avenue by which a person or group can perceive itself in a way that could not otherwise occur. In the process of the dialogue and in responding to questions or objections, one gains insights into one's inner self and into one's belief system in ways that might be totally new and in doing so deepens one's own understanding. This process is analogous to the manner by which we can deepen our understanding of our own culture by entering into dialogue with another culture or cultures. This expanded knowledge of one's own faith should lead to a change of behavior, a more loving attitude. The purpose of dialogue is not simply to gain knowledge but for all the participants to learn and change accordingly. In the case of dialogue among Christian churches the aim of dialogue might be to bring about structural union. But Christians in dialogue with Buddhists, Muslims, Hindus, or any member of a non-Christian religion should first strive to know the dialogue partners as accurately as possible and try to gain an understanding of their beliefs in a sympathetic fashion. Such dialogue should begin by seeking to learn what is shared in common as well as the differences between them. Dialogue should seek to find agreement with one's partner as far as possible on a subject without violating one's integrity. Usually what is shared in common is more extensive than what might have been anticipated. But it is also important to learn what the differences are. Swidler informs us that these differences may occur in one of several forms:

1. Complementary, as for example a stress on the prophetic rather than the mystical;

2. Analogous, as for example the notion of God in the Semitic religions and of *sunyata* in Mahayana Buddhism; or

3. Contradictory, in which the acceptance of one entails the rejection of the other, as for example the Judeo–Christian notion of the inviolable dignity of each individual person and the now largely disappeared Hindu custom of *suttee*, widow-burning.[99]

Swidler notes that the differences in the first two categories should not simply be acknowledged, but because they are complementary or analogous, they should be cherished because by discerning them one extends his or her own understanding of reality and how to live accordingly.

There are many possible subjects of dialogue. In some ways the spiritual area is the most attractive, at least for those with a more interior or mystical frame of mind. Such an approach promises a great deal of commonality because mystics appear to meet on a high level of unity with the Ultimate Reality, however it is described, including even the more philosophical systems such as Neoplatonism. Using Christian terms, to experience the living God is not only to experience a power that is to be proclaimed to all nations but it is to realize that the mystery of the Godhead will always be more than we have experienced. To experience the mystery of God in an authentic fashion is to know with certainty that we are experiencing it only partially. All the major religious traditions seem to agree concerning such religious experience—that God, Allah, Brahman, Sunyata, the Tao—can be known only in part. If this is so, then Christians should be open to discovering "other parts." In other words, there is much to learn about the Godhead in learning how others perceive this mystery.

Dialogue with Judaism

The historically unique relationship between Catholicism and Judaism provides a special opportunity for dialogue, and such dialogue can be an example of the call to dialogue with the other world religions. As is well-known, the postbiblical history of Christian–Jewish relations has been until recently filled with hostility and atrocities. During the Crusades, Jews were slaughtered, and in the fourteenth and fifteenth centuries they were exiled from their homes in England, France, Portugal, and Spain. Beginning in Venice in the sixteenth century and then reaching throughout Europe, Jews were forced to live in ghettoes without the rights of citizenship. And of course no episode regarding the Jews has had a more profound effect on the conscience of Christians than the Holocaust, the Nazi extermination of six million Jews during World War II. As Küng has written, "After Auschwitz there can be no more excuses. . . . Christendom cannot avoid a clear admission of its guilt."[100]

The Declaration on the Relationship of the Church to Non-Christian Religions contains a statement on Jewish–Christian relations titled *Nostrate Aetate* (In Our Age).[101] Though this statement is rather brief it contains several very important principles. It maintains, for example, that the Covenant God made with the people of Israel, as recorded in their Scriptures, is irrevocable. The statement also affirms that the Christian Church is a partner in the Covenant with the God of Israel, although, as discussed previously, the exact relationship between what Christians refer to as the Old Israel and the New Israel has yet to be established. Finally, in this document the Catholic Church explicitly rejects any thought of Jewish collective guilt for the death of Jesus and all theories that might suggest the contemporary Jewish people as anything less than the chosen people of a divine Covenant.

The major obstacle to dialogue between Jews and Christians lies in the fact that for all practical purposes there simply has been no communication between them for almost 2,000 years. In June of 1985, the Vatican's Commission for Religious Relations with the Jews issued a document, "The Jews and Judaism in Preaching and Catechesis," to promote a greater and more informed awareness of Judaism in the religious education of Roman Catholics. The text of this document can be found in *Ecumenical Trends*, published by the Greymoor Ecumenical Institute.[102] The document reminds us of the dialogue begun at Vatican II and adds important nuances of historical and biblical awareness that can greatly enhance the Jewish–Christian relationship. Nevertheless, it remains true that the dialogue between Jews and Christians that began with the publication of *Nostra Aetate* (In Our Age) in 1965 is still in an embryonic stage. As I wrote in *Roman Catholicism: Yesterday and Today* in 1992,

> If Christians and Jews can replace vague notions and stereotyped images about what it is that genuinely concerns their respective communities and work out joint approaches to their common religious and societal problems, they will have taken a positive step in the direction suggested at Vatican II in *Nostra Aetate* that called for "mutual knowledge and reciprocal respect."[103]

Dialogue with Other Christians

In the 1963 draft of the *Dogmatic Constitution on the Church* there was a claim of exclusivity between the Church of Christ and the Roman Catholic Church. However, the final text states, "The Church of Christ subsists in the Roman Catholic Church."[104] This suggests that Eastern Orthodoxy and Protestant Christianity are members of Christ's mystical body. The *Decree on Ecumenism* produced a major breakthrough in this regard with the acknowledgment of the "ecclesial reality" of Christian churches other than the Roman Catholic Church. The decree uses the terms *churches* and *ecclesial communities* to refer to all other Christian churches. This acknowledgment marks a basic change in Roman Catholic thinking, especially in regard to Protestant Christianity. Eastern Orthodox Christianity has always been considered a valid and fruitful church by Roman Catholicism, possessing true bishops, priests, and sacraments. But the Catholic attitude toward Protestantism was one that viewed such churches merely as a religious phenomenon. In other words, Protestants were seen as religious individuals on whom God had somehow bestowed his grace but whose *corporate life* as members of Protestant communities was devoid of grace. They were saved despite their Protestant affiliation. Since Vatican II, official recognition has been given to the fact that by their baptism other Christians are really, even if not fully, incorporated in the Church of Christ. As Sullivan writes,

> If other Christian bodies are rightly called "churches and ecclesial communities," they also must participate, in varying degrees, in the reality of Christ's church. Furthermore, they participate in the saving function of Christ's church inasmuch as it is in these churches and communities that people are brought to Christian faith and receive the sacraments of salvation. Protestant Christians are not saved in spite of, or independently of, the churches to which they belong, but rather through the ministry of the word and sacrament which their own churches provide for them.[105]

The distinction between those communities that Vatican II refers to as "churches" and those that it called "ecclesial bodies" is based on the principle that there is not the full reality of church where, "because of the lack of the sacrament of orders, there is not the full reality of the Eucharist."[106] Nevertheless, the council insisted it was using the term "ecclesial" correctly. The commission responsible for the *Decree on Ecumenism* defined its use of the term in the following way:

> It must not be overlooked that the communities that have their origin in the separation that took place in the West are not merely a sum or collection of individual Christians. On the contrary, they are constituted by social ecclesiastical elements which they have preserved from our common patrimony, and which confer on them a truly ecclesial character. In these communities the one sole Church of Christ is present, albeit imperfectly, in a way that is somewhat like its presence in particular churches, and by means of their ecclesiastical elements the Church of Christ is in some way operative in them.[107]

Vatican II teaches that the fullness of the means of salvation is found only in the Catholic Church. But the Catholic Church now recognizes that other Christian communities are used by God as instruments of salvation for those who belong to them in good faith. God gives his gifts to Protestant Christians in their corporate ecclesial life and not merely in their individual encounters with God.[108] Also, liturgical actions in Protestant churches are now understood in such a way that "these actions can truly engender a life of grace, and can rightly be described as capable of providing access to the community of salvation."[109] The council makes very clear the Catholic acceptance of the fact that in regard to other Christian churches, "the Spirit of Christ has not refrained from using them as a means of salvation."[110]

Among other recommendations, Vatican II encourages dialogue with other Christian communities. Formal dialogues have been undertaken between Roman Catholicism and Lutheran, Episcopalian, Presbyterian, and other Christian churches, including the Eastern Orthodox church. These meetings have been very fruitful. Differences have been honestly discussed and in some instances overcome, such as the basic agreement on the meaning of justification reached by the Catholic Church and the Lutheran World Federation. The results of these dialogues have often been mutually enriching, even though there is still much work to be done from a theological point of view. But there has been a good beginning.

Dialogue in a Global Society

At the present Catholics and all persons of good will are being called from the age of monologue to the age of dialogue. In the past it was possible, if not unavoidable, for most human beings to live out their lives in isolation from those who were not a part of their community. Such is no longer the case. Because of transit and modern communication, large elements of the globe become present to us. We do indeed live in a "global society." We can no longer avoid "the other," even though we can close our minds and hearts to them and look at them with fear and resentment. But we are called as human beings to true dialogue, to a search for understanding. It is only by struggling out of a self-centered monologue into dialogue with "others" as they really are, and not as we have perceived them from afar, that we can really grow. Religions and ideologies must enter into dialogue with full force to help ensure not only mutual understanding and a deeper self-awareness, but perhaps even more important a global responsibility that will help make the future one of peace and harmony for all of God's creation.

SUMMARY

The future of Roman Catholicism and its relationship to other Christian churches has been solved to a great extent by Vatican II. In regard to the other world religions the problem has centered on whether or not the Church has understood those religions to have experienced revelation. In the past the stress on the uniqueness and finality of revelation in Jesus often excluded the possibility of any true revelation in the non-Christian religions. The traditional understanding of revelation, which has been taught by Catholics and Protestants alike, was formulated with great clarity by St. Thomas Aquinas. The world religions were understood to have a "natural" knowledge of God, but not a revealed knowledge of Him or Her. Such "natural" knowledge was not of saving benefit. The modern understanding of revelation is quite different. The traditional view began to break down irreparably at the beginning of the twentieth century because of the impact of nineteenth-century theology, biblical criticism, modern science, and the comparative study of religion. The world religions are now thought to possess revealed knowledge. Catholic scholars no longer equate divine revelation solely with Holy Scripture or divine doctrine. The highly conceptual understanding of divine revelation has been superseded, and revelation is now understood as more than propositional truth. Revelation is now understood as a divine self-disclosure. God does not merely reveal truths about Godself, God reveals Him- or Herself. Although it is still necessary to say that the revelation of Christ is final, it is now possible to add that divine revelation is an ongoing reality among human beings.

The official teaching of the Church may be summarized in the following way. All religions are related to Christ insofar as salvation is concerned. Apart from this relationship they have no salvific power because the salvation of the human race comes only through Jesus. This teaching is very much akin to that of Rahner and his notion of "anonymous Christianity." Other religions contain many authentic values even though they contain certain "errors" from a Christian perspective. They do contain elements of supreme truth, and divine grace works in and through them. Because Catholics must support true religious freedom, their relationship with other traditions should be characterized by acceptance, collaboration, and dialogue. The *Declaration on the Relationship of Christianity to Non-Christian Religions* teaches that the Church must be open to all forms of dialogue, imbued with the spirit of justice and love, and must engage in a common search for moral and spiritual enrichment. Much can be gained by all participants in such authentic dialogue.

Study Questions

1. What is meant by "salvation history"? Is this a new concept? How does it relate to secular history?

2. Explain the traditional understanding of revelation. Why has it been so readily acceptable to Christians?

3. Describe and evaluate the modern view of revelation. What brought about this rather amazing change in the traditional position? Is this view acceptable to all Christians today?

4. Why did Rahner use the term "anonymous Christian"? Does his theory violate the freedom of non-Christians?

5. According to Rahner, are all human beings offered God's grace? Explain.

6. Why does Rahner teach that all grace is related to the Church and not simply to Jesus's saving act? Is his theory in accordance with the teachings of the Church?

7. Küng, Lindbeck, and de Lubac object to Rahner's theory of the "anonymous Christian." What were the specific objections of each? Do you agree with these objections?

8. Should Catholic parishes promote dialogue (1) with other Christians? (2) with members of non-Christian religions? How can this be accomplished?

Epilogue

In the aftermath of Vatican II, and with the coming of the third millennium, the Catholic Church remains rooted in its biblical foundations and continues to be guided by the Holy Spirit. Until Vatican II, complete uniformity was found in the Church. This is no longer true. As long as the Church lived in a European-cultured setting, such uniformity was more or less acceptable. But today approximately 70 percent of all Catholics live in the Southern hemisphere, generally speaking in the developing world. This presents new questions and interesting challenges for the Church. The passage from uniformity to pluriformity is now evident. In *Evangelii Nuntiandi* (Announcing the Good News or Evangelization in the Modern World) Pope Paul VI spoke of the need for the incarnation of the Church in diverse cultures and of the need for legitimate pluriformity. He saw this not as a threat to unity but as an enrichment, as a God-given expression of unity in diversity.

The passage from uniformity to pluriformity will continue to produce tensions between local churches and Rome. This is seen in the call for democratization of Church structures and for a greater sense of collegiality at all levels of Church life. And though inculturation is accepted in principle by the hierarchy of the Church, it brings with it a number of problems, including the possibility of "cultural relativism," which the Church cannot accept. Problems presented by those who are not Catholic also must be faced, as is seen in the case of biblical scholars who attack the very basis of the Catholic understanding of Jesus. And there is a great need for Catholics to deepen their witness to Christ by communicating with members of other world churches and with nonbelievers as well. Such dialogue can be mutually beneficial.

New questions will continue to arise in theology and ethics. Much give and take will be involved, not only theologically but in all areas of the Christian life. The changes brought about by history and technology have profound meaning and consequences for the Church and its mission. The word "catholic" names an aspiration to become, in the fullest sense of the word, a universal Church that concerns itself with every culture, every crisis, and every human opportunity, in a prophetically open fashion. This new era of the Church was inaugurated by Vatican II, which will go down in history as the first council representing a truly universal church, rooted on every continent. The majority of the council fathers have passed from the world scene, but the Church lives on, thinks on, and develops further. Vatican II represents the transition from the second to the third millennium, which, it is hoped, will be one of mutual respect and dialogue. And as I wrote in the epilogue to *Roman Catholicism: Yesterday and Today,*

> The church in the year 2100 will undoubtedly look very different in its outward appearance than it does today, although the substance of the faith will be the same. The next one hundred years will be challenging and exciting, and filled with difficult and tense moments, which is nothing less than a sign of life and a confirmation that the Holy Spirit will be with the church always.[111]

Endnotes

Chapter 1

1. Flannery, "Pastoral Constitution on the Church," 947.
2. Flannery, "Constitution on Sacred Liturgy," 107 n.30.
3. The full text and a commentary by Fitzmeyer of "Historical Truth of the Gospels" is given in *Theological Studies* 25 (1964): 386–408.
4. Meier, *A Marginal Jew.*
5. L. Johnson, *Real Jesus*, 133.
6. McBrien, *Catholicism*, 435.
7. Brown, *Crises Facing the Church*, 33–37.
8. Ibid., 34.
9. Ibid., 36.
10. O'Collins, *Christology*, 113–52.
11. Norris, *Christological Controversy*, 159.
12. McBrien, *Catholicism*, 482.
13. O'Collins, *Christology*, 200–201.
14. St. Thomas Aquinas, *Summa Theologica*, vol. 3: 1, 2.
15. Ibid., 48, 3 response.
16. Ibid., 49 nn.4, 1, 3, 2.
17. O'Collins, *Christology*, 206–07.
18. Brown, *Crises Facing the Church*, 6.
19. See note 3.
20. Rahner, "Two Types of Christology," 213–23.
21. Flannery, "Pastoral Constitution on the Church," 922 n.22.
22. Ibid., 932.
23. Ibid., nn.2, 10, 25, 45.
24. Flannery, "Declaration on the Relationship of the Church to Non-Christian Religions," 738–42 nn.2–4.
25. Denziger, *Enchiridion Symbolorum*, 672.
26. Kasper, *Jesus the Christ*, 104–11. In this section, Kasper analyzes two other titles attributed to Jesus: Son of Man and Son of God.
27. Boff, *Jesus Christ Liberator.*
28. Sobrino, *Christology at the Crossroads.*
29. Carr, *Transforming Grace*, 164–65.
30. Ibid., 168.

31. Ibid., 169.

32. E. Johnson, *She Who Is*.

33. E. Johnson, *Consider Jesus: Renewal in Christology*.

34. E. Johnson, *She Who Is, 167*.

35. Knitter, *One Earth, Many Religions,* 17.

36. Ibid.

37. Borg, *Jesus in Contemporary Scholarship*, 162.

38. Funk, "Cross Examination," E1, E5.

39. Funk, Hoover, and the Jesus Seminar, *Five Gospels*, 8.

40. An English translation is available in Charles H. Talbert, ed., *Reimarus*.

41. den Heyer, *Jesus Matters*.

42. Meier, *A Marginal Jew*, 1: 21–40.

43. Ibid., 1 and 1: 340, 682, 778.

44. Ibid., 1: 41–166.

45. L. Johnson, *Real Jesus*, 128.

46. Ibid., 21.

47. Funk, Hoover, and the Jesus Seminar, *Five Gospels*, 37.

48. Meier, *A Marginal Jew*, 139. (For his treatment of the Rag Hammadi material read pages 123–39.)

49. L. Johnson, *Real Jesus*, 22.

50. Funk, Hoover, and the Jesus Seminar, *Five Gospels*, 7.

51. Ibid., 7.

52. Ibid., 8.

53. Ibid., 2.

54. Ibid., 3.

55. L. Johnson, *Real Jesus*, 25.

56. Schillebeeckx, *God, the Future of Man*; and *Jesus*.

57. Schnackenburg, *God's Rule and Kingdom*.

58. Viviano, *Kingdom of God in History*.

59. Funk, Hoover, and the Jesus Seminar, *Five Gospels*, 4.

60. See Riesner, "Jesus as Preacher and Teacher," 185–210.

61. Funk, Hoover, and the Jesus Seminar, *Five Gospels*, 4, 5.

62. L. Johnson, *Real Jesus*, 26.

63. Hays, "Corrected Jesus," 43–48.

64. Theiring, *Jesus and the Riddle of the Dead Sea Scrolls*.

65. Spong, *Born of a Woman*.

66. Borg, *Jesus*.

67. Crossan, *Historical Jesus*.

68. L. Johnson, *Real Jesus*, 29–56.
69. Meier, *A Marginal Jew*, 22.
70. Ibid., 31.
71. Ibid., 198.
72. Funk, Hoover, and the Jesus Seminar, *Five Gospels*, 2.
73. Ibid., 2, 3.
74. Ibid., 398
75. Ibid.
76. An excellent analysis of the Resurrection can be found in Dunn, *Evidence for Jesus*, 53–76.
77. McBrien, *Catholicism*, 435.
78. Ibid.
79. L. Johnson, *Real Jesus*, 140.
80. Meier, *A Marginal Jew*, 199.
81. Ibid.

Chapter 2

1. Marty, "State of Disunion," 115: 43.
2. Coleman, "Who Are the Catholic Fundamentalists?", 115: 42–47.
3. Kennedy, *Tomorrow's Catholics, Yesterday's Church*, 8.
4. Ibid., 13.
5. Granfield, *Limits of the Papacy*, 13.
6. Sigmund, *Nicholas of Cusa and Medieval Political Thought*, 91.
7. Ibid., 310.
8. Granfield, *Limits of the Papacy*, 62.
9. Zinelli, "Acta synodalia sacrosancti concilii oecumenici," 57: 775.
10. Mansi, ed., *Sacrorum consiliorum nova et amplissima collectio*, 683B.
11. Flannery, "Dogmatic Constitution on the Church," 381.
12. Ibid., 374–76.
13. Pope Paul VI. Text referring to the establishment of the Synod of Bishops. *Acta apostolicae sedis.*
14. National Council of Catholic Bishops, "Challenge of Peace," 13.
15. Flannery, "Decree on the Bishops' Pastoral Office in the Church," 564–610.
16. Ibid., 372–76.
17. Ibid., 361–63.
18. Ibid., 367–68.
19. Ibid., 368–69.
20. Flannery, "Dogmatic Constitution on the Church," 382–84.
21. Green, "Pastoral Governance Role of Diocesan Bishop," 49: 480.

22. See Lynch, "Co-Responsibility in the First Five Centuries," 48.

23. *Code of Canon Law,* 66–67.

24. Beal, "Toward a Democratic Church," 66.

25. Flannery, "Dogmatic Constitution on the Church," 384–87.

26. Corecco, "Aspects of the Reception of Vatican II in Code of Canon Law," 252.

27. Flannery, "Dogmatic Constitution on the Church," 390–91.

28. Flannery, "Decree on the Bishops' Pastoral Office," 579–80.

29. Flannery, "Dogmatic Constitution on the Church," 394–96.

30. Congregation for Bishops, *Directory on the Pastoral Ministry of Bishops*, 204.

31. Castillo, "Origin of the Priest Shortage."

32. Schoenherr Report, "Study of U.S. Diocesan Priesthood Statistics," 206.

33. Bernier, *Ministry in the Church*, 46–47.

34. Schnackenburg, *Church in the New Testament.*

35. McBrien, *Catholicism*, 769–70.

36. Schillebeeckx, *Church with a Human Face*, 140.

37. Ibid., 153.

38. Bernier, *Ministry in the Church*, 137.

39. Flannery, "Decree on The Ministry and Life of Priests," 872–75.

40. Flannery, "Dogmatic Constitution on the Church," 385–87.

41. Iserloh, "Die Confessio Augustana," 32.

42. Schillebeeckx and Metz, eds., *Right of a Community to a Priest.*

43. Sherry, "Shortage? What Vocation Shortage?" 41: 29–31.

44. Hoge, *Future of Catholic Leadership*, 18.

45. Coleman, "Future of Ministry," 144: 248–49.

46. Flannery, "Dogmatic Constitution on the Church," 394–96.

47. Leddy, Remi de Roo, and Roche, *In the Eye of the Catholic Storm*, 45.

48. O'Meara, *Theology of Ministry*, 166.

49. Flannery, "Decree of the Apostolate of the Laity," 777.

50. Doyle, *Church Emerging from Vatican II*, 237–44.

51. Bernier, *Ministry in the Church*, 255–57.

52. Butler, "Second Thoughts on the Ordination of Women."

53. Flannery, "Dogmatic Constitution on the Church," 387.

54. Bishops' Committee on the Permanent Diaconate, "Permanent Deacons in the United States," 13.

55. Flannery, "Decree on Renewal of Religious Life," 612–14.

56. Dolan, *American Catholic Experience*, 438.

57. McBrien, *Ministry*, 38.

58. Ibid., 38, 39.

59. Flannery, "Dogmatic Constitution on the Church," 361.

60. Ibid., 390–91.

61. Flannery, "Ministry and Life of Priests," 880.

62. Flannery, "Dogmatic Constitution on the Church," 390.

63. Flannery, "Pastoral Constitution on the Church, 942.

64. Flannery, "Dogmatic Constitution on the Church," 393–94.

65. Ibid., 396.

66. Ibid., 381.

67. Granfield, *Limits of the Papacy*, 113.

68. Greeley, *Catholic Myth*, 144–45.

69. Ibid., 145.

70. Murnion, "Community Called Parish," 183.

71. Ibid., 183–90.

72. Ibid., 188.

73. Pope Paul VI, encyclical "Ecclesiam Suam."

74. Coleman, "Not Democracy but Democratization," 226.

75. Ibid., 229.

76. D'Antonio et al., *American Catholic Laity in a Changing Church*, 109–11.

77. Granfield, *Limits of the Papacy*, 107–68.

78. Granfield, "Legitimation and Bureaucratization of Ecclesial," 92.

79. Flannery, "Dogmatic Constitution on the Church," 389.

80. Ibid., 394.

81. *Code of Canon Law,* 204, #1.

82. Bianchi and Ruether, "Toward a Democratic Church," 257.

Chapter 3

1. Rahner, "Towards a Fundamental Theological Interpretation of Vatican II."

2. Shorter, *Toward Theology of Inculturation*, 11.

3. Arrupe, "Letter to the Whole Society on Inculturation."

4. Shorter, *Toward Theology of Inculturation*, 29–30.

5. Ibid., 14.

6. Buhlmann, *Church of the Future*, 7.

7. Cf. Flannery, "Dogmatic Constitution on the Church," vol. 1, 364–65; 376–78. Also cf. Flannery, vol. 2, 742–43.

8. Shorter, *Toward a Theory of Inculturation*, 144.

9. Fitzpatrick, *One Church, Many Cultures*, 71.

10. Shorter, *Toward a Theology of Inculturation*, 158.

11. Ibid., 158.

12. Trigault, *China that Was*, 159.

13. Pope John Paul II, "Address to the Participants at the Gregorian University."

14. Pope Pius XII, "Address to Pontifical Mission Aid Societies."

15. Pope John XXIII, encyclical *Princeps Pastorum* (1959), quoted in Shorter, *Toward a Theology of Inculturation*, 187.

16. Flannery, "Pastoral Constitution on the Church," 958.

17. Ibid., 962, 963.

18. Flannery, "Dogmatic Constitution on the Church," 376.

19. Shorter, *Toward a Theology of Inculturation*, 68.

20. Flannery, "Decree on the Church's Missionary Activity," 1: 824.

21. Ibid., 825.

22. Flannery, "Constitution on the Sacred Liturgy," 1: 14.

23. Ibid., 13.

24. Ibid.

25. Chapungco, *Liturgies of the Future*.

26. Shorter, *Toward a Theory of Inculturation*, 194.

27. Pope Paul VI, "Allocution to the Convocation of the Bishops of Africa in Kampala, Uganda."

28. Pope Paul VI, "On Evangelization in the Modern World."

29. Ibid., 742.

30. Ibid., 743–44.

31. Pope John Paul II, letter to Agostino Cardinal Casaroli.

32. Ibid., 5.

33. Ratzinger, with Messor, *Ratzinger Report*, 37.

34. Pope John Paul II, "Address to Pontifical Council for Culture."

35. Hillman, *Polygamy Reconsidered*.

36. Schreiter, *Constructing Local Theologies*.

37. Flannery, "Decree on the Church's Missionary Activity," 1: 39–40.

38. Symposium of Bishops of Africa and Madagascar, *Acts of the Fifth Assembly of SECAM, ACCRA*, 225.

39. Geertz, *Interpretation of Cultures*.

40. Schreiter, *Constructing Local Theologies*, 31.

41. Ibid.

42. Ibid., 37.

43. Flannery, "Dogmatic Constitution on the Church," 1: 381–82.

44. Pope John Paul II, "Speech to the Roman Curia on Dec. 20, 1990."

45. Komonchak, "Theology of the Local Church," 49.

46. Second General Council of Latin American Bishops, "Church in Transformation of Latin America," 23.

47. Ibid., 175.

48. Cleary, *Crisis and Change*, 104–05.

49. Gallo, "Basic Ecclesial Communities," 99.

50. Boff, *Church*, 8.

51. Pope Paul VI, *Evangelii Nuntiandi*, 2: 724.

52. Ibid., 738–40.

53. For a collection of some of Archbishop Romero's pastoral letters and sermons, see *Voice of the Voiceless*.

54. Gutiérrez, *A Theology of Liberation*, 90.

55. Ratzinger, *Instruction on Certain Aspects of the Theology of Liberation*, 3.

56. L. Boff and C. Boff, *Liberation Theology*, 19.

57. Ibid., 20.

58. Ferm, *Third World Liberation Theologies*, 112–13.

59. Congregation for the Doctrine of the Faith, *Instruction on Christian Freedom and Liberation*.

60. Cenkner, ed., *Multicultural Church*.

61. Cf. Jennessey, *American Catholics*; and Dolan, *American Catholic Experience*.

62. Fitzpatrick, *One Church, Many Cultures*, 117.

63. Ibid.

64. Herberg, *Protestant, Catholic, Jew*, 285–89.

65. The final draft "Challenge of Peace" appears in *Origins* 13: 1–32. The document was also published in booklet form by the U.S. Catholic Conference, Washington, D.C.

66. McBrien, *Caesar's Coin*, 197.

67. Burns, *Roman Catholicism*, 201.

68. National Council of Catholic Bishops, "On Catholic Social Teaching and U.S. Economy."

69. Curran, *Toward an American Catholic Moral Theology*, 183.

70. Greeley, *American Catholics since the Council*.

71. Greeley, *Confessions of a Parish Priest*.

72. Coleman, *An American Strategic Theology*.

73. Newbigin, *Foolishness to the Greeks*, 3.

74. Tracy, "Ethnic Pluralism and Systematic Theology," 91.

75. Gleason, *Keeping the Faith*, 200–201.

76. Power, "Communion within Pluralism in the Local Church," 89.

77. Ibid., 97.

78. Ibid., 100.

79. Sandoval, *On the Move*.

80. Both of these letters can be obtained from the National Council of Catholic Bishops, U.S. Catholic Conference, 1312 Massachusetts Ave., N.W., Washington, D.C. 20005.

81. National Council of Catholic Bishops, "Hispanic Presence: Challenge and Commitment," in pastoral letter *On Hispanic Ministry,* 4.

82. Ibid., 5.

83. Jaffe, Cullen, and Boswell, *Changing Demography of Spanish Americans.*

84. Ibid., 22.

85. Phan, "Contemporary Theology and Inculturation," 120–23.

86. Elizando, *Galilean Journey,* 104. See also "Mestizaje as a Locus of Theological Reflection," 104–23.

87. Phan, "Contemporary Theology and Inculturation," 122.

88. See Goizueto's "Theology as Intellectually Vital Inquiry."

89. See, for instance, Isasi-Díaz and Tarango, *Hispanic Women.*

90. Shorter, *Toward a Theology of Inculturation,* 14.

Chapter 4

1. Daniélou, *Holy Pagans of the Old Testament.*

2. Martyr, *First Apology,* 244–45.

3. Ibid., 272.

4. Ignatius of Antioch, "Philadelphians," 108.

5. Irenaeus, *Adversus Haereses,* 7: 906–07.

6. Clement of Alexandria, "Pedagogus," 8: 299.

7. Origen, "In Jesu Nave," 11: 841.

8. St. Cyprian, "Unity of the Catholic Church," 49.

9. St. Augustine, "De Baptismo Contra Donatistas," bk. 7, chap. 1, 43: 223–25.

10. Concerning St. Augustine's understanding of the axiom "There is no salvation outside the Church," cf. Willems, *Reality of Redemption,* 105–06.

11. St. Augustine, "De Baptismo Contra Donatistas," bk. 4, chap. 18, 43: 170.

12. Ibid., 196–97.

13. Fulgentius of Ruspe, "De Fide."

14. Cf. Willems, *Reality of Redemption,* 106.

15. Denziger, *Enchiridion Symbolorum,* 479.

16. Ibid.

17. Ibid., 1647.

18. Cf. the letter to Archbishop Richard Cushing of Boston.

19. Flannery, "Dogmatic Constitution on the Church," 1: 367–68.

20. Coomaraswany, *Am I My Brother's Keeper?,* 10.

21. Lindbeck, *Future of Roman Catholic Theology,* 22–24.

22. Schlette, *Towards a Theology of Religions,* 68.

23. Ibid., 70.

24. Rahner, "History of the World and Salvation History," 97–102.

25. Ibid., 109–10.

26. Schlette, *Towards a Theology of Religions*, 63–107.

27. Cf. St. Thomas Aquinas, *Summa Theologica*, vol. 1., q. 12, arts. 12, 13; Pegis, *On the Truth of the Catholic Faith*, bk. 1, chaps. 5–8, 69–76; cf. also Seckler, "Salvation for the Non-Evangelized," 9 (autumn 1961): 168–73.

28. Cf. George W. Forell, *Protestant Faith*, 53–56.

29. Cf. Robert D. Young, *Encounter with World Religions*, 45–50.

30. Denziger, *Enchiridion Symbolorum*, 1647.

31. The modernity of the distinction of "special" and "general" revelation has at times been called into question. However, as John Baillie points out, the full development of the distinction is modern, even though it was hinted at by earlier writers. Cf. Baillie and Martin, *Revelation*, 18.

32. Flannery, "Declaration on the Relationship of the Church to Non-Christian Religions," 738–39.

33. See Lindbeck, *Future of Roman Catholic Theology*, 36–38; Also cf. Tillich, *Systematic Theology*, 152–55.

34. Moran, *Theology of Revelation*.

35. Baum, "'Religions' in Contemporary Roman Catholic Theology," 42–43.

36. Flannery, "Dogmatic Constitution on the Church," 367.

37. Ibid., 365.

38. Ibid., 367.

39. Ibid.

40. Ibid., 368.

41. Ibid., 367–68.

42. Flannery, "Relationship of the Church to Non-Christian Religions," 740–41.

43. Sullivan, *Salvation outside the Church?*, 155.

44. *Acta Synodalia Concilii Vaticani II*, 3: 1, 206.

45. Sullivan, *Salvation outside the Church?*, 155.

46. Ibid.

47. Kraemer, *Christian Messenger*, 1963.

48. Hick and Knitter, *Myth of Christian Uniqueness*.

49. Dupuis, *Jesus Christ at the Encounter of World Religions*.

50. Rahner, "World and Salvation History," 5: 99–114.

51. Rahner, "Thoughts on the Possibility of Belief Today," 5: 3–22.

52. Rahner, *A Rahner Reader*, 185.

53. Rahner, "Thoughts on the Possibility of Belief Today," 28.

54. Rahner, "Dogmatic Notes on 'Ecclesiological Piety,'" 5: 359.

55. Rahner, *On the Theology of Death*, 95.

56. Ibid., 88.
57. Ibid., 90.
58. Rahner, "Dogmatic Notes on 'Ecclesiological Piety,'" 357.
59. Rahner, "Membership of the Church According to the Teaching of Pius XII's Encyclical, 'Mystici Corporis Christi,'" 45.
60. Ibid., 67.
61. Ibid., 73.
62. Ibid., 77–79.
63. Ibid., 81.
64. Ibid., 82.
65. Ibid., 83.
66. Ibid., 84–85.
67. Ibid., 85.
68. Ibid., 87.
69. Rahner, "Christianity," 1: 308.
70. Rahner, "Dogmatic Notes on 'Ecclesiological Piety,'" 361.
71. Rahner, "Christianity and the Non-Christian Religions," 133.
72. Rahner, "Dogmatic Notes on 'Ecclesiological Piety,'" 361.
73. Rahner, "Christianity and the Non-Christian Religions," 119–21.
74. Ibid., 125.
75. Flannery, "Dogmatic Constitution on the Church," 23.
76. Küng, *Church*, 317.
77. Ibid.
78. Ibid., 318.
79. Ibid.
80. Lindbeck, *Future of Roman Catholic Theology*, 36.
81. Cf. Sullivan, *Salvation outside the Church?*, 175.
82. Paninder, "Salvation of Other Men," 196.
83. Flannery, "Relationship of the Church to Non-Christian Religions," 738.
84. Ibid., 738–42.
85. Flannery, "Decree on the Church's Missionary Activity," 822–23.
86. Ibid., 829–31 and 834–35.
87. Ibid., 816–17.
88. Ibid., 825 and 834–35.
89. Flannery, "Relation of Christianity to the Non-Christian Religions," 738–42.
90. Ibid., 738–39.
91. Ibid.
92. Ibid., 738–40 and 742.

93. Flannery, "Dogmatic Constitution of the Church," 367–69.

94. Pope John Paul II, "Redemptoris Missio," *Origins*, vol. 20, no. 34 (31 January 1995): n.55.

95. Ibid., n.56.

96. Pope Paul VI, "Ecclesiam Suam," n.78.

97. Swidler et al., *Death or Dialogue*, 57.

98. Ibid.

99. Ibid., 64.

100. Küng, *On Being a Christian*, 169.

101. Flannery, "Relationship of the Church to Non-Christian Religions," 743–49.

102. Vatican's Commission for Religious Relations with the Jews, "Jews and Judaism in Preaching and Catechesis."

103. Burns, *Roman Catholicism*.

104. Flannery, "Dogmatic Constitution on the Church," 2: 357.

105. Sullivan, *Salvation outside the Church?*, 147–48.

106. Cf. the Decree on Ecumenism in Flannery, *Documents of Vatican II*, 456.

107. *Acta Synodalia Concilii Vaticani II*, 3: 2, 335.

108. Ibid., 455.

109. Ibid.

110. Ibid.

111. Burns, *Roman Catholicism*, 217.

Further Reading

The following books are recommended for further reading. Adventurous readers may read the other, often more specialized resources given in the chapter notes.

CHAPTER 1

Brown, Raymond E. "How Much Did Jesus Know? *Jesus, God and Man: Modern Biblical Reflections.* Milwaukee, WI: Bruce, 1967.

——. *Crises Facing the Church.* New York: Paulist Press, 1975.

Fitzmeyer, Joseph A. *A Christological Catechism: New Testament Answers.* New York: Paulist Press, 1981.

——. *Scripture and Christology: A Statement of the Biblical Commission with a Commentary.* New York: Paulist Press, 1986.

Johnson, Elizabeth. *Waves of Renewal in Christology.* New York: Crossroad, 1990.

Johnson, Luke Timothy. *The Real Jesus.* San Francisco: Harper, 1996.

Kreig, Robert A. *Story—Shaped Christology: The Role of Narratives in Identifying Jesus Christ.* New York: Paulist Press, 1988.

Lane, Dermot A. *The Reality of Jesus: An Essay in Christology.* New York: Paulist Press, 1975.

———. *Christ at the Center: Selected Issues in Christology*. New York: Paulist Press, 1991.

Macquarrie, John. *Jesus Christ in Modern Thought*. London: SCM Press, 1990.

Meier, John, P. *A Marginal Jew*. Vol. I. New York: Doubleday, 1991.

———. *A Marginal Jew*. Vol. II. New York: Doubleday, 1994.

O'Collins, Gerald. *Interpreting Jesus*. New York: Paulist Press, 1981.

———. *Christology: A Biblical, Historical, and Systematic Study of Jesus*. New York: Oxford University Press, 1995.

Pannenberg, Wolfhart. *Jesus: God & Man*. Translated by L. L. Wilkins and D. A. Priebe. London: SCM Press, 1968.

Rahner, Karl. *Foundations of the Christian Faith*. Translated by W. V. Dych. London: Darton, Longman and Todd, 1978.

Sanders, E. P. *The Historical Figure of Jesus*, London: Penguin Press, 1978.

Sobrino, Jon. *Christology at the Crossroads*. London: SCM Press, 1978.

CHAPTER 2

Bianchi, Eugene C., and Rosemary Radford Ruether, eds. *A Democratic Catholic Church*. New York: Crossroad, 1992.

Bernier, Paul. *Ministry in the Church*, Mystic, CT: Twenty-Third Publications, 1992.

Bokenkotter, Thomas. *A Concise History of the Catholic Church*. Rev. and expanded ed. New York: Doubleday Image Books, 1990.

Cunningham, Lawrence, ed. *The Catholic Faith: A Reader*. New York: Paulist Press, 1988.

D'Antonio, William, James D. Davidson, Dean R. Hoge, and Ruth A. Wallace. *American Catholic Laity in a Changing Church*. Kansas City, MO: Sheed and Ward, 1989.

Dolan, John P. *Catholicism: An Historical Survey*. Woodbury, NY: Baron's Educational Series, 1968.

Doyle, Dennis. *The Church Emerging from Vatican II*. Mystic, CT: Twenty-Third Publications, 1992.

Gilkey, Langdon. *Catholicism Confronts Modernity: A Protestant View*. New York: Seabury Press, 1975.

Granfield, Patrick. *The Limits of the Papacy*. New York: Crossroad, 1987.

Hoge, Dean. *Future of Catholic Leadership: Responses to the Priest Shortage*. Kansas City, MO: Sheed and Ward, 1987.

Kennedy, Eugene. *Tomorrow's Catholics, Yesterday's Church*. San Francisco: Harper and Row, 1988.

McBrien, Richard P. *Catholicism: New Edition*. San Francisco: Harper, 1994.

McKenzie, John L. *Authority in the Church*. New York: Sheed and Ward, 1966.

O'Meara, Thomas F. *Theology of Ministry*. New York: Paulist Press, 1983.

Osborne, Kenan R. *Ministry: Lay Ministry in the Roman Catholic Church: Its History and Theology*. New York: Paulist Press, 1993.

Rausch, Thomas P. *The Roots of the Catholic Tradition*. Wilmington, DE: Michael Glazier, 1986.

Schillebeeckx, Edward. *Church with a Human Face*. New York: Crossroad, 1985.

CHAPTER 3

Boff, Leonardo. *Church: Charisma and Power*. New York: Crossroad, 1985.

Buhlmann, Walter. *The Church of the Future*. Maryknoll, NY: Orbis Books, 1986.

Cenker, William, ed. *The Multicultural Church*. New York: Paulist Press, 1996.

Chapungo, Arthur. *Liturgies of the Future*. New York: Paulist Press, 1989.

Cleary, Edward L. *Crisis and Change*. Maryknoll, NY: Orbis Books, 1985.

Coleman, John A. *An American Strategic Theology*. Ramsey, NJ: Paulist Press, 1982.

Costa, Ray O. *One Faith, Many Cultures*. New York: Orbis Books, 1988.

Elizondo, Virgil. *The Galilean Journey: The Mexican-American Promise*. Maryknoll, NY: Orbis Books, 1983.

Fitzpatrick, Joseph J. *One Church, Many Cultures*. Kansas City, MO: Sheed and Ward, 1987.

Geertz, Clifford. *The Interpretation of Cultures*. New York: Basic Books, 1973.

Hillman, Eugene. *Polygamy Reconsidered.* Maryknoll, NY: Orbis Books, 1975.

Sandoval, Moises. *On the Move: A History of the Hispanic Church in the United States.* Maryknoll, NY: Orbis Books, 1990.

Schreiter, Robert. *Constructing Local Theologies.* Maryknoll, NY: Orbis Books, 1986.

Shorter, Aylward. *Toward a Theology of Inculturation.* Maryknoll, NY: Orbis Books, 1992.

CHAPTER 4

DiRoia, J. A. *The Diversity of Religions: A Christian Perspective.* Washington, D.C.: Catholic University of America Press, 1992.

Dupuis, Jacques. *Jesus Christ at the Encounter of World Religions.* Maryknoll, NY: Orbis Books, 1991.

Fransen, Piet. *Divine Grace and Man.* Translated by Georges Dupont. New York: New American Library, 1965.

Hillman, Eugene. *Many Paths.* Maryknoll, NY: Orbis Books, 1989.

Knitter, Paul. *One Earth, Many Religions.* Maryknoll, NY: Orbis Books, 1995.

Küng, Hans. *Christianity and the World Religions: Paths of Dialogue with Islam, Hinduism, and Buddhism.* Garden City, NY: Doubleday, 1986.

Moran, Gabriel. *Theology of Revelation.* New York: Herder and Herder, 1966.

Neuner, Joseph, ed. *Christian Revelation and World Religions.* London: Burns and Oates, 1967.

Pope John Paul II. *Redemptoris Missio* (The Mission of Redemption). *Origins* 20 (31 January 1991): 541, 543–68.

Rahner, Karl. *On the Theology of Death.* New York: Herder and Herder, 1965.

——. "History of the World and Salvation History." In *Theological Investigations.* Vol. 5. Baltimore: Helicon, 1966.

——. "Christianity and the Non-Christian Religions." In *Theological Investigations.* Vol. 5. Baltimore: Helicon, 1966.

Sullivan, Francis A. *Salvation outside the Church? Tracing the History of the Catholic Response*. New York: Paulist Press, 1992.

Swidler, Leonard, John B. Cobb, Jr., Paul F. Knitter, and Monika K. Hellwig. *Death or Dialogue: From the Age of Monologue to the Age of Dialogue*. Philadelphia: Trinity Press International, 1996.

Willems, Boniface. *The Reality of Redemption*. New York: Herder and Herder, 1970.

Selected Bibliography

Acta Synadolia Council Vatican II 3: 1,1206.

Acta Romans Societatis Jean. Rome: Curia Praepositi Generalis, 1979.

Arrupe, Pedro, S.J. "Letter to the Whole Society on Inculturation." In *Aixala*. Vol. 3. 1172–81.

Baillie, John, and Hugh Martin, eds. *Revelation*. New York: Macmillan, 1937.

Baum, Gregory. "The 'Religions' in Contemporary Roman Catholic Theology," *Journal of Religious Thought* 25 (1969): 42–43.

Beal, John. "Toward a Democratic Church: The Canonical Heritage." In *A Democratic Catholic Church*. Edited by Eugene C. Bianchi and Rosemary Radford Ruether. New York: Crossroad, 1992.

Bernier, Paul. *Ministry in the Church*. Mystic, CT: Twenty-Third Publications, 1992, 46–47.

Bishops' Committee on the Permanent Diaconate. *Permanent Deacons in the United States*. Washington, D.C.: U.S. Catholic Conference, 1985.

Boff, Leonardo. *Jesus Christ Liberator: A Critical Christology for Our Time*. Maryknoll, NY: Orbis Books, 1978.

——. *Church: Charisma and Power*. New York: Crossroad, 1985.

Boff, Leonardo, and Clodovis Boff. *Liberation Theology*. San Francisco: Harper and Row, 1986.

Borg, Marcus. *Jesus: A New Vision: Spirit, Culture and the Life of Discipleship*. San Francisco: Harper and Row, 1987.

——. *Jesus in Contemporary Scholarship*. Valley Forge, PA: Trinity Press, 1994.

Brown, Raymond E. *Crises Facing the Church*. New York: Paulist Press, 1975.

Buhlmann, Walter. *The Church of the Future*. Maryknoll, NY: Orbis Books, 1986.

Burns, Robert A. *Roman Catholicism: Yesterday and Today*. Chicago: Loyola University Press, 1992.

Butler, Sara. "Second Thoughts on the Ordination of Women." *Worship* 63 (2 March 1989): 157–65.

Carr, Anne. *Transforming Grace: Christian Tradition and Women's Experience*. San Francisco: Harper-Collins, 1988.

Castillo, Dennis. "The Origin of the Priest Shortage: 1942–1962." *America* 167 (24 October 1992): 302–14.

Cenkner, William, ed. *The Multicultural Church*. New York: Paulist Press, 1996.

Chapungco, Anscar. *Liturgies of the Future*. New York: Paulist Press, 1989.

Cleary, Edward L. *Crisis and Change*. Maryknoll, NY: Orbis Books, 1985.

Clement of Alexandria. "Pedagogus." Vol. I. 6 Vol. In *Patrologiae cursus completus, series Graeca* Vol. 8. Edited by J. P. Migne. 161 vols. Paris, 1857–1866, 299.

Code of Canon Law, The. Grand Rapids, MI: William B. Erdmans, 1983.

Coleman, John. "The Future of Ministry." *America* 144 (1981) 248–49.

——. *An American Strategic Theology*. New York: Paulist Press, 1982.

——. "Who Are the Catholic Fundamentalists?" *Commonweal* 115 (27 January 1989): 42–47.

——. "Not Democracy but Democratization." In *A Democratic Catholic Church*. Edited by Eugene C. Bianchi and Rosemary Radford Ruether. New York: Crossroad, 1992.

Congregation for Bishops. *Directory on the Pastoral Ministry of Bishops*. Ottawa: Publication Service of the Canadian Catholic Conference, 1974.

Coomaraswany, Amanda. *Am I My Brother's Keeper?* New York: John Day, 1947.

Corecco, Eugenio. "Aspects of the Reception of Vatican II in the Code of Canon Law." In *The Reception of Vatican II*. Edited by Guiseppi Alberigo, Jean-Pierre Jossua, and Joseph A. Komonchak. Washington, D.C.: Catholic University of America Press, 1987, 252.

Crossan, John Dominic. *The Historical Jesus: The Life of a Mediterranean Jewish Peasant*. San Francisco: Harper, 1991.

Crowley, Paul, ed. "Theology as Intellectually Vital Inquiry: The Challenge of/to U.S. Hispanic Theologians." *Proceedings of the Forty-Sixth Annual Convention of the Catholic Theological Society of America*. Washington, D.C., Catholic University Press of America, 1991.

Curran, Charles. *Toward an American Catholic Moral Theology*. Notre Dame, IN: University of Notre Dame Press, 1987, 183.

Daniélou, Jean. *The Holy Pagans of the Old Testament*. Translated by Felix Faber. Baltimore: Helicon Press, 1957.

D'Antonio, William, James D. Davidson, Dean R. Hoge, and Ruth A. Wallace. *American Catholic Laity in a Changing Church*. Kansas City, MO: Sheed and Ward, 1989.

den Heyer, C. J. *Jesus Matters*. Valley Forge, PA: Trinity Press International, 1996.

Denziger, Henry. *Enchiridion Symbolorum, Definitionum, et Declarationum de Rebus Fidei et Morum* (Handbook of Creeds, Definitions and Declarations Concerning Matters of Faith). Edited by Adolf Schonmetzer, S.J. 36th ed., no. 3434. New York: Herder and Herder, 1976.

——. *Enchiridion Symbolorum, Definitionum, et Declarationum de Rebus Fidei et Morum* (Handbook of Creeds, Definitions and Declarations Concerning Matters of Faith). Edited by Karl Rahner. 31st ed. Freiburg, Germany: Herder, 1957.

Dolan, Jay P. *The American Catholic Experience: A History from Colonial Times to the Present*. Garden City, NY: Image Books, 1985.

Doyle, Dennis. *The Church Emerging from Vatican II*. Mystic, CT: Twenty-Third Publications, 1992, 237–44.

Dunn, James D.G. *The Evidence for Jesus*. Philadelphia: Westminster Press, 1985.

Dupuis, Jacque. *Jesus Christ at the Encounter of World Religions*. Maryknoll, NY: Orbis Books, 1991.

Elizando, Virgil. *"Mestizaje* as a Locus of Theological Reflection." In *Frontiers of Hispanic Theology in the United States.* Edited by Allan Figueroa Deck. Maryknoll, NY: Orbis Books, 1992.

———. *The Galilean Journey: The Mexican-American Promise.* Maryknoll, NY: Orbis Books, 1983.

Ferm, Dean William. *Third World Liberation Theologies: An Introductory* Survey. Maryknoll, NY: Orbis Books, 1983.

Fitzmeyer, Joseph. "The Historical Truth of the Gospels." *Theological Studies* 25 (1964): 386–408.

Fitzpatrick, Joseph J., S.J. *One Church, Many Cultures.* Kansas City, MO: Sheed and Ward, 1987.

Flannery, Austin, O.P., ed. "The Constitution on the Sacred Liturgy." In *Vatican Council: The Conciliar and Post Conciliar Documents.* Vol. I. Northport, NY: Costello, 1992.

———. "Declaration on the Relationship of the Church to Non-Christian Religions." In *Vatican Council: The Conciliar and Post Conciliar Documents.* Northport, NY: Costello, 1992.

———. "Decree of the Apostolate of the Laity." In *Vatican Council: The Conciliar and Post Conciliar Documents.* Northport, NY: Costello, 1992.

———. "Decree on the Bishops' Pastoral Office in the Church." In *Vatican Council: The Conciliar and Post Conciliar Documents.* Northport, NY: Costello, 1992.

———. "Decree on the Church's Missionary Activity." In *Vatican Council: The Conciliar and Post Conciliar Documents.* Vol. I. Northport, NY: Costello, 1992.

———. "Decree on the Ministry and Life of Priests." In *Vatican Council: The Conciliar and Post Conciliar Documents.* Northport, NY: Costello, 1992.

———. "Decree on Renewal of Religious Life." In *Vatican Council: The Conciliar and Post Conciliar Documents.* Northport, NY: Costello, 1992.

———. "The Dogmatic Constitution on the Church" In *Vatican Council: The Conciliar and Post Conciliar Documents.* Northport, NY: Costello, 1992.

———. "Pastoral Constitution on the Church in the Modern World." In *Vatican Council: The Conciliar and Post Conciliar Documents.* Northport, NY: Costello, 1992.

Forell, George W. *The Protestant Faith*. Englewood Cliffs, NJ: Prentice-Hall, 1960.

Fulgentius of Ruspe. "De Fide." 5. Vol. 25 of *Patrologiae cursus completus, series Latin*. 221 vols. Edited by J. P. Migne. Paris, 1844–1864, 65:704.

Funk, Robert. "Cross Examination." Interview by Mary Source. *Los Angeles Times* (24 February 1994): E1, E5.

Funk, Robert W., Roy W. Hoover, and The Jesus Seminar. *The Five Gospels: What Did Jesus Really Say?* San Francisco: Harper, 1996.

Gall, Jeannie. "Basic Ecclesial Communities: A New Model of Church." In *One Faith, Many Cultures*. Edited by Ray O. Costa. Maryknoll, NY: Orbis Books, 1988.

Geertz, Clifford. *The Interpretation of Cultures*. New York: Basic Books, 1973.

Gleason, Philip. *Keeping the Faith: American Catholicism Past and Present*. Notre Dame, IN: University of Notre Dame Press, 1987.

Goizueto, Roberto. "Theology as Intellectually Vital Inquiry: The Challenge of/to U.S. Hispanic Theologians." Proceedings of the Forty-Sixth Annual Convention of the Catholic Theological Society of America, Paul Crowley, ed. Washington, D.C.: Catholic University of America Press, 1991, 58–69.

Granfield, Patrick. *The Limits of the Papacy*. New York: Crossroad, 1987.

——. "Legitimation and Bureaucratization of Ecclesial Power." In *Power in the Church*. Edited by James Provost and Walf Concilius. Edinburgh: T. & T. Clark, 1986.

Greeley, Andrew. *American Catholics since the Council*. Chicago, IL: Thomas More Press, 1985.

——. *Confessions of a Parish Priest*. New York: Simon and Schuster, 1986.

——. *The Catholic Myth*. New York: Charles Scribner's Sons, 1990.

Green, Thomas. "The Pastoral Governance Role of the Diocesan Bishop: Foundations, Scope, and Limitations." *Jurist* 49 (1989): 480.

Gutiérrez, Gustavo. *A Theology of Liberation*. Maryknoll, NY: Orbis Books, 1973.

Hays, Richard. "The Corrected Jesus." Review of *The Five Gospels*. *First Things* (May 1994): 43–48.

Herberg, Will. *Protestant, Catholic, Jew*. New York: Doubleday, 1955.

Hick, John, and Paul Knitter, eds. *The Myth of Christian Uniqueness: Towards a Pluralistic Theology of Religions*. Maryknoll, NY: Orbis Books, 1987.

Hillman, Eugene. *Polygamy Reconsidered*. Maryknoll, NY: Orbis Books, 1975.

Hoge, Dean. *Future of Catholic Leadership: Responses to the Priest Shortage*. Kansas City: Sheed and Ward, 1987.

Ignatius of Antioch. "Philadelphians." In *Early Christian Fathers*. Translated and edited by Cyril Richardson. Vol. I of *The Library of Christian Classics*. 26 vols. Philadelphia: Westminster Press, 1953.

Irenaeus, *Adversus Haereses*, 3. 24 vol. *Patrologiae cursus completus, series Graeca* (Complete Course on Patrology: Greek Series). 161 vol. Edited by J. P. Migne. Paris, 1857–1866, 906–07.

Isasi-Díaz, Ada Maria, and Yoland Tarango. *Hispanic Women: Prophetic Voice in the Church*. San Francisco: Harper and Row, 1988.

Iserloh, Erwin. "Die Confessio Augustana als Anfrage an Lutheraner und Katholiken im 16. Jahrhundert und Heute" (Concerning the Augustans Confession as Understood by Lutherans and Catholics in the 16th Century and Today). *Catholica* 33 (1979): 32.

Jaffe, A. J., Ruth M. Cullen, and Thomas D. Bosnell. *The Changing Demography of Spanish Americans*. New York: Academic Press, 1980.

Jennessey, James, S.J. *American Catholics: A History of the Roman Catholic Community in the United States*. New York: Oxford University Press, 1981.

Johnson, Elizabeth. *Consider Jesus: Waves of Renewal in Christology*. New York: Crossroad, 1990.

———. *She Who Is: The Mystery of God in Feminist Theological Discourse*. New York: Crossroad, 1992.

Johnson, Luke Timothy. *The Real Jesus*. San Francisco: Harper Collins, 1996.

Kasper, Walter. *Jesus the Christ*. New York: Paulist Press, 1976.

Kennedy, Eugene. *Tomorrow's Catholics, Yesterday's Church*. San Francisco: Harper and Row, 1988.

Knitter, Paul. *One Earth, Many Religions*. Maryknoll, NY: Orbis Books, 1995.

Komonchak, Joseph A. "The Theology of the Local Church; State of the Question." In *The Multicultural Church*. Edited by William Cenkner, O.P. Mahwah, NJ: Paulist Press, 1996.

Kraemer, Hendrick. *The Christian Message in a Non-Christian World.* Grand Rapids, MI: Kregel, 1963.

Küng, Hans. *The Church.* New York: Sheed and Ward, 1967.

——. *On Being a Christian.* New York: Doubleday, 1976.

Leddy, Mary Jo, Bishop Remi de Roo, and Douglas Roche. *In the Eye of the Catholic Storm.* Toronto: Harper Collins, 1992.

Letter to Archbishop Cushing of Boston. *American Ecclesiastical Review* 77 (1952): 307–11.

Lindbeck, George. *The Future of Roman Catholic Theology.* Philadelphia: Fortress Press, 1970.

Lynch, John E. "Co-Responsibility in the First Five Centuries: Presbyterial Colleges and the Election of Bishops." In *Who Decides for the Church?* Edited by James Coriden. Washington, D.C.: Canon Law Society of America, 1971.

Mansi, J. D., ed. *Sacrorum consiliorum nova et amplissima collectio* (New and Amplified Collection of the Sacred Councils). Arnhem and Leipzig: Welter, 1927.

Marty, Martin E. "The State of Disunion." *Commonweal* 115 (29 January 1988): 43.

Martyr, Justin. *The First Apology in Early Christian Fathers.* Translated and edited by Cyril Richardson. Vol. I of *The Library of Christian Classics.* 26 vols. Philadelphia: Westminster Press, 1953.

McBrien, Richard. *Catholicism.* San Francisco: Harper Collins, 1994.

——. *Ministry.* San Francisco: Harper and Row, 1987.

——. *Caesar's Coin.* New York: Macmillan, 1987.

McCool, Gerald A., ed. *A Rahner Reader.* New York: Seabury Press, 1975.

Meier, John. *A Marginal Jew: Rethinking the Historical Jesus.* 2 vols. to date. New York: Doubleday, 1991–1994.

Moran, Gabriel. *Theology of Revelation.* New York: Herder and Herder, 1966.

Murnion, Philip J. "The Community Called Parish," In *The Catholic Faith: A Reader.* Edited by Lawrence Cunningham. New York: Paulist Press, 1988.

National Council of Catholic Bishops. "The Challenge of Peace." *Origins* 13: 13.

Newbigin, Lesslie. *Foolishness to the Greeks.* Grand Rapids, MI: Eerdmans, 1986.

Norris, Richard A., ed. and trans. *The Christological Controversy.* Philadelphia: Fortress Press, 1980.

O'Collins, Gerald, S.J. *Christology: A Biblical, Historical and Systematic Study of Jesus.* New York: Oxford University Press, 1995.

O'Meara, Thomas F. *Theology of Ministry.* New York: Paulist Press, 1983.

Origen, "In Jesu Nave." Vol. 3. In *Patrologiae cursus completus, series Graeca.* Edited by J. P. Migne. 161 vols. 11. Paris, 1857–1866, 841.

Paninder, Geoffrey. "The Salvation of Other Men." In *Man and His Salvation.* Edited by E.J. Sharpe and J. R. Hinnels. Manchester: Manchester University Press, 1973.

Pegis, Anton C., ed. *On the Truth of the Catholic Faith (Summa Contra Gentiles).* Garden City, NY: Image Books, 1955.

Phan, Peter C. "Contemporary Theology and Inculturation in the United States." In *The Multicultural Church.* Edited by William Cenkner. New York: Paulist Press, 1996.

Pope John Paul II. "Letter to Agostino Cardinal Casaroli." *L'Osservatore Romana* 7 (28 June 1982): 6.

——. "Address to the Participants at the Gregorian University on the Occasion of the 400th Anniversary of the Arrival of Father Matthew Ricci in China." Speech given on October 25, 1982. In *Acta Romana: Societatis Jesu.* Vol. 18. Rome: Curia of the Society of Jesus, 3 (1983): 740–47.

——. "Speech to the Roman Curia on Dec. 20, 1990." *Acta Apostolica Sedis* 83 (1991): 746.

——. Address to Pontifical Council for Culture. *L'Osservatore Romano* (28 June 1982): 4–11.

——. "Redemptoris Missio" (The Mission of Redemption). *Origins* 20 (31 January 1995): n.55.

Pope Paul VI. *Encyclical "Ecclesiam Suam"* (His Church). Huntington, IN: Our Sunday Visitor Press, 1964, 1–40.

——. "Allocution to the Convention of the Bishops of Africa in Kampala, Uganda." *Acta Apostolical Sedis* 66 (1969).

——. *Evangelii Nuntiandi* (Announcing the Good News or Evangelization in the Modern World). In *Vatican Council: The Conciliar and Post Conciliar Documents.* Vol. II. Edited by Austin Flannery, O.P. Northport, NY: Costello, 1992.

Pope Pius XII. "Address to Pontifical Mission Aid Societies." *Acta Apostolicae Sedis* (1944): 210.

Power, David. "Communion Within Pluralism in the Local Church: Maintaining Unity in the Process of Inculturation." In *The Multicultural Church*. Edited by William Cenkner. New York: Paulist Press, 1995, 79–101.

Rahner, Karl. "Membership of the Church According to the Teaching of Pius XII's Encyclical 'Mystici Corporis Christi.'" *Theological Investigations*. Vol. 2. Translated by Karl H. Kruger. Baltimore: Helicon Press, 1963.

——. *On the Theology of Death*. New York: Herder and Herder, 1965.

——. "Christianity and the Non-Christian Religions," *Theological Investigations*. Vol. 5. Translated by Karl H. Kruger. Baltimore: Helicon Press, 1966.

——. "Dogmatic Notes on 'Ecclesiological Piety.'" *Theological Investigations*. Vol. 5. Translated by Karl H. Kruger. Baltimore: Helicon Press, 1966.

——. "History of the World and Salvation History." *Theological Investigations*. Vol. 5. Translated by Karl H. Kruger. Baltimore: Helicon Press, 1966.

——. "Thoughts on the Possibility of Belief Today," *Theological Investigations*. Vol. 5. Translated by Karl H. Kruger. Baltimore: Helicon Press, 1966.

——. "Christianity." In *Sacramentum Mundi*. New York: Herder and Herder, 1969.

——. "Two Types of Christology." In *Theological Investigations*. Vol. 13. New York: Seabury Press 1975.

——. "Towards a Fundamental Theological Interpretation of Vatican II." In *Vatican II: The Unfinished Agenda*. Edited by Lucien Richard, O. M. I., with Daniel T. Harrington, S.J., and John W. O'Malley, S. J. New York: Paulist Press, 1987.

Ratzinger, Joseph. *Instruction on Certain Aspects of the Theology of Liberation*. Boston: St. Paul's Editions, 1984.

Ratzinger, Joseph, with Vittorio Messor. *The Ratzinger Report*. San Francisco: Ignatius Press, 1985.

Regional Catholic Bishops Statement on Land Issues, "Strangers and Guests," *Origins* 10 (June 26, 1980): 81–96.

Riesner, Rainer. "Jesus as Preacher and Teacher." In *Jesus and the Oral Gospel Tradition*. Edited by Henry Wansbrough. Sheffield, England: Sheffield Academic Press, 1991.

Robinson, James M. *A New Quest for the Historical Jesus.* Missoula, MO: Scholars Press, 1959.

Romero, Oscar. *Voice of the Voiceless.* Maryknoll, NY: Orbis Books, 1985.

Sandoval, Moises. *On the Move: A History of the Hispanic Church in the United States.* Maryknoll, NY: Orbis Books, 1990.

Schillebeeckx, Edward. *God, the Future of Man.* New York: Sheed and Ward, 1968.

———. *Jesus: An Experiment in Christology.* New York: Seabury Press, 1979.

———. *Church with a Human Face.* New York: Crossroad, 1985.

Schillebeeckx, Edward, and J. B. Metz, eds. *The Right of a Community to a Priest.* New York: Crossroad, 1980.

Schlette, Heinz Robert. *Towards a Theology of Religions.* New York: Herder and Herder, 1966.

Schnackenburg, Rudolf. *God's Rule and Kingdom.* London: Nelson, 1963.

———. *The Church in the New Testament.* New York: Herder and Herder, 1965.

Schoenherr Report. "Study of U.S. Diocesan Priesthood Statistics: 1966–2005." *Origins* 20 (1990): 206.

Schreiter, Robert. *Constructing Local Theologies.* Maryknoll, NY: Orbis Books, 1986.

Schweitzer, Albert. *The Quest of the Historical Jesus: A Critical Study of Its Progress from Reimarus to Wrede.* Translated by William Montgomery. New York: Macmillan, 1968. (Original published 1906.)

Seckler, Max. "Salvation for the Non-Evangelized," *Theology Digest* 9 (autumn 1961): 168–73.

Second General Council of Latin American Bishops. *The Church in the Present-Day Transformation of Latin America in the Light of the Council.* 3rd ed. Washington, D.C.: National Conference of Catholic Bishops, 1979.

Sherry, Robert. "Shortage? What Vocation Shortage?" *The Priest* 41 (1985): 29–31.

Shorter, Aylward. *Toward a Theology of Inculturation.* Maryknoll, NY: Orbis Books, 1992.

Sigmund, Paul E. *Nicholas of Cusa and Medieval Political Thought.* Cambridge, MA: Harvard University Press, 1963.

Sobrino, Jon. *Christology at the Crossroads*. Maryknoll, NY: Orbis Books, 1978.

Spong, John. *Born of a Woman: A Bishop Rethinks the Birth of Jesus*. San Francisco: Harper, 1992.

St. Augustine. "De Baptismo Contra Donatistas" (Concerning Baptism against the Donatistas). Book VII. *Patrologiae cursus completus, series Latina* (Complete Course of Patrology: Latin Series) I. Vol. 28. Edited by J. P. Migne. (221 vols.). Paris, 1844–1864, 43: 223–25.

St. Cyprian. "The Unity of the Catholic Church." *Ancient Christian Writers*. Vol. 25. Translated by Maurice Bévenot. Westminster, MD: Newman Press, 1957.

St. Thomas Aquinas. *Summa Theologica*. Vols. 2 and 3. Rome: Marietti, 1952.

Sullivan, Francis. *Salvation outside the Church?* New York: Paulist Press, 1992.

Swidler, Leonard, John B. Cobb, Jr., Paul Knitter, and Monica Hellwig. *Death or Dialogue? From the Age of Monologue to the Age of Dialogue*. Philadelphia: Trinity Press International, 1996.

Symposium of Bishops of Africa and Madagascar. *Acts of the Fifth Assembly of SECAM, ACCRA*. Kinshasa, Zaire, 1978.

Tacitus Annals. Loeb Classical Library. 4 volumes. Cambridge, MA: Harvard University Press, 1932.

Talbert, Charles H., ed. *Reimarus: Fragments*. Philadelphia: Fortress Press, 1970.

Theiring, Barbara. *Jesus and the Riddle of the Dead Sea Scrolls, Unlocking the Secrets of His Life Story*. San Francisco: Harper, 1992.

Tillich, *Systematic Theology*. Vol 3. Chicago: University of Chicago Press, 1963.

Tracy, David. "Ethnic Pluralism and Systematic Theology; Reflections." *Concilium* 101 (1977): 91.

Trigault, Nicholas. *The China that Was*. Translated by Louis J. Gallagher. Milwaukee, WI: Bruce, 1942.

United States Bishops Conference. Pastoral letter "The Challenge of Peace: God's Promise and Our Response." Final draft. *Origins* 13 (19 May 1983): 13.

United States Bishops Conference. Pastoral letter "On Catholic Social Teaching and the U.S. Economy." Final draft. *Origins* 16 (27 November 1986): 411–55.

Vatican's Commission for Religious Relations with the Jews. "The Jews and Judaism in Preaching and Catechesis." *Ecumenical Trends* 14 (October 1985): 1383–44.

Viviano, Benedict T. *The Kingdom of God in History*. Wilmington, DE: Michael Glazier, 1988.

Willems, Boniface. *The Reality of Redemption*. New York: Herder and Herder, 1970.

Young, Robert D. *Encounter with World Religions*. Philadelphia: Westminster Press, 1970.

Zinelli, Bishop. "Acta synodalia sacrosancti concilii oecumenici. Vaticani II" (*Synodal Acts of the Sacred Ecumenical Council, Vatican II*). Vol. 3, part 1, 247. *Acta apostolicae sedis* 57 (1965): 775.

Index